TELEVISION INDUSTRIES

TELEVISION INDUSTRIES

Edited by
Douglas Gomery and Luke Hockley

 Publishing

First published in 2006 by the
BRITISH FILM INSTITUTE
21 Stephen Street, London W1T 1LN

The British Film Institute's purpose is to champion moving image
culture in all its richness and diversity across the UK, for the benefit
of as wide an audience as possible, and to create and encourage debate.

Cover design: Squid Inc.
Cover image: *Law & Order: Special Victims Unit* (Dick Wolf, USA, 1999–, NBC Universal Television/
Wolf Films/NBC Universal Television/Studios USA Television/Universal Network Television),
Christopher Meloni and Mariska Hargitay

Set by Fakenham Photosetting Limited, Fakenham, Norfolk
Printed in the UK by St Edmundsbury Press, Bury St Edmunds, Suffolk

British Cataloguing-in-Publication Data
A catalogue record for this book is available from the British Library

ISBN 1–84457–107–6 (pbk)
ISBN 1–84457–106–8 (hbk)

Contents

(Grey box case studies are indicated in brackets)

Preface

DOUGLAS GOMERY AND LUKE HOCKLEY

Television Industries is the last volume in the series that will eventually make up *The Television Book*. As such, it might be expected to pull together some of the issues and themes of previous volumes, summarise the state of television studies and generally bring the series to a graceful conclusion. In reality there is a different desire at the heart of this project. Its intellectual history lies in the early days of television studies in ground-breaking production studies such as *Hazell: The making of a TV series* (Alvarado and Buscombe, BFI 1978) and later work such as *Boys from the Blackstuff: The Making of a TV Drama* (Millington and Nelson, Comedia 1986). These books attempted to get behind the seemingly impervious surface of which the seamless flow of television programmes is composed and to expose how, and why, these programmes came into being, as did studies such as *MTM 'Quality Television'* (Feuer, Kerr and Vahimagi) and *Made for Television*: *Euston Films Limited* (Alvarado and Stewart, 1985). While not a production study, this book also attempts to provide an insight into the inner workings of the television industry. As such its central concern is with processes, not texts or techniques or histories, which other volumes in this series deal with in detail.

Broadcasters work hard at making their job look easy and fun. Ask a typical producer what it's like working in the industry and likely as not you'll get a string of anecdotes about near-misses on location and gaffs of the rich and famous that never made it to air, each tale adding to the excitement of being close to the magic of the media circus, with its intoxicating mixture of glamour and power. In reality, broadcasting is just an industry, albeit a significant one. It's heavily regulated, technologically complex and expensive, driven by financial concerns and increasingly international markets.

This provides the focus for the current book which attempts to offer some insight into the macro-extrinsic elements of the industry: the policy and regulatory frameworks, the swiftly changing world of video production technology, all of which supply the backdrops against which broadcasters shape and sell their products. Looking inside the industry we can find what might be termed macro-intrinsic elements. These company-wide concerns include elements such as international programme sales and the importance of programme tie-ins, while at the micro-intrinsic level we have the working practices of scheduling, budgeting, selling advertising air-time and so forth. Where issues may be familiar to readers (for example, debates around public service broadcasting), the entries aim to be explanatory and fresh. Of course, it is not possible to cover every aspect of what is a complex and ever changing industry. Nonetheless, the aim is to provide a starting point for students and new scholars as they start to research into the nature of the broadcasting industry.

Of course, the above categories are not independent of each other. In any complex interlocked system it is inevitable that one area will flow into another. Hence this volume is cross-referenced and guides readers as they tease out for themselves some of the complexity of this industry. Where readers would like more information *The Television History Book*, *Television Studies* and *Contemporary World Television* address many topics in more detail than can be provided here. Some issues cut right across the areas. At the time of writing, midway through 2005, the BBC has announced 4,000 job losses in a major restructuring exercise. There has already been a one-day strike and other longer strikes are planned. Here the perspective provided by the broadcasting unions is essential, hence the inclusion in this volume of entries examining the role of the unions in shaping the current terrain of UK broadcasting and their core concern of diversity in the broadcasting workforce in a multicultural Britain.

There are several other elements that are distinctive about this volume. Perhaps the most striking of these is its blend of contributions from the UK and US. The US more than the UK dominates the globe in terms of the supply of television programmes. Some of its brands are known across the world, such as CNN. By contrast, the BBC is distinctive in offering a well-understood brand with a reputation for impartiality and quality. Our intention has been to provide an insight into our own countries' broadcasting practices that is of interest not only to readers on both sides of the Atlantic but also to readers from other countries, many of whom will be consumers of products from America and the BBC. However, it is not just the geography of origin that is significant in these contributions – the range of voices from full-time academics to diehard broadcasters also provides some interesting takes on current developments. The tone of the entries also varies; some have a detached academic style, while others write more anecdotally. We hope that the cumulative effect of this is to give an insight into the differing, yet valid, perspectives afforded by working in the broadcasting and education industries.

This volume doesn't adopt a polemical position about issues such as cross-media ownership. Instead it presents for the reader's consideration a point of view, sometimes several points of view, which provide a starting point for further reflection and exploration. As a result, we suspect that this volume will raise as many questions as it provides answers. As the final volume in the series it doesn't provide a fullstop, nor should it. Instead it aims to make a contribution to the continuing debates in the now well-established world of television studies with fresh perspectives on some familiar, and some not so familiar, landscapes.

June 2005

ACKNOWLEDGMENTS

Our thanks go firstly and importantly to Andrew Lockett and Ann Simmonds at the BFI for their advice and support in the evolution of this project. We both thank the contributors and give to all a huge heart-felt thank you as this volume would not exist without their generosity of spirit and professionalism. Luke thanks Manuel Alvarado for his help in formulating the conceptual shape of this volume, and Mary McDonnell for her continuous support. Douglas thanks Marilyn Moon for the shaping of all his work and for her example of how best to analyse complex industries. All of what Douglas contributed was inspired by Marilyn's example in a wholly different, but actually quite similar, industry in the US, health care.

Notes on Contributors

Richard Adams is the Creative Director of YooMedia, the UK's fastest-growing interactive TV and wireless entertainment company. He is also Visiting Professor of Digital Media at Salford University and a director of Earcom Ltd, an audio and music design consultancy based in London. He has worked in digital media and interactive TV for over ten years and is a member of BAFTA.

Patricia Aufderheide is Professor in the School of Communication at American University, Washington D.C. and co-director of the university's Center for Social Media.

Peter Dean is currently the Deputy Head of Media, Art and Design at the University of Luton, and has a background in computer science. While leading the Media Production programme at Luton, his teaching has focused on the theory and practice of new media. Current research interests include the production of dynamic content-rich websites and the regulation of the new media.

David Docherty has written extensively on media for the past twenty years. After achieving a PhD in Sociology and an MSc in International Relations from the London School of Economics, he joined the British Film Institute as a Research Fellow. During his time at the BFI, he published books on the UK cinema audiences and historical accounts of Channel 4 and London Weekend Television. He joined the BBC, where he became the first Director of New Media and Deputy Director of Television. He left the BBC to join Telewest Broadband as MD Broadband, before becoming Chief Executive of interactive media company, YooMedia. He is a published novelist, a Research Fellow of Leeds University, and Pro-Chancellor and Chairman of the Board of the University of Luton.

Philip Drake is Lecturer in Film and Media at University of Paisley, Scotland. He has written on celebrity, performance, memory and film music, and on cities. He has recent chapters in *Film Stars: Hollywood and Beyond* (Manchester University Press, 2004), edited by Andrew Willis, *Memory and Popular Film* (Manchester University Press, 2003), edited by Paul Grainge, and *Hollywood Comedians: The Film Reader* (Routledge, 2003), edited by Frank Krutnik. He has forthcoming articles on media and intellectual property, and celebrity and political discourse, and is co-editor of a forthcoming special edition of the journal *Cultural Politics* on the cultural politics of celebrity. He is currently finishing a book on the political economy of stardom in contemporary Hollywood cinema.

Christine Fanthome began her career at Thames Television, where she worked in a variety of positions, including senior researcher, associate producer, reporter and continuity scriptwriter. After taking an MA and a PhD in Media and Communication at London University she now works as a consultant and writer. Her publications include *Channel 5 – the Early Years* (University of Luton Press, 2003).

Douglas Gomery teaches Media Studies at the University of Maryland and is Resident Scholar at the Library of American Broadcasting. His book *Who Owns the Media?: Competition and Concentration in the Mass Media* (Lawrence Erlbaum Associates, 2000) earned the Picard Prize in 2001, and *Shared Pleasures* (University of Wisconsin Press, 1992) the Theatre Library Association Award in 1993; he has published a dozen other books.

Luke Hockley is Associate Dean – Media, at the University of Sunderland. His recent publications include 'Detective Films and Images of the Orient: A Post-Jungian Reflection', in *Post-Jungian Criticism: Theory and Practice* (State University of New York Press, 2004), edited by James S. Baumlin, Tita French Baumlin and George H. Jensen, and 'BSkyB', in *BFI Television Handbook 2005: The Essential Guide to UK TV* (BFI, 2005), edited by Alistair D. McGown. His forthcoming book, *Frames of Mind*, will be published by John Libby Media later this year.

Richard Kilborn is Senior Lecturer in the Department of Film and Media Studies at the University of Stirling, Scotland. He has also lectured at the University of Munich and at Northwestern University (Chicago). He is particularly interested in film and television documentary and has written, with John Izod, *Confronting Reality: An Introduction to Television Documentary* (Manchester University Press, 1997) and *Staging the Real: Factual TV Programming in the Age of 'Big Brother'* (Manchester University Press, 2003).

Stephen Lax is a Lecturer in Communications Technology at the University of Leeds. He is a member of the Digital Radio Cultures in Europe research group and on the steering group of the UK Radio Studies Network. He coordinated the ESRC 'Informed or Forewarned' Seminar Series at the Institute of Communication Studies from 1996 to 1998. He is author of *Beyond the Horizon: Communications Technologies Past Present and Future* (University of Luton Press, 1997) and editor of *Access Denied in the Information Age* (Palgrave, 2001).

Philip Lodge lectures in Communication in the School of Communication Arts at Napier University, Edinburgh. He is programme leader for the MSc Creative Advertising and the online MSc International Communication, and has a particular interest in the intellectual history of the communication discipline and development of communication theory.

Sheila Lodge is Dean of the Faculty of Arts, Humanities and Social Sciences at UHI Millennium Institute, Scotland, and has a long-standing interest in the role of advertising in Scottish culture.

Kathryn C. Montgomery is Professor of Communication at American University, Washington, D.C., where she also serves as Co-Director of the Center for Social Media. Prior to her appointment at AU in the autumn of 2003, she was President of the Center for Media Education (CME), a D.C.-based non-profit organisation she co-founded in 1991. She is the author of *Target: Prime Time – Advocacy Groups and the Struggle over Entertainment Television* (Oxford University Press, 1989). Montgomery received her PhD in Film and Television from the University of California, Los Angeles.

Susan Murray is Assistant Professor of Culture and Communication at New York University. She is the author of *Hitch Your Antenna to the Stars!: A History of Early*

Television and Broadcast Stardom (Routledge, 2005) and the co-editor of *Reality TV: Remaking Television Culture* (New York University Press, 2004).

Philip M. Napoli is an Associate Professor in the Schools of Business at Fordham University and Director of the Donald McGannon Communication Research Center. His books include *Foundations of Communications Policy: Principles and Process in the Regulation of Electronic Media* (Hampton Press, 2001), *Audience Economics: Media Institutions and the Audience Marketplace* (Columbia, 2003) and *Media Diversity and Localism: Meaning and Metrics* (Lawrence Erlbaum Associates, in press).

Clara Pafort-Overduin lectures at the Department of Theatre, Film and Television Studies at Utrecht University. She teaches film history, European film and television repertory. She is the former co-ordinator of the undergraduate Theatre, Film and Television programme. She is currently working on a book about Dutch film in the 1930s.

Adrian Page is an Academic Leader at London Metropolitan University, where he teaches Film Studies. He is the author of *Cracking Morse Code: Semiotics and Television Drama* (University of Luton Press, 2000). He is currently writing a book chapter for the University of Wales Press on the television series *Nip/Tuck*.

Julian Petley is Professor of Film and Television in the School of Arts at Brunel University, principal editor of the *Journal of British Cinema and Television* and joint chair of the Campaign for Press and Broadcasting Freedom. His most recent publication is *Culture Wars: The Media and the British Left* (Edinburgh University Press, in press), jointly authored with James Curran and Ivor Gaber.

Patricia Phalen has experience in media planning and television audience research. She is co-author, with James Webster and Lawrence Lichty, of *Ratings Analysis: The Theory and Practice of Audience Research* (Lawrence Erlbaum Associates, 2000) and, with James Webster, *The Mass Audience: Rediscovering the Dominant Model* (Lawrence Erlbaum Associates, 1996). Research interests include the socio-economics of mass media and audience analysis.

Graham Roberts is a Senior Lecturer at the Institute of Communications, Leeds, and Director of the university's Louis Le Prince Centre for Cinema, Photography and Television. His publications include *Stride Soviet, History and Soviet Non-Fiction Film* (I. B. Tauris, 1998), *The Man* *with the Movie Camera* (I. B. Tauris, 2000), *The Historian and Television* (University of London Press, 2001) and *European Cinema in the Television Age* (Edinburgh University Press, 2006).

John Sedgwick works as a media economist/historian at London Metropolitan University. His research publications have been in the area of film history and concerned with providing an empirical methodology for understanding of how the film business worked at various historical junctures in both the UK and the US.

Tony Stark has over twenty years' experience of making documentaries for British and American broadcasters. He has produced films in a range of styles: from crafted historical documentaries to observational, investigative and presenter-led approaches. Three of his programmes have been recognised at international film festivals, including a BAFTA nomination in 2002.

Michael Svennevig is Director of the Research Centre for Future Communications at the University of Leeds' Institute for Communications Studies. He previously worked for audience research departments of the BBC and the former Independent Broadcasting Authority. He has also worked in the market research industry and has run his own media research company.

Janice Turner is editor of BECTU's union magazine *Stage, Screen & Radio*, and is the union's diversity official. In 2003 she organised 'Move on up', the union's diversity initiative in partnership with the film and broadcasting industry, for which the Trades Union Congress awarded BECTU the TUC Equality Award.

Garry Whannel is Professor of Media Cultures and Director at the Centre for International Media Analysis at the University of Luton. He is the author of *Media Sport Stars, Masculinities and Moralities* (Routledge, 2001) and has been researching on the theme of media and sport for over twenty years.

John Willis began his career at Yorkshire Television, where he won a string of awards for his hard-hitting documentary programmes, including *Johnny Go Home* (British Academy Award) and *Rampton – The Secret Hospital* (International Emmy). Later he became Controller of Documentaries and Current Affairs, and started the acclaimed documentary series *First Tuesday*. In 1988, he joined Channel 4 Television as Controller of Factual Programmes, introducing new documentary stands like *Cutting Edge*, *True Stories* and *Secret History*. In 1993, he was promoted to Director of Programmes and oversaw a number of successful programmes and films in several genres, including *Father Ted*, *Rory Bremner*, *The Politician's Wife* and the movies *Four Weddings and a Funeral* and *Trainspotting*. After Channel 4, he became Chief Executive of United Productions as it rapidly expanded in both factual programmes and drama, with successes including *Hornblower*, *Oliver Twist* and several Paul Watson documentaries. He represented United on the Boards of both Channel 5 and Independent Television News. When Granada Media bought United, John moved to become Managing Director of both United Productions and London Weekend Television and, subsequently, Managing Director of Granada's International Production.

In 2001, he won the prestigious Royal Television Society Gold Medal for Creative Contribution to Television. In June 2002, he moved to Boston to join WGBH, America's biggest public television station, as Vice-president in charge of national programmes. Their award-winning programmes include *Frontline*, *Nova*, *American Experience* and *ExxonMobil Masterpiece Theatre*. In June 2003, he joined the BBC as Director of Factual and Learning with responsibility for BBC factual production across all channels. Since then his department has been responsible for award-winning productions like *The Secret Policeman*, *Dunkirk*, *One Life* and *Pompeii*.

TELEVISION AS BUSINESS

The Economics of Television – UK

On 2 November 1936 the BBC opened the world's first regular service of high-definition television from Alexandra Palace in north London. The programmes reached only the 20,000 homes within a thirty-five-mile range of the transmitter. The first sets cost about £100, more than a year's wages for many British workers in those days. On 1 September 1939, two days before Britain declared war on Germany, a Mickey Mouse cartoon was being shown when the television service was suddenly blacked out for defence reasons. It was feared that the signals could act as direction-finders for enemy aircraft. That same Mickey Mouse cartoon was shown on 7 June 1946 when BBC television re-opened.

As in the United States, television in Britain diffused almost like a contagion during the 1950s. In 1949 only 1 per cent of British households possessed a television set, receiving broadcasts from one broadcaster (the BBC). Commercial television arrived on 22 September 1955, with the inauguration of the ITV network of independent, British-owned regional companies, and by 1960 over 75 per cent of British households possessed a receiver (Bowden and Offer, 1999). BBC2 commenced broadcasting on 20 April 1964, using the new 625-line system, which eventually replaced the original 'high-definition' 405 lines, thus making the picture quality of British television superior to that of the US, with its 525 lines. The first scheduled colour programming began on BBC2 on 1 July 1967 (the Wimbledon Tennis Tournament), and by 1976 colour sets outnumbered black and white. Rupert Murdoch introduced the revolutionary, multichannel Sky satellite television provider on 6 February 1989, and today 82 per cent of adults live in homes with more than one television set, receiving programmes from five main terrestrial channels – BBC1, BBC2, ITV1, Channel 4 and Five – in analogue or digital form (collectively referred to as public service broadcast (PSB) channels in that their licences specify that they meet certain specified obligations to the general public as television viewers) and a host of satellite and cable channels in digital form only. Significantly, even though there has been increasing competition for consumers' leisure time in recent years, the hold of television on viewers has actually increased from, on average, 25.6 hours per household per week in 1993 to 26.1 hours in 2003. Television continues to be central to people's lives and their sense of well-being (Ofcom, 2004).

In examining the economics of the industry in Britain, it is important to distinguish between the reasons how and why programmes are made, and the heterogeneous preferences of viewers. One way of doing this is to consider the nature of television programmes as a commodity-type with a distinct set of characteristics (which distinguish it from other commodity-types such as movies (see Sedgwick, 2000), radio, or theatre), that have been shaped jointly and dynamically over time by a *system of provision* comprising broadcasters, programme-makers, programme distributors, viewers, critics and the state.

Each television programme may be conceived of as a discrete and unique bundle of characteristics. Where many of these characteristics are shared with other programmes, it is common to refer to these programme clusters as genres. In the

Early television set

UK, the following genre categories are commonly used – news, current affairs, parliamentary, arts and classical music, children's, religious, general factual, educational, drama, films, entertainment/music, sport (Ofcom, 2004). Of course, within each category lies a series of sub-genres and within them sub-sub-genres, for example, drama includes soaps as a sub-genre, and there are different types of soaps. It is possible to imagine programmes organised into sub-sub-genres arranged along a continuum such that programmes near to one another make up a 'neighbourhood' of similarity. The neighbourhoods overlap with respect to certain characteristics, but as the characteristics vary along the continuum the degree of similarity diminishes until the programmes in 'distant' neighbourhoods have little in common. Economists refer to this as *horizontal product differentiation*. The clustering of viewers that goes with these programme neighbourhoods suggests that numerous *taste publics* exist.

Economists refer to qualitative differences within commodity-types/product groups as *vertical product differentiation*. An investigation of audience viewing figures indicates that the distribution of viewers among broadcast programmes is highly unequal. Clearly, some programmes – and indeed

genres – are very much more popular than others. Table 1.1 lists the top twenty programmes screened on British television for the week ending 29 May 2005. The list is dominated by three soaps – two produced and broadcast by ITV1 (*Coronation Street* and *Emmerdale*) and one by BBC1 (*EastEnders*) – multiple episodes of which are broadcast each week, with repeats broadcast during the same evening on digital channels (available via satellite, cable and Freeview) owned by the two broadcasters, and in the case of *EastEnders* an omnibus edition appearing on BBC1 on Sunday afternoons. It is important to note that the three soaps are not scheduled to compete head-to-head: in effect the two broadcasters collude to allow fans to view all three soaps, with each complementing the other in meeting a joint demand for the sub-genre, rather than serving as a rival, and thus, substitute goods. The reader will also note that very few of the genres listed earlier are to be found in Table 1.1 and that just two channels dominate it. Indeed, the only non-BBC1/ITV1 programme in the list is Channel Four's reality programme *Big Brother*, which takes the joint twentieth berth. Of the remaining two terrestrial channels, the most popular programme on BBC2 was the motor TV magazine *Top Gear* with 3.67 million viewers and on Five *CSI:*

Table 1.1 The top twenty programmes on British television during w/e 29 May 2005

Rank	Programme	Day	Time	Sub-genre	Broadcaster	Audience (millions)
1	Coronation Street	Monday	19.30	Soap	ITV	11.61
2	Coronation Street	Monday	20.30	Soap	ITV	10.69
3	EastEnders	Monday	20.00	Soap	BBC1	10.50
4	EastEnders	Tuesday	19.30	Soap	BBC1	9.96
5	UEFA Champions League Football	Wednesday	19.00	Sport	ITV	9.50
6	Coronation Street	Friday	19.30	Soap	ITV	9.24
7	Emmerdale	Monday	19.00	Soap	ITV	9.03
8	EastEnders	Thursday	19.30	Soap	BBC1	9.00
9	Emmerdale	Tuesday	19.00	Soap	ITV	8.89
10	Coronation Street	Friday	20.39	Soap	ITV	8.77
11	EastEnders	Friday	20.00	Soap	BBC1	8.57
12	New Tricks	Monday	21.00	Police drama	BBC1	8.25
13	Heartbeat	Sunday	20.00	Police drama	ITV	7.81
14	Emmerdale	Thursday	19.00	Soap	ITV	7.73
15	Emmerdale	Friday	19.00	Soap	ITV	7.33
16	Holby City	Tuesday	20.00	Weekly soap	BBC1	7.11
17	Doctor Who	Saturday	19.00	Sci-fi drama	BBC1	6.86
18	Emmerdale	Sunday	19.00	Soap	ITV	6.54
19	The Last Detective	Sunday	21.00	Police drama	ITV	6.37
20	The Bill	Thursday	20.00	Soap	ITV	6.04
20	Big Brother	Friday	21.00	Reality	Channel Four	6.04

Source: BARB, 2005

Crime Scene Investigation with 3.37 million viewers. Table 1.1 also indicates that broadcasters place the most popular programmes in those time slots – between 6.00 and 10.00 hours on weekdays – when the most viewers are watching. Indeed, for each of the five terrestrial channels almost all of their weekly top thirty programmes fall within this peak period (BARB, 2005). These broadcast tactics can be understood in terms of market clearing – the means by which the industry adjusts supply to the distinct levels of audience demand for different programmes. One final observation is that, unlike the market for movies in the UK, the top-ranking television programmes are all British productions.

Interestingly, the viewing figures for the most popular terrestrial television programmes dwarf those enjoyed by broadcasters who supply programmes through digital technology only. While the thirtieth-ranking broadcast from each of the five principal terrestrial channels drew weekly viewing figures respectively of 3.67, 1.4, 3.31, 1.33 and 0.99 millions during the week ending 29 May 2005, the best viewing figures achieved by prominent digital channels were 589,000 (BBC3 – repeat of *EastEnders*), 256,000 (BBC4), 269,000 (CBBC), 137,000 (Discovery), 227,000 (Hallmark), 1,011,000 (ITV2 – *Extra Time for Footballers' Wives*), 430,000 (ITV3 – repeat of *The Last Detective*), 429,000 (Living TV), 884,000 (Sky One), 222,000 (Sky Movies), 944,000 (Sky Sports) (BARB, 2005).

Television programmes are made by production organisations that may be: a) part of an in-house vertically integrated supply chain controlled by the broadcaster; b) contracted by the broadcaster to make specified products; or c) contracted to a distributor whose function it is to interest broadcasters in their product(s). The broadcaster may partly or wholly finance the production, or alternatively take no stake in the production, acquiring it from the open market through a distributor by paying a price based upon an internationally agreed range of territorial prices for the rights to screen the product for a given duration (Hoskins *et al.*, 1997; TBI, 2004). Thus, broadcasters assemble portfolios of programmes so as to meet their corporate goals, such as market share and/or commercial viability, while conforming to the regulatory framework by meeting series of obligations placed upon them.

Unlike most products, and with the exception of pay-as-you-view television, which is very small in the UK, television programmes do not require that viewers pay a price to consume them. Rather, viewers are excluded from consumption if they do not have the necessary means of receiving broadcast signals, or are not allowed access to them because they have not paid the requisite subscription fee. This means that broadcasters generate revenues either through receipt of a statutory levy from viewers (such as the licence fee in Britain, used to finance the BBC), advertising charges, fixed price subscrip-

tions to particular packages of broadcaster channels or overseas sales – of growing importance, with the BBC taking approximately a 50 per cent share of UK export televisual revenues in 2002 (Steemers, 2004, ch. 4). Regarding advertising, the programmes broadcast on commercial terrestrial television can be conceived of as quasi-gifts from advertisers to viewers, with the intention that the latter absorb the information/message manifest in those advertisements placed around and during the programme they choose to watch.

Table 1.2 charts the market share of the terrestrial channels and digital channels (including those owned by public service broadcasters) since 1981. It is clear that BBC1 and ITV1 have lost market dominance over the period. ITV1 in particular has lost ground, losing 20 percentage points of its share since the onset of digitalisation in 1991, compared to the 10 percentage points lost by BBC1. Since 1991, the supply side of the market has become increasingly fragmented as the share taken by digital television has not only grown to over a quarter by 2004, but is divided among a host of channels, of which the weekly viewing figures are available for the fifty main entertainment channels from the BARB website. As is evident from the earlier analysis comparing the most popular programmes on digital television with the thirtieth-ranking broadcast from each of the five principal terrestrial channels, the numbers of viewers attracted to individual digital programmes are small in comparison. However, cumulatively, larger numbers of viewers are being attracted to digital channels, suggesting the existence of niche taste publics spread across the highly varied provision. Given that digital television by early 2004 was being accessed by only 53 per cent of British households, it is likely that the share of market absorbed by digital television channels will increase, but it is uncertain how this will be divided between PSB digital channels available on Freeview and non-public service broadcasters that require viewers to pay a subscription to receive their programmes.

The market power of the BBC and ITV has been further undermined by the efforts of government to introduce competition into the industry by introducing legislation to constrain the extent of *vertical integration*. The Broadcasting Act of 1990 required terrestrial channels to acquire 25 per cent of their programmes from independent producers, and was followed in 1996 by legislation that introduced a 10 per cent quota on their digital-only channels. As an extension of this, the BBC, in its current proposals to the government concerning the renewal of its charter, has announced that it intends extending the range of contestable funding to independent suppliers, to an additional 25 per cent of its programming (Ofcom, 2005).

The structural changes that have been identified through discussion of Table 1.2 are reflected in the sources of the

Table 1.2 Annual shares of television viewing by individuals, 1981–2004

Year	Broadcast Channels					Digital broadcasters[b]
	BBC1	BBC2	ITV1	Channel Four	Channel 5	
1981	39	12	49			
1986	37	11	44	8		
1991	34	10	42	10		4
1996	33.5	11.5	35.1	10.7	2.3[a]	10.1
2001	26.9	11.1	26.7	10	5.8	19.6
2004	24.7	10	22.8	9.7	6.6	26.2

Notes: a. This figure is recorded for 1997; b. BARB labels this category as 'Other' and includes the partly state-funded Welsh-language channel SC4.

Source: BARB

Table 1.3 Total TV industry revenues by source (£ millions, 2002 prices)

Year	1998	1999	2000	2001	2002	2003
Net Advertising Revenue	3,077	3,241	3,591	3,442	3,147	3,148
Licence Fee	1,725	1,843	1,883	1,965	2,224	2,233
Subscription	1,451	1,697	2,186	2,613	2,968	3,148
Other	238	337	408	792	648	951

Source: Ofcom, 2004, fig. 6

revenues earned by the broadcasters set down in Table 1.3. The most startling observation is the growth of digital television subscriptions, overtaking first the licence fee as a source of finance in 1999, and then net advertising revenues in 2003. Moreover, the share of advertising revenues received by digital channels increased from 15 to 21 per cent during the five years 1998 to 2003, in keeping with growing viewer numbers. Taken together, these figures tell a story in which the digital sector income has risen from 30 per cent of total industry revenue in 1998 to 48 per cent in 2003, while attracting just over a quarter share of the viewing audience (see Table 1.2). In competitive terms it is clear that digital television has had a profound effect on the terrestrial sector, particularly the commercial channels ITV1, Channel Four and Channel 5, whose combined share of industry revenues has plummeted from 42 to 27 per cent over the six years. While licence fee revenues have actually risen by 28 per cent over this period, as a share of industry revenue they too have fallen, but much more gently, from 28 to 24 per cent (Ofcom, 2004).

The principal reason for the growth of digital television in the UK has been the business strategy developed by BSkyB, based on developing channels dedicated to sport and film genres. Although the various Sky channels collectively attracted only a 6 per cent audience share in 2003, the broadcaster accounted for 25 per cent of the industry's total spend on programmes (amounting to 80 per cent of that spent by the digital sector) in order to achieve this, reflecting a strategy that has resulted in a growth of subscription and advertising income that now amounts to 20 per cent of industry revenues. This disproportionality between the size of its audience on the one hand and its levels of programme expenditure and revenue on the other, contrasts markedly with the figures for the BBC, which in 2003 received only 28 per cent of industry revenue, but represented 32 per cent of the industry's total spend on programmes, in attracting a 38 per cent share of the audience. The figures for ITV, Channel Four and Channel Five were much closer to the ratio of 1:1:1 for these three indicators. Clearly, different business models are in operation. Sky spends considerably more per viewer than the industry average, while the BBC spends less, suggesting that the BBC is more efficient at turning programme budgets into audience numbers. However, Sky's strategy is based on turning audience figures into revenue, and in this it is much more successful than any of the other principal broadcasters (Ofcom, 2004, fig. 10).

The British television market is highly competitive, with each of the terrestrial channels attempting to maintain market share in the face of the growth in demand for digital television. Together, on average, their spend in real terms on programmes has increased by 15 per cent over the period 1998 to 2003. However, this masks considerable differences between the channels, as ITV1 and BBC1 have spent, respectively, 19 and 18 per cent more on programmes during these years, compared to 8, 10 and 3 per cent, respectively, for BBC2, Channel Four and five, which helps to explain the dominant position of ITV1 and BBC1 when measured by peak-hour viewing figures. Given the decline in market share experienced by these two most popular channels, both ITV1 and BBC1 have seen their spend (£ millions, in 2002 prices) for each percentage point of audience share rise sharply from £21.77 million to £34.42 million and £22.52 million to £30.19 million, respectively. However, these figures need to be put into perspective since Sky is spending ten times that amount to attract a much smaller market share (Ofcom, 2004, figs 19, 21, 29 and para. 5.2).

John Sedgwick

RECOMMENDED READING

BARB (Broadcasters' Audience Research Board) (2005), at <www.barb> (accessed in June).

Bowden, S. and Offer, A. (1999), 'Household appliances and systems of provision', *Economic History Review*, 52, pp. 563–7.

Hoskins, C., McFadyen, S. and Finn, A. (1997), *Global Television and Film*, Oxford: Oxford University Press.

Ofcom (2004), The Communications Market 2004 – Television, August 2004, at <www.ofcom> (accessed in June 2005).

Ofcom (2005), Review of Television Production Sector, May 2005, at <www.ofcom> (accessed in June).

Sedgwick, J. (2000), *Popular Filmgoing in 1930s Britain: A Choice of Pleasures*, Exeter: Exeter University Press.

Steemers, J. (2004), *Selling Television: British Television in the Global Marketplace*, London: BFI.

TBI (Television Business International) (2004), *Television Yearbook 2003*, London: TBI.

The Economics of Television – US

In the US, television is an industry – that is a set of related businesses. These businesses do one of the three following things, most do at least two, many do all three.

1. They make programming, principally in their Hollywood studios. This is where prime-time hits come from. So when one sees the highest-rated show of 2004, one saw *CSI: Crime Scene Investigation*. But this show was fashioned by the CBS Productions division of the Paramount studio, a Viacom subsidiary, and distributed and shown on the CBS network, also a Viacom subsidiary.

2. They distribute programming. That is what a network does. Most viewers watch network shows from broad-based ones like CBS and NBC and Fox – all broadcast and delivered by cable and satellite directly to the home – to small cable and satellite-only ones like CNN, the Discovery Channel, the Food network, the Golf network and the Home and Garden network – worth more than a hundred others. Here the economies of scale work to spread the cost invested in production across as many presentation venues as possible. That is, if a show like *CSI* costs $1.5 million to make a single episode, if shown on 220 owned or affiliated CBS stations then the cost per station becomes manageable. This has been a key concept in US television – networking. Here is where the power rests and so most major producers also own a channel (or series of channels) to guarantee the savings accumulated from economies of scale.

3. Finally, broadcast stations, cable systems and satellite to home services present scheduled programmes from which viewers can choose. Here, because of legal reasons and technological constraints, there is a limited number of channels from which to choose. A broadcast station must have a licence issued by the Federal Communications Commission. A cable system must be granted a franchise by local government in the same manner as the local entity grants rights of ways for water delivery, phone service or electricity. Because of limited satellite spacing options, there exist but two satellite to home services in 2004: Rupert Murdoch's News Corporation's DirecTV, and the smaller Echostar service. Cable may have been subscribed to by 85 per cent of households in the US in 2004, but most of what people watched came from NBC, CBS, ABC or Fox. Finally, it was possible for consumers to buy copies of movies and older TV series on VHS video or DVD.

Organised this way, the television business has long been one of the most profitable in the US, and one that commands vast sums of attention of the peoples of the US – about six hours per day on average. Thus the monies paid for access (broadcasting alone is free if one lives within sixty miles of the station's transmitter tower) and advertising far exceed the costs, and generate profit in the millions, if not billions of dollars per year.

Thus, while the industry seems to have many players, the four major television networks – Disney's ABC, General Electric's NBC, Viacom's CBS and News Corporation's Fox – in 2004 accounted for more than half of prime-time television viewing. They were the dominant businesses in the TV industries and thus the most powerful forces in TV economics.

Almost as powerful and certainly as profitable were the holders of many local cable franchises. In 2004 that was Comcast (one-third of the households in the US) and Time Warner (one-sixth). With their ownership of networks – such as Time Warner's ownership of CNN – they dominated cable networks as well. Indeed, in the spring of 2004 Comcast tried to buy Disney to gain access and control of the ABC network and the popular and profitable sports cable networks called ESPN.

Finally, News Corporation's DirecTV dominated satellite to home transmission. The corporation, better known for its Fox network, really was a world power in satellite to home service, and used its 20th Century-Fox studio to generate programming shown around the world via satellite.

The production, distribution and presentation of broadcast television and radio, and home video and cable television requires substantial investment and frequently generates vast profits. When, in early 2004, Comcast bid to purchase Disney, the offer exceeded $50 billion, and made headlines around the world. Cable TV operations form the core of the $19 billion revenues per year of the Time Warner media empire. General Electric's NBC and Microsoft spend billions of dollars to create the twenty-four-hour news operation, MSNBC. Both GE and Microsoft represented, in the early twenty-first century, two of the five largest companies in any business in the US.

These, and past and future examples, tell us that, while TV seems to the viewer a cornucopia of pleasure production, the television industries to Wall Street certainly represent a set of profitable businesses, with entrepreneurs looking to make and indeed making fortunes.

Television economics can best be studied by looking at its structure and conduct. First, scholars analyse the basic structure of a set of profit-maximising firms. Who are they? How big are they? Do some dominate? Second, since the structure directly influences the corporation's conduct or behaviour, scholars then ask: how do firms set prices? How do they decide to distribute what they sell?

First, we begin by asking about media ownership: who owned the largest stake in the television industries in the US as the twenty-first century commenced? Here diversified companies dominated, as can be surmised from above: General Electric's NBC, Disney ABC, Viacom's CBS, News Corporation's Fox network and satellite business, Time Warner's cable business and Comcast's cable businesses. Thus, we have a classic oligopoly – a few corporations dominating the TV industries, and thus setting up barriers to entry to potential new competitors. It costs so much to mount a new network or service that, as Rupert Murdoch showed, it is easier to buy and assemble the parts of a diversified media empire than start one from scratch.

At the core of the structure of the television industries in the US in 2004 were powerful and influential media conglomerates. Gone are the separate industries of film, TV and cable. The prototype is now to have as many of these businesses under one corporate umbrella as possible. For example, media conglomerate Time Warner covers all bases.

In cable television, it not only has the second highest number of subscribers, but is also owner of WTBS-The Superstation, TNT, CNN, Black Entertainment Television, HBO and Cinemax. Warner Bros. is one of Hollywood's major studios, both for its profitable motion pictures and plethora of television series. It has kept spreading its umbrella and in 2000 it merged with the Internet's AOL, but within three years failed to fit the Internet into the core TV industry. How the Internet will take a place within or alongside the TV industries in the future remains an unanswered question.

Once we have established the basic oligopolistic structure of an industry, we ought to look at how companies behave in the marketplace. For the television industry in the US it is best to recognise two distinct classes of revenue collection:

Direct payment: People pay directly for access to cable and satellite TV, and to purchase VHS or DVD copies.

Indirect payment: On the other hand over-the-air television is full of advertising. Indeed, so-called premium channels, like HBO, cost extra to subscribe to because they do not have advertising. In 2004 it was still advertising that created the bulk of the revenues. Billions of dollars per year were paid by third parties just to buy the time in thirty-second hunks to hawk their wares or services.

With these two sources of revenues, and networking and re-running to cut programme costs, profits are considerable for the dominant owners. But there is a degree of competition as all seek to gain the largest share of the audience that advertisers desire, or simply to have more subscribers with access to cable or satellite delivery, and then to continually encourage them to pay more for premium channels.

In an oligopoly, the essence of the conduct is that the number of firms is small enough that all can be cognisant of the conduct of their rivals and react accordingly. Take the case of the major television networks. When NBC offers a new comedy at a particular time of a particular day, its rivals, ABC, Fox and CBS, counter-programme. This does lead to some experimentation, but all too often also to a numbing sameness where similar programmes face off against each other, whether news, soap operas or situation comedies.

To make the most possible money as a group, oligopolists ought to – for some matters at least – co-operate, and they do. They work together to fashion positive governmental policies towards their industry, and thus to keep out potential competitors. Nothing unites a media oligopoly more than a threat from the outside. Simply put, oligopolists tend to seek and agree upon an informal set of rules for 'competition'. This translates into seeking government rules to help them preserve their position as a member of the oligopoly – and keep outsiders out.

Will this oligopolistic structure and conduct last? I think it will. The Internet has made little impact as of 2004, as the AOL–Time Warner failed merger illustrated so well. The 1996 Communications Act favoured the oligopolists and, unless those rules are amended, only some radical new technology can lead to change. But often even that does not. For example, a quarter-century ago the widespread adoption of cable TV promised greater competition and a greater choice of TV services. The broadcast network oligopoly expanded but the bottleneck of a few networks has continued.

Better images through digital television might offer some hope of breaking the oligopolistic deadlock in the TV industry. But as the 20th century ended and these sharper pictures came to the home, it certainly looked as though they would be supplied by existing enterprises. DirecTV led the way, although by 2004 few citizens of the US had purchased the digital receiver needed to actually see the superior pictures.

Thus, let me end by isolating three economic principles that will drive and unite the TV industries in the US well into the twenty-first century.

1. Diversification will remain important as media conglomerates continue to hedge regarding the ever changing marketplace by establishing subsidiaries operating in all and every media market. Diversification into all media segments spreads the risk. Single-line media companies will become rarer and rarer. For example, in the US, in 2004, there existed only one channel among the hundred or so on cable or satellite delivery that was independent of a major media conglomerate – the Weather Channel. Media conglomerates, led by Viacom, News Corporation, General Electric and Time Warner, can take a loss in one business as they reap profits from other company activities. New companies will find it harder and harder to enter the business.

2. There will continue to be economies of scale. That is, do not look for the networks to disappear. The optimal market for selling a product is the entire planet. Once the costs of initial product (usually high) are sunk, the marginal cost of selling an additional item is small. Hence as one expanded the market, one could extract enormous profits. The major companies will seek to dominate US and world distribution.

3. Finally, there will continue to be vertical integration. The major companies will seek to own significant stakes in production, distribution and presentation. Two motivations are common to all forms of vertical integration. First, media businesses desire to reduce costs of sales. The vertically integrated corporation literally sells to itself, and thus does not need a large sales staff or vast accounting depart-

ments. But a more important motivation is market access. A vertically integrated firm need not worry about being shut out of any key market – anywhere in the world.

Douglas Gomery

RECOMMENDED READING

Compaine, Benjamin and Gomery, Douglas (2000), *Who Owns the Media?*, Mahwah, NJ: Erlbaum.

Parsons, Patrick R. and Frieden, Robert M. (1998), *The Cable and Satellite Television Industries*, New York: Allyn & Bacon.

Walker, James and Ferguson, Douglas (1998), *The Broadcast Television Industry*, New York: Allyn & Bacon.

Sponsorship and the Funding of Television – UK

When the original statutory documents regulating British broadcasting were being drafted – first in 1922 and then again in 1926 – there was concern at the commercialised and deregulated character of radio in the US, and a consequent determination to isolate broadcasting from the influence of advertisers, especially in the form of sponsorship. The view that sponsorship would determine which programmes were made, and that this was a bad thing, continued to shape successive reports, white papers and broadcasting acts until 1990.

Ever since the mid-1960s, when sponsorship of sporting events, and later art and cultural events, began to grow, there have been plenty of programmes featuring the visible presence of sponsors' banners, with the sponsorship revenue going to the event promoter rather than the broadcaster. Minor sports, seeing television as the key to obtaining sponsorship, were prepared to sell television rights at bargain prices. Some events supported by sponsorship took to offering ready-made coverage at cost or less than cost, to secure television exposure for the sponsor. In the cultural sphere, award ceremonies with title sponsors began to proliferate – with the Man Booker Prize and the Whitbread Prize merely the best known of a growing pack.

For much of this time, the BBC has been in slow retreat in its attempts to marginalise the presence of sponsors' names. Major sports like football were too important as elements in BBC–ITV competition to be dictated to by broadcasters. The BBC was ultimately unsuccessful in attempting to keep sponsors' names out of the heart-of-the-action, meeting their Waterloo in 1983, when they were forced to allow sponsors' logos on footballers' shirts. The growing visibility of sponsors' names from this point on made the restrictions on programme sponsorship appear hypocritical to some.

ITV CHANGES THE RULES

During the 1980s the Thatcherite transformation of the political landscape began to have its impact on broadcasting policy. Deregulation, privatisation and enterprise became prominent themes, underpinning the plans for satellite television, the auctioning of ITV franchises and the replacement of the IBA by the new 'lighter touch' ITC. Channel Four had already had a major impact in enabling the establishment of a thriving independent production sector; and attention turned to means of financing the envisaged expansion of broadcast hours, channels and platforms that has characterised the last decade.

In April 1989 the IBA informed ITV contractors of a relaxation in its sponsorship code. The first sponsorship after this ruling was Powergen's sponsorship of the weather forecast (Dyja, 1991, p. 57). Under the 1991 ITV Code, all categories of programmes apart from news, current affairs and religious broadcasts could now be sponsored (Longdon, 1992, p. 43).

After the introduction of sponsorship on ITV, the new source of revenue grew rapidly. The £5 million revenues of 1990 grew to £50 million by 1995 (MAPS, 1995). By 2001, television sponsorship was still growing at around 30 per cent a year. *Big Brother 1* obtained around £300,000 in sponsorship from Southern Comfort. *Big Brother 2* got nearer £5 million from BT Cellnet. But, the *Observer* suggested, few in the industry expected it to overtake traditional advertising and it then represented only 3 per cent of Carlton's income (*Observer*, 2001). Although some had argued for sponsorship as a way of funding programmes that might otherwise not be made, experience suggests that sponsorship goes predomi-

Big Brother

nantly to popular programming – *Coronation Street* and major football tournaments were among the early beneficiaries.

Concerns grew that the 'break bumpers' were simply extra advertisements which, of course, is exactly what they are. An update to the ITC Code of Programme Sponsorship, published in October 2000, attempted to preserve a distinction between sponsorship and advertising by asserting that a key principle of the Code was the distinction between sponsor credits and advertising. The Code aimed to ensure that credits were not used to extend the time allowed for advertising. They sought to prevent sponsor credits being used for 'the type of selling propositions that should be confined to advertisements, and further to ensure that credits achieve their primary objective of creating an association between the sponsor and the programme being sponsored' (ITC, 2000).

The ITC also hoped that the Code would ensure that sponsors did not influence the content or scheduling of programmes in such a way as to affect the editorial independence and responsibility of the broadcaster. However, as sponsorship grows as a form of revenue, it has clear potential to influence the types of programmes that are planned, simply by its availability or non-availability.

BBC REMAINS ALOOF?

Sponsorship of programmes remained barred on the BBC, but of course the BBC continued to broadcast events (both sport and non-sport) that had sponsorship. The changed conditions for ITV focused attention on some of the BBC's practices. For example, in 1990 Lloyds Bank agreed to sponsor the BBC's Young Musician of the Year, an event felt by some to have infringed the BBC guidelines since it was not an outside event but one specially created by the BBC (Dyja, 1991).

Ironically, in 2000, in its response to the White Paper, *A New Future for Communications*, the BBC noted that 'the public interest requires clearly defined restrictions on programme sponsorship on commercial television and radio, to prevent a blurring between the editorial content of a programme and any commercial promotion associated with it'.

When Ofcom was established, it was proposed that the BBC should be under an obligation to comply with the programme standards codes issued by Ofcom with the exception of accuracy and impartiality, which would continue to be regulated solely by the BBC governors, and advertising and sponsorship, seen as not relevant to the BBC.

The debate leading to the renewal of the BBC's Charter raises issues of how the BBC might be financed, but many favour the retention of the licence fee, and resistance to the introduction of other forms of revenue. For example, the Creators' Rights Alliance (which brings together sixteen major organisations representing over 85,000 copyright creators and content providers throughout the media) examined the alternatives to the licence fee (selling off bits of the BBC, advertising, sponsorship, subscription, state funding, different methods of taxation) and said that 'we strongly believe that the licence fee is the only viable way to fund the BBC' (Creators' Rights Alliance, 2004).

The Creators' Rights Alliance offered a textbook defence of the principle of 'an independent public broadcaster that is able to deliver free-to-air, high quality programmes across all broadcast media, that has creative and cultural values at its heart and that is rigorous in its defence of democracy and freedom from interference by government' (Creators' Rights Alliance, 2004).

SPONSORSHIP ROUTINISED

On ITV, meanwhile, sponsorship has become routinised and commonplace. Granada's total sponsorship revenue in 2002 was £19 million. The expansion of new media began to offer means of enhanced exposure for sponsors. ITV secured a £3 million sponsorship deal with Travelex, the foreign exchange specialist, for exclusive sponsorship of the football World Cup. The deal included sponsorship of all TV coverage, ITV's World Cup website and branding on all ITV's World Cup marketing. Also in 2002, Walkers Snacks became a sponsor of ITV's children's programme *SM:TV*, Coca-Cola continued its sponsorship of the Premier League, and Cadbury's extended its

sponsorship of *Coronation Street*. The new genre of consumption-oriented property transformation shows proved to be magnets for sponsors with sponsorship of *Better Homes* by Direct Line and *Home on Their Own* by Vanish.

Early sponsorships such as Powergen's sponsoring of the weather forecast did not necessarily have strong links between programme content, or target audience, and sponsor. However, increasingly, sponsors have sought programmes and audiences that play a co-ordinated role in marketing strategy. The soft drink Tizer had become stuck with an 'old-fashioned' image but in 1999 its £500,000 one-year sponsorship of ITV1's Saturday morning pop music programme *cd:UK* transformed its fortunes, making it cool with the sixteen to twenty-four age group. Like advertising in general, sponsorship is drawn to particular demographics, a trend that has already appeared to have an impact on Channel Four's programme strategies. Some minorities have more commercial value than others.

Garry Whannel

RECOMMENDED READING

Dyja, Eddie (1991), *BFI Film and Television Handbook* (London: BFI, 1991), p. 57.

Sturgess, Brian, 'Television Sponsorship', in Tim Congdon (ed.), *Paying for Broadcasting, the Handbook* (London: Routledge, 1992), p. 43.

Coronation Street

SPORTS SPONSORSHIP

Sports sponsorship has demonstrated, over four decades, means by which sponsorship of events can provide added value. The now ubiquitous post-event interviews, invariably shot with a backdrop of sponsors' logos, are there not to enlighten viewers, but to increase the amount of brand-name exposure. The introduction of sponsorship of television programmes has interesting implications for an event, such as a sporting competition already gaining sponsorship in its own right. Advertisers can now choose to sponsor the television coverage rather than the event – good news for commercial

Lance Armstrong, Tour de France 2002

television, but bad news for sport. For television, sponsored break bumpers can be used as a means of carrying an audience through advertising breaks, by use of questions and answers, or running jokes.

In 2002, ITV and retailer Halfords signed a sponsorship deal for ITV's coverage of the *Tour de France 2002*. Halfords is a leading retailer of car parts and accessories and, more significantly for this sponsorship, bicycles. Cycling has never been a major sport in the UK and obtained little television coverage until the 1980s when Channel Four introduced a series of city centre sprints. They followed this up with daily coverage of the Tour de France, and during the 1990s the coverage won both viewers and acclaim. For 2002, the event, now broadcast by ITV, was scheduled for more than fifty-two hours of live coverage and highlights for three weeks in July.

The deal, negotiated by Carlton Digital Sales and Mindshareworld, involves specially produced five-second sponsorship credits book-ending all *Tour de France 2002* programming on ITV1 and ITV2 and five-second break bumpers leading into and out of the advertising breaks. One significant feature of such sponsorships is the way in which mutual and self-promotion is mobilised in press releases and launches, instore promotions, press coverage and programme publicity. ITV and Halfords were happy to take the opportunity to blow each other's trumpets. Brian Barwick, ITV Controller of Sport, commented, 'This important sponsorship deal is an ideal partnership for both ITV and Halfords, a name synonymous with cycling in the UK, (ITV, 2002). A Halfords Development Manager, reciprocated that

> We are proud to be associated with ITV1 and ITV2's coverage of the Tour De France, and to help bring it to the thousands of cycling enthusiasts who follow the event. As the most important event in the cycling calendar, it makes sense for the largest name in UK cycling to sponsor the coverage. (ITV, 2002)

Garry Whannel

The Funding of Television – US

The manner in which a television system is funded largely depends on its historical relationship with the state and whether or not broadcasting has been envisioned as a public or private entity. It is also a result of they way that broadcasting's perceived relationship to the economy, culture, politics and national identity was understood at the time that it first became institutionalised. In general, there are three primary models of systems that have developed over time – commercial, public service and state-run. With increased convergence and globalisation, however, public and commercial hybrids are becoming increasingly common.

The system that exists in the US is obviously commercial and has been since the early years of radio broadcasting. During the 1920s, alternative funding structures for radio were discussed, with many organisations and individuals backing a mixed system that would allow a range of stations to exist, including governmental, commercial and amateur. It was often argued that, although a system run by the government alone could be problematic, an organisational structure that allowed for an element of public control and participation would be a healthier structure than that of a commercial system. Others argued that a commercial system was an inherently American system. As Susan Smulyan points out, 'Support of broadcast advertising was treated almost as a matter of patriotic pride, while broadcast advertising itself was made to appear as a natural extension of a capitalist economy' (Smulyan, p. 77). Despite the fact that vigorous debates on these issues were still ongoing, the Radio Act of 1927 along with the act that followed in 1934, succeeded in legitimating an already developing private system supported by advertising and regulated by the government. The act, however, contained a caveat that required broadcasters to serve 'the public interest, convenience, and necessity' in exchange for their use of the airwaves, which were viewed as a public resource. Interpreting how this clause, which was similar to ones in acts regarding public utilities, applies to commercial broadcasting would prove to be a vague and often thorny process throughout the history of broadcasting. Although it was intended as a way to rein in the worst capitalist tendencies of advertisers and broadcasters, the public interest requirement was so vague (some would interpret it as what the public is interested in watching) that it had little bite. Instead, commercial and programming excesses were most often restrained by advertisers themselves, who feared alienating or offending audiences.

Although the government was charged with protecting the public interest, it also enabled a small number of corporations to invest heavily in broadcasting, squelch much of their competition and eventually form an oligopoly. In network radio, sponsors hired advertising agencies to produce programmes for them, which meant that commercial messages would eventually become part and parcel of the programme text. At first, indirect advertising techniques were considered more tasteful than direct advertising, so many programmes promoted the name of their sponsors in more subtle ways. A common way to do this would be to label an act or programme with a name that includes the name of the sponsor's product (A&P Gypsies or the *Eveready Hour*). During radio's 'Golden Age', however, more and more direct advertising appeared; advertisers would either incorporate product plugs into the narrative or push them directly during breaks and at the beginning and end of a programme. This would continue to be the case early in the history of television, at least until a different system of exchange developed in the mid- to late 1950s. Magazine style or participation advertising came into use,

allowing the networks to have more creative control and to disperse advertising investment and risk among multiple sponsors. Now networks would hire production companies to produce a programme and then they would sell advertising around it. This type of advertising still predominates in US television, as networks and stations sell thirty- to sixty-second spots on either a local or national level. While networks can make additional income from programmes that they've invested in and local affiliates can also profit from network compensation, it is advertising that makes the system run. What this means, then, is that US broadcast television, more than anything else, is in the business of selling audiences to advertisers. The implication of this for programming is something that continues to be discussed and debated.

Advertising is a large part of cable television's funding story as well. However, cable networks have an additional profit-making mechanism – subscription fees. Basic cable channels, such as MTV, CNN and ESPN, charge local cable system operators between 5 and 10 cents per subscriber per month for the right to carry their service. Premium or pay channels like HBO and Showtime sell no advertising whatsoever and instead charge viewers relatively high fees for monthly access to their programming. In exchange for such a high cost, these channels offer uninterrupted programming that is difficult to find anywhere else on cable or broadcast. Sometimes this means providing viewers with controversial or uncensored content and at others it may mean offering limited-access programmes, such as boxing events or early television runs of Hollywood films.

The mandate of public service broadcasting differs greatly from that of commercial broadcasting. While commercial broadcasters seek to attract audiences and please advertisers, public service broadcasters are expected to provide uplifting and educational programming, serve minority audiences with diverse tastes and screen shows that display or explore national cultures. Michele Hilmes argues that the public service model proliferated around the globe not only out of a sense of nationalism but also out of a particular disdain for the crass commercialism of the US system: 'From the beginning, as the nations of the world constructed their radio broadcasting systems, they did so with one eye cast over their shoulder, worried about keeping American influences – notably advertising – firmly out of their cultural and economic space' (Hilmes, 2002, p. 368).

The British Broadcasting Corporation provides *the* model for public service broadcasting. At first, it looked somewhat similar to the way broadcasting was developing in the US at the time. As a patent pool of private companies, the BBC (then called the British Broadcasting Company), during the 1920s, had a government-sanctioned monopoly on programming and the building of stations (much like RCA). However, by 1927 concerns over the effects of commercialism and pri-

MADISON AVENUE

Madison Avenue, a broad boulevard in New York City running parallel to the more famous Fifth Avenue, is home to the biggest and most powerful advertising agencies in the US. To TV professionals it is the centre of the advertising business. And the television industry relies on millions of dollars from advertisers to make its programmes possible.

In the TV world of the twenty-first century, Madison Avenue struggled to validate the effects of TV advertising. Advertisers wanted not only to deliver a message to consumers, but also to persuade them to actually go and buy the products or services. With new media available, Madison Avenue professionals were constantly rethinking the role of advertising and TV, how best to use TV, acting as agencies (for their corporate clients), planning and buying TV time.

With so many new channels, the debate centred on the prospects for a new form of measurement for ratings. Nielsen new portable people meter technology simultaneously measures multiple forms of media use. In 2004, Nielsen had been testing the device's ability to simultaneously measure TV use, coupled with use of the Internet and, for the first time, counting out-of-home usage, for example, in public spaces such as airports.

Nielsen, the generators of the data upon which Madison Avenue bases its advertising plans, also sought to integrate portable people meters (devices used by Nielsen in the home to indicate who is in the room when the television is on) with consumer product-usage scanner panels. Madison pros want to encode TV commercials so that advertisers can finally track the progress from ad to purchase.

The politics surrounding the deployment of the portable people meter are twofold: first, because major TV companies have been reluctant to shift the way their audiences are measured (and consequently how they are bought and sold); and,

second, because the TV networks historically have underwritten the primary cost of media measurement.

While agencies have been exploring ways of developing surrogate measures of attentiveness, the industry still lacked, in 2004, a standard approach. Some Madison Avenue agencies developing such customer research are using unconventional syndicated data, such as Marketing Evaluations Inc.'s TV Q scores, as a proxy for viewer involvement, or attentiveness. This survey seeks to measure star power, attentiveness to the show and, thus, the ability to make the audience stick around to see the ads.

The development of standardised measures of advertising persuasiveness will be difficult, especially since it blurs the role of advertising messages and the responsibility of TV programmers. Some Madison Avenue agencies have been using techniques developed for measuring the impact of ad messages prior to their airing. This 'copy-testing' then gives Madison Avenue the ability to argue that TV is the best vehicle of persuasion – far better than print or even the Internet.

The lack of good testing has contributed to a bias within agencies towards a greater reliance on TV ads and at media agencies towards heavier weighting towards TV ad spending. So, for example, it would be typical for a Madison Avenue shop to budget only 8 or 9 GRPs (gross rating points) per week for a magazine ad campaign as compared to a minimum of 50 GRPs per week for a typical TV ad campaign. This is what advertisers ultimately buy, the size of the audience, so Madison Avenue loves the Super Bowl, TV's most popular programme of the year.

Thus, with all the changes – and more in the future with TiVo and other digital devices – TV is still king on Madison Avenue.

Douglas Gomery

---

vate interests led the BBC to be transformed into a publicly owned, non-profit corporation that would answer to a board of governors who were charged by the state to look after the public and national interests. Not allowed to accept any form of advertising, broadcasting in the UK was to be funded by listener-paid licence fees to the government, thereby preventing commercial interests from dictating programming decisions. These basic tenets of the BBC system would remain in place as the corporation moved into television during the post-war era. The values inherent in the BBC Charter have resulted in regional and national programming intended to appeal to diverse segments of the population. The BBC currently has ten radio channels, four broadcast television channels and an additional four digital-only television channels.

More recently, the corporation has ventured into international commercial services, such as the advertising-supported cable channel BBC America, but profits are kept separate from its domestic public services and are used to 'keep the licence fee low' while improving programme offerings.

The last broadcasting system is the state-run model. Although it shares some similarities with public service broadcasting, its connection to the interests of the state is much more manifest. Strictly controlled and organised by the government, television in countries such as China and the USSR used to consist only of state-approved content. This type of system, however, is becoming increasingly rare as many countries have introduced some form of commercial broadcasting into their midst. Satellite services such as Sky have entered nations formerly closed off from much Western programming and its impact has been wide-ranging and complex. In particular, the link between public service broadcasting and the preservation of national identity is shifting as commercial broadcasting works to be local as it simultaneously exists as global. It seems as though, while many countries have instituted limits on imported programming in order to preserve and strengthen national production, they are still finding it more and more difficult to stave off commercial interests altogether.

Susan Murray

RECOMMENDED READING

Corner, John (1991), *Popular Television in Britain: Studies in Cultural History*, New York: BFI.

Hilmes, Michele (2002), *Only Connect: A Cultural History of Broadcasting*, Belmont, CA: Wadsworth Publishing.

McChesney, Robert W. (1994), *Telecommunication, Mass Media, and Democracy: The Battle for Control of U.S. Broadcasting, 1928–1935*, New York: Oxford University Press.

Streeter, Thomas (1996), *Selling the Air: A Critique of the Policy of Commercial Broadcasting in the United States*, Chicago, IL: University of Chicago Press.

TV Moguls and Executives

Four men dominated the television industry in the US during the early days of the twenty-first century. They represent the four major networks: (Fox's Rupert Murdoch, ABC Disney's Michael Eisner, the unknown Sumner Redstone of CBS and NBC's Robert Wright. They divide into two groups: those who own their networks – Murdoch and Redstone – and those who simply manage it. They were not the only moguls but it was they who exercised the most power.

RUPERT MURDOCH

In 1985 the billionaire Australian-born press lord began to fashion a US-based corporate mass media colossus. At the heart of his empire-building was the establishment of a fourth over-the-air television network – Fox. By the mid-1990s Murdoch had established Fox as a contending TV network, and had remade his media empire from one centred in newspapers and magazines to an electronic-oriented corporation positioned at the very heart of the upcoming information and entertainment superhighway.

In 1985 Rupert Murdoch began a serious quest to create a fourth television network. But he did not initially move directly into the television industry in the United States, but rather into television's source of programming, Hollywood. In March of that year Murdoch agreed to buy half of 20th Century-Fox, the movie and television production studio, from Denver oilman, Marvin Davis. Murdoch's closely held News Corporation Ltd paid $250 million for half of 20th Century-Fox's parent company, then fully owned by Marvin Davis. This proved the first step in Murdoch's advance into television in the US.

Murdoch's next step was to acquire a core of television stations in the largest cities in the United States. For more than $1 billion, News Inc., Murdoch's parent corporation, purchased the six Metromedia independent television stations, then not affiliated with any network. The six (one per market) are located in New York City (the largest television market in the United States), Los Angeles (the second largest), Chicago (third largest), Washington, DC (eighth), Dallas (ninth) and Houston (tenth). In toto, nearly one in five homes with television sets in the United States could tune into one of these stations, providing the largest reach for any set of stations outside of those owned by ABC, CBS and NBC.

By the late 1980s, having acquired the remaining half of 20th Century-Fox studio, Rupert Murdoch stood ready to launch his new TV network. A fourth television network had become possible because the Federal Communications Commission had, during the 1980s, placed a plethora of new TV stations on the air around the US. Now that Murdoch owned a major Hollywood studio and an important set of television stations, his first move was to place Barry Diller in charge of his new empire, which he had renamed Fox Inc. Diller had the perfect background to run the new film and television empire. He knew how the major networks operated; at ABC TV in the 1970s Diller had pioneered the successful made-for-television 'Movie of the Week' series. He also knew Hollywood. At the Paramount Pictures Hollywood studio factory during the late 1970s and early 1980s Diller had created a consistent string of box-office successes.

Murdoch and Diller initially hit it off and began to work closely together. The first attempts, in particular *9 to 5*, failed badly, as did a game show/beauty contest entry, *Dream Girl, U.S.A.*, and the much heralded late-night entry, *The Joan Rivers Show*. But from a base of Sunday-night programming only, the Fox network added more nights and developed hits like *Married … with Children, America's Most Wanted, Beverly Hills 90210* and *Melrose Place*. In 1993 the Fox network began, on a limited basis, telecasting seven nights a week.

But the key breakthrough show came with *The Simpsons*, which premiered in January 1990. Soon *The Simpsons* had become not only the new Fox television network's first top-rated series, but also the initial popular culture fad of the 1990s. By 1992 Fox's television network was making money.

But we ought not to think that this new network represented Murdoch's sole thrust into television. Fox's production of television programmes for the other three television networks was thriving (including *LA Law*), and its television 'evergreens', such as *M*A*S*H*, were making millions of dollars in TV syndication. Fox's *A Current Affair* was hated by critics but drew such good ratings and cost so little that it drew millions more into Fox's bottom line.

As Fox approached the twenty-first century, it represented the optimum globalised mass media operation. The term 'movie studio' no longer adequately described its power and influence and multiplicity of activities. Murdoch had to make one significant change in the way he did business, moving his base (and citizenship) to the United States in general, to Hollywood in particular. The Communications Act of 1934 requires the owner of a United States television station to be a United States citizen.

In 1994 he outbid CBS for the rights to National Football League games, a contract that CBS had had for nearly four decades. In a remarkably short period of time the Fox television network, and its allied media investments, have made Rupert Murdoch one of the most powerful and most important persons in the creation of mass popular culture. This achievement ranks with the creation of NBC, CBS and ABC, all of which required far more time to reach the status Fox did in only half a dozen years.

SUMNER REDSTONE

Sumner Redstone represents one of the least known and most powerful media moguls of the late 20th century. In his capacity as dominant owner and chief executive officer of Viacom Inc., Redstone lords over Hollywood's Paramount Pictures television and motion picture factory, a handful of cable TV networks, including MTV and VH1, and a vast array of cable franchises. He has a CEO who runs things out front – Mel

Sumner Redstone

Karmizan – but it is Redstone who owns the majority of the company and has the final say. As chief of Viacom, Redstone oversees the company that owns many popular cable TV channels, including MTV, the Movie Channel, Showtime and Nickelodeon, the world's largest producer of children's programming. Viacom also owns several cable TV systems, some radio and TV stations, and a production and syndication business that has the lucrative syndication rights to mega-hit TV series such as *Roseanne* and *The Cosby Show*.

The takeover of Viacom was not easy. Viacom had survived an earlier takeover attempt by financier Carl Icahn. When Viacom executives attempted to buy their own company, Redstone became embroiled in a bitter, six-month takeover war that forced him to raise his offer three times. Redstone even brushed off investment bankers and did much of the negotiating himself. He bought into Viacom to share in the success of other entertainment companies, realising the only way to enter new segments of the TV industry was through investing in other companies. Rather than break up Viacom and spin properties, as many bankers expected, he built Viacom into one of the world's top TV corporations.

By the mid-1990s MTV, for example, had expanded far beyond its original base in the US and was reaching more than 200 million households in some eighty countries. Under Redstone, Viacom took MTV to Europe, Latin America, Australia and Russia. In the autumn of 1991, the MTV network formed a joint venture with an Asian satellite company to beam MTV into Hong Kong, China, Korea and Taiwan.

He was an acquirer. In 1993 he bought Paramount. As television reached the era of multiple networks, more than NBC or CBS, Viacom stood at the intersection of technological, economic, political, social and cultural change and desired to be at the forefront of the information and entertainment revolution promised for the twenty-first century.

MICHAEL EISNER

Since 1984, Michael Eisner has made Disney a success; the same cannot be said for his record running ABC. But keep things in perspective. Eisner hardly started from a base of zero or with an altogether new enterprise. He took a company which was under-performing and began to fully exploit its rich assets during one of the greatest peacetime economic expansions on record. Eisner brought a rich base of experience to Disney, but after twenty years was under attack to do even better. Eisner expanded efforts to make the Disney Channel a pay cable TV power. With a seemingly infinite set of cross-promotional exploitation, by 1990, with 5 million subscribers (of some 60 million possible cable households), the Disney Channel began to make money. It was from this base that Eisner bought ABC, but by the beginning of the twenty-first

Michael Eisner

century was unable to achieve synergy with his studio. Yet in just less than a decade of owning ABC he was never able to make it the power it had been in the 1980s. He was fired in 2005.

ROBERT C. WRIGHT

Robert C. Wright succeeded legendary Grant Tinker as president of NBC when NBC was acquired by General Electric. A law graduate, Wright had entered the GE corporate ladder as a staff attorney but quickly moved to the decision-making side, first through plastic sales (1978–80), then into housewares and audio equipment (1983–4) and in 1984 to the presidency of GE Financial Services. Wright caught the eye of Jack Welch, the creator of the modern General Electric corporate colossus and soon became a Welch protégé. Before heading NBC, Wright's experience in television was limited to a three-year break from GE to be executive vice-president of Cox Communications' cable operations (1980–3). In appointing Wright to network work, president GE boss Jack Welch looked to Wright to increase NBC's bottom-line operating profit. Wright did not disappoint, cutting the budget by $200 million and staff by 25 per cent, while keeping revenues increasing so profits rose rapidly. He took NBC into deals with cable TV, most notably the cable financial-talk channel CNBC.

He was a GE lifer. Like mentor Jack Welch, Robert Wright came from a Catholic household (from suburban Long Island), the son of an engineer, so Wright could talk engineer Welch's language. Like Welch, Wright had not gone to an Ivy League college and was devoted to GE for a whole career.

Neither watched much television and worked as 'type A' personalities.

But to GE, NBC is a highly profitable but small division of a major manufacturer based in the United States. And though Robert Wright's corporate strategy was to start with cable, by 2003 he had purchased Universal Studios, vertically integrating to match his rivals above.

All these moguls are white men, well educated with considerable business skills. They operate just like moguls in other industries. There are many other moguls but they lack the power of the four above. Cable TV has Brian Roberts of Comcast and Richard Parsons of Time Warner. Murdoch took over DirecTV in 2004. And all are heads of major studios so they issue the bulk of what the public buys in video and DVD. The lone exception is Japan's Sony, owned from Tokyo, but run and managed in Los Angeles.

While much has been made of diversity in the media moguldum, only Richard Parsons is a man of colour. And there is not a woman among them. This is typical of US business. We can see this in the autobiographies of Redstone and Eisner, testimonies to their ego, power and drive. They would do well in any industry, but have the aptitude to see how the television system works, and how they can dominate it. They all believe in owning a studio and a TV network. They all believe in vertically integrating. They all dabble in cable, but cast their major chips in the major networks. They all represent the trends of the workings of the television business of the beginning of the twenty-first century.

Douglas Gomery

RECOMMENDED READING

Eisner, Michael (1998), *Work in Progress*, New York: Random House.
Redstone, Sumner (2001), *A Passion to Win*, New York: Simon and Schuster.

Pay-per-view Programming

Historically, TV has tended to be advertiser-funded. This has meant that companies have bought air-time and have screened filmed commercial messages in timed slots within the broadcast entertainment content, giving rise to the ubiquitous commercial break. In the UK a government-controlled licence fee has funded a large part of the TV sector but the launch of the ITV network also saw the appearance of advertiser-funded networks and programming. Given the amount of regulation surrounding TV broadcasting and the limited worthwhile slots available, it is no surprise that TV advertising has grown into a major industry. It is clear, however, that there is only so much advertising money and so many worthwhile advertising slots in each territory. This has meant that the amount of revenue raised from advertising has been largely finite. Almost from their inception, TV companies rapidly began to explore ways of increasing the average revenue from each viewer. A possible solution to this has been to offer pay-per-view TV (PPV TV).

Pay-per-view TV is a system whereby viewers pay extra one-off fees to access special or premium content, such as a major sports event. This is different to pay TV, which is a term that is used to describe subscription-based services, usually bundles of channels. This said, the two do have distinct bearings on each other. On pay TV an event is shown at a set time only and in this respect is different to video-on-demand (VOD) where a viewer watches the content when they want. The theory is that, if extra special premium content is offered as a special one-off event, then viewers will pay an extra amount to watch it. In fact, it is clear that viewers will subscribe to a TV service for entertainment but will also pay to go to a football match, make a trip to the cinema to see a film or watch a video. As the rise of the video store in the 1980s proved, people would not only pay for extra content, they would also travel to get it. So, the logic goes, if a TV company could deliver the content directly to your TV set without you having to leave the house, then it should be even more popular than the video-store experience.

Early and very primitive PPV TV services were trialled as far back as the 1950s in the US, but it was in the 1970s with the rise of cable TV that the PPV TV concept finally became a viable consumer proposition, particularly in the US. The expansion of cable networks there meant that there was a significant rise in infrastructure costs. The hope was that advertising revenue from the extra channels that could be offered would help to recover the expensive infrastructure costs. However, as the number of ad slots increased, their value diminished. Even so, PPV TV became a commercially attractive proposition and in the US the size of the network TV market peaked in 1986. At that time, competition from cable TV, PPV TV and VCRs began to decrease market share. The major US broadcast networks had a 91 per cent share of prime-time audiences during 1978–9. This dropped to 75 per cent in 1986–7 and to 61 per cent in 1993–4 (WikiPedia, 2004).

Similarly, brands and franchises began to examine ways of maximising their TV revenue through PPV TV. It became clear that if a sports event, for example, a world championship boxing match, attracted high viewing figures, then it would be a valuable property for the boxing authorities. This led to organisations questioning how much TV stations were paying for the rights to screen their events. It became clear that PPV events might be one way to extract maximum value from these events and to cut the TV stations out of the loop. After all, if 100,000 people try to buy one of only 20,000 tickets to a live event at $50 each, then there is a potential revenue of $400,000 to be made by allowing the disappointed ticket buyers to pay to watch the event on PPV TV. Similarly, movie companies whose revenues had been hit by the rise of TV also saw this as a way of increasing distribution. It was no surprise then that the first forays into PPV TV concentrated on sports events and films.

According to the website of the Museum of Broadcast Communications, based in Chicago (Museum of Broadcast Communications, 2004),

> In 1974 [Coaxial Communication] inaugurated the first true PPV service in Columbus, Ohio. The service, called Telecinema, provided movies priced at $2.50 per title. Telecinema shortly succumbed to pay cable's better revenue stream. Warner Cable introduced Columbus to another short-lived PPV service via its interactive QUBE system in 1978. Not until late 1985 did two satellite distributed national PPV services appear. Viewer's Choice was launched on 26 November 1985, and Request Television was launched a day later. By 1995, nine PPV networks were in operation in the United States. Several of them had expanded their service to multiple channels (called 'multiplexing'). Viewer's Choice and Request Television remained the two leading PPV networks in terms of cable system carriage and subscriber count. More than 800 systems carried Request Television to over 11 million addressable subscribers, and nearly 600 systems carried Viewer's Choice to 12 million addressable subscribers. 1994 figures showed 22 million addressable PPV cable households (37% of all cable households) in the United States.

This was not confined to the US. As satellite and cable systems launched in other parts of the world so the models created in the US market became the norm. In the UK in 1995, a boxing match featuring Mike Tyson was attracting a paying audience of 1.52 million people, generating an income of £41 million a fight. Even in a highly regulated, licence-fee-driven market such as the UK, PPV was a potentially lucrative system.

In recent years, new technologies and advanced digital systems have opened up new vistas for the PPV TV market. The arrival of digital TV means that many more channels can be compressed and broadcast than was previously possible; systems such as Sky in the UK carry several hundred channels at once, along with additional interactive services. This, in com-

THE UK MARKET

In the UK, the pay-per-view TV market has grown rapidly over the years. Sky has offered many events, from boxing matches to football matches to movies and musical concerts. Cable companies have followed suit and have shown many similar events with varying degrees of success. The recent introduction of digital technologies seems to have given a significant boost to the market and indeed the UK has been the fastest-growing digital TV market in the world, boasting upwards of 50 per cent penetration of digital TV by household.

With the advent of digital TV, more people have become used to paying for extra content, particularly movies. There are now over 9 million homes capable of accessing PPV content via the Front Row services on cable and Box Office on Sky. Both Sky and the cable companies have used their hundreds of TV channels to create NVOD services where the same film is broadcast at short intervals on separate channels; so, for example, a viewer can choose to watch at 10pm, 10.10pm, 10.20pm and so on.

This has led to viewers becoming used to accessing PPV services and, interestingly, this has not resulted in a drop of earnings in other areas; in fact, it has been quite the opposite as overall revenues have increased. This shows that, at least in the UK, viewers will pay for convenient access to big events on top of their increasing subscriptions.

A recent report by Mintel suggests,

Continued growth in subscriptions and pay per view appears inevitable. The market has demonstrated minimal effects in terms of increased churn in response to price growth well ahead of inflation, presenting platform providers with the incentive to further increase subscriptions, particularly in view of the anticipated continuation of only a modest recovery in advertising revenue.
Independent TV (Industrial Report), Mintel, 2004

As Sky+ and other PVRs are bought, the broadcasters are looking at delivering PPV movies direct to the PVR. In the case of Sky+, customers can buy a PPV movie from Box Office and, using the PVR, they can then watch the movie any time they want within a twenty-four-hour period, as well as being able to use the PVR functionality such as rewind, pause and so on. It is clear that this alone is not massively different from VCR functionality but Sky+ integrates with the EPG and this effectively allows the viewer to create his or her own TV channel. By as far back as Christmas 2003, the Sky+ service already had more than 250,000 customers and, according to the *Guardian* newspaper (Dodson, 2004), the rate is still growing extremely fast.

PPV TV in the UK seems to be a success so far but it remains to be seen as to whether TV can change totally to a pay model. Indeed, it may be undesirable to do so and even socially unacceptable.

Richard Adams

---

bination with smarter, more powerful set-top box decoders, has led to the emergence of a plethora of near video-on-demand (NVOD) services, which are closer to the idea of TV when the viewer wants it. So far, the main content has been movies, sports, music events and adult channels.

Video-on-demand is also being rolled out around the world. There are still technical issues with such systems and the commercial models are still not totally satisfactory but even so some services have launched. HomeChoice, available in certain areas of London, is one such system. Using a broadband Internet connection, the viewer can watch any programme they want when they want it by choosing from a menu. When the viewer presses play, the programme starts and the viewer can pause, stop, rewind and fast-forward the content at their leisure. This is one way forward for pay TV and it may be that one day all TV will be TV on demand, with all the implications that this carries for pay TV.

Another new technology that may fundamentally change the pay TV market is the personal video recorder (PVR), the biggest brand of which in the US is TiVo and in the UK is Sky+. In essence, this is a hard disk onto which TV content is recorded, giving the viewer control over the programme in a similar way to the digital versatile disc (DVD). PVRs can be set to record entire series and even learn to anticipate your choices and record them without you intervening. In the case of Sky+, the recorder controls are integrated with the electronic programme guide (EPG) so that by browsing the guide on-screen, a viewer can choose to record any programme or event with just one click of a button.

TiVo

It is clear that PPV TV will have a big part to play in the future of TV. As TV has evolved, more and more PPV systems have emerged. From the early days of occasional PPV movies on the Qube system in the US to the NVOD systems of Sky, viewers are consuming more and more extra paid-for content. Sports, arts, adult content and movies have all largely been the premium content of choice but it is also possible that standard TV content will become part of PPV systems. For example, there is no reason why a major series may not be moved over to pay models, with filler content on schedule channels acting as advertisements for the on-demand premium content. Whatever the future, one thing seems to be clear, the cost of choice and control for the viewer will not be cheap.

Richard Adams

RECOMMENDED READING

Gauntlett, David and Hill, Annette, (1999), *TV Living: Television, Culture and Everyday Life*, London: Routledge.

Schwalb, Edward M. (2003), *ITV Handbook: Technologies and Standards*, Indianapolis: Prentice-Hall Professional Technical Reference.

Whitaker, Jerry (ed.) (2000), *Interactive Television Demystified*, New York and London: McGraw-Hill.

TELEVISION TECHNOLOGY

BBC Online*

On 23 August 2003 Tessa Jowell, the Secretary of State for Media, Culture and Sport, gave a speech at the Edinburgh Television Festival announcing a review of the BBC's online provision, to be led by Philip Graf, the former chief executive of Trinity Mirror. She commented that:

> Reviews are vital to ensure that promises are kept, and that accountability is visible. There will be ample opportunity for everyone to put their case. We want to look at quality and value for money, how the online services fit with the BBC's public service remit, the services' impact on competition and on the general development of the BBC's online services. (Department for Culture, Media and Sport, 2003)

This was the first review of BBC Online since the original approval for licence fee money to be used for a BBC online presence was granted in 1997–8. While this review will have a major impact on the future development of BBC Online, and the wider UK online market generally, it also needs to be seen in the wider context of the 2006 review of the BBC's Royal Charter. The terms of reference for the review specifically link Graf to the charter review.* It is likely that the BBC's online services will be at the heart of the debate as most interested parties cite the development of online services as a reason for either retaining or abolishing the licence fee. Inevitably, the issue has also acquired greater sensitivity following the publication of the Hutton Report and the formation of Ofcom. The regulation of the BBC has rarely been such a foreground issue.

From the earliest days of personal computers and public digital networks the BBC has experimented with the distribution of digital material. Following 'The Mighty Micro', a

prescient documentary presented by Dr Christopher Evans and broadcast in the early 1980s, the BBC Computer Literacy Project and the BBC Micro (Wikipedia, 2003) successfully raised the public profile of personal computer technology. With the expansion of domestic Internet access in the mid-1990s it was inevitable that the BBC should look at providing web access to its content. The BBC's comprehensive web presence was approved by the Department of Media, Culture and Sport (DCMS) in November 1997. This was for an initial period of one year and was subject to public consultation. Following this, permanent approval was granted in October 1998. Within this consent, key objectives (BBC) were set:

- To act as an essential resource offering wide-ranging, unique content.
- To use the Internet to forge a new relationship with licence-fee payers and strengthen accountability.
- To provide a home for licence-fee payers on the Internet and act as a trusted guide to the new media environment.

These objectives were expanded into a comprehensive specification for the service, much of which was concerned with leveraging BBC content into the new medium with the aim of establishing the BBC as a genuine tri-media organisation. A number of the requirements serve to illustrate the distinctiveness of the BBC's web presence. For example, the BBC site navigation design was required to focus on the needs of the user, maximise ease and speed of use and minimise download times. This is a fairly purist approach to web design and is much easier to achieve within the context of a licence-fee-funded site, free from the constraints of the two common revenue-generating mechanisms – subscription and advertising content. A subscription model imposes a heavy overhead through registration and authentication and the associated security/trust issues. Advertising content consumes valuable screen area and its high visibility (for example, pop-up windows, pop-under windows and flickering animation) is focused on revenue generation not ease of use. Potentially, this gives the BBC an intrinsic advantage over websites that compete in the same content areas but are operated commercially.

---

* There is some possibly confusing terminology in this area. Over recent years, the BBC has developed the BBCi brand to cover services delivered as interactive television through the satellite, cable and digital terrestial platforms, as well as services delivered via the Internet. On 6 May 2004 these services were split and BBCi now refers to interactive television services only with the BBC Internet services labelled as bbc.co.uk. This chapter is solely concerned with Internet-delivered services.

---

*The terms of reference for the Graf review include, 'consider, in the context of the approaching review of the BBC's Charter, what the role of BBC Online might be within the BBC's overall service'.

The figure above (Sky News homepage, 6 August 2004) demonstrates the balance of content and advertising dictated by the commercial imperative and is in marked contrast to the figure below (BBC News homepage, 6 August 2004).

Since the initial DCMS approval, the BBC has developed into one of the major names in the UK Internet market. In March 2004 the BBC website reached 45 per cent of the 23 million Internet-using adults in the UK. Only MSN, Google, Yahoo! and Microsoft have a greater UK reach (BBC). In this environment, and at a time of increased scrutiny of the licence fee, it is unsurprising that the BBC has attracted a considerable amount of criticism from other interested parties, most of whom have a financial interest in the same market.

The British Internet Publishers Association (BIPA) was formed as an umbrella organisation representing a number of major commercial Internet publishers. It argues that the BBC competes unfairly with its members and that this should be stopped. The choice of name for this group is interesting as it challenges the technological determinism that underpins the BBC's approach to Internet distribution. The BBC sees the Internet as the next natural technological development in broadcasting. Institutionally, it has always embraced technological change, moving from radio to monochrome television to colour television and on to digital television and DAB – it is taken as axiomatic that the BBC should expand into Internet distribution. It describes itself as a tri-media organisation, seeing radio, television and the Internet as potentially equal broadcasting mechanisms.

The Graf Report was published on 5 July 2004 and was generally well received by the interested parties, although the British Internet Publishers Alliance expressed some reservations (Graf, 2004). The report made a number of recommendations:

- The BBC considers aligning online services to the framework for online public purposes and strategic priorities.
- BBC Online must actively seek to engage and communicate its purposes and strategic objectives to its audiences and the wider market.
- BBC Online continues to act as a home and guide to the Internet for those who require it; it must, however, develop a more consistent and transparent approach to linking to

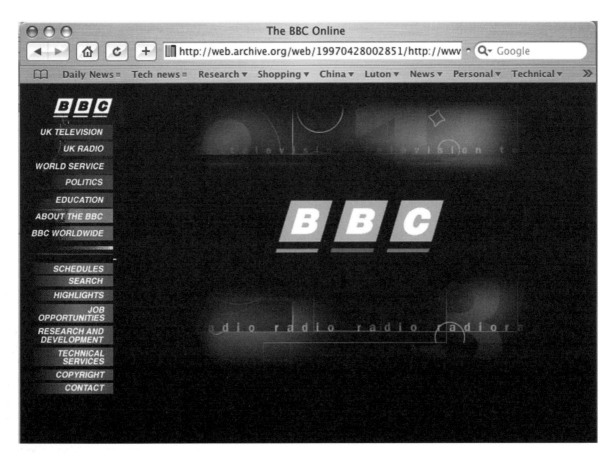

BBC homepage, 28 April 1997

all relevant sources (commercial and public) and ensure that its search tool prioritises user experience over BBC content.

- The remit and strategic objectives should be directly underpinned by a financial and performance measurement system, which clearly links the BBC's remit and strategic objectives, through BBC-wide new media objectives down to divisional priorities. This improved clarity should work to encourage focus and further efficiencies (2004, p. 9)

Interestingly, Graf found that the central allegation made by some commercial publishers, namely that BBC Online has had a negative impact on the commercial Internet publishing market and reduced competition, could not be substantiated.

> Given the nature and complexity of BBC Online's services, and the evidence available to the review, the analysis of the market impact of BBC Online does not 'prove' or 'disprove' the hypothesis that BBC Online has had no adverse market impact. (2004, p. 58)

The British Internet Publishers Alliance welcomed the report but highlighted Graf's concerns that the presence of BBC Online may have deterred investment in commercial projects and opportunistic expansion into areas of limited public service such as Fantasy Football and What's On listings. Hugo Drayton, Chairman of BIPA, said: 'BIPA welcomes the Graf Report and Recommendations as an important landmark in calling the BBC to account – but if they fail to deliver, BIPA recommends that this role should pass immediately to OFCOM' (BIPA, 2004).

This returns us to an issue that is at the heart of the debate. Graf makes two specific recommendations that concern the role of the BBC governors. First, the regulation of BBC Online should be reinforced by the appointment of two governors with specific expertise in new media and competition law. Second, the governors should be supported by access to independent analytical advice on the market impact of BBC Online. This highlights the much more general issue of BBC governance that has arisen post-Hutton. The rationalisation of regulation introduced by the Communications Act 2003 with the creation of Ofcom, the questions raised by the governors' handling of the

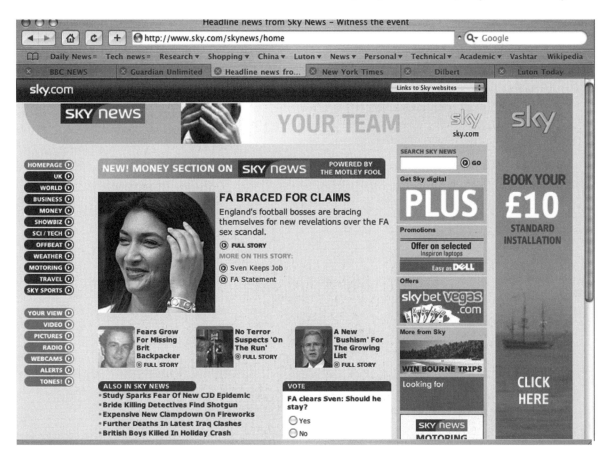

Sky News homepage, 6 August 2004

Gilligan affair and the post-Hutton resignations, together with the imminent Charter Review have all coincided to focus attention on the role of the governors. There is a perception that the governors are not sufficiently independent of the BBC management to be able to hold it to account. The Graf recommendations implicitly acknowledge this and are a clear signal to the BBC that its governance must be capable of preventing the fears of commercial Internet publishers being realised. Drayton draws attention to this with the suggestion that Ofcom could take over the role of the governors.

BIPA also expresses concerns about the level of resources allocated to BBC Online:

BIPA has no doubt that this has been the case [adverse impact on competition] and we welcome the fact that Graf has identified this as a real concern, made worse by indiscriminate commissioning policies, overabundant budgets and resources, and relentless cost-free cross-promotion. (BIPA, 2004)

The BBC responded to the criticisms of its commissioning policy immediately. Ashley Highfield, the BBC's Director of New Media and Technology, announced the closure of five BBC websites (What's On, Fantasy Football, Games Portal, Surfing Portal and the Pure Soap site) as the Graf report was published.

BBC News homepage, 6 August 2004

These sites were recognised as having a market impact greater than their public value (BBC News Online, 2004).

However, the envious view of the resources allocated to BBC Online and the use of cross-promotion is harder to justify. If the BBC is to exist as a genuine tri-media organisation funded by the licence fee, then the licence-fee payers are entitled to access the content they have paid for through all appropriate media channels. BBC Online enables access to a vast amount of legacy content that could not be made available solely through radio and television. Care should also be taken to identify the marginal cost of making content available online once fixed costs have been incurred in generating content primarily for radio or television. On this basis, it could be seen as good value, given its reach.

It is also unrealistic to expect the BBC to avoid cross-promotion of its services. Much of the online material is related to radio and television material and often provides an opportunity for interaction with the audience. There is inevitable cross-promotion in this. Even where the online content is self-contained but provides a public service then the promotion of that service on radio and television must also be a public service.

It is not yet possible to assess the overall impact that the Graf Report will have on BBC Online and the commercial Internet publishing market. The Secretary of State, Tessa Jowell, has given the BBC four months to respond to the report by redefining the remit of BBC Online (Department for Culture, Media and Sport, 2004). The service is very much on probation. Any expansion into new content areas will be carefully scrutinised by commercial providers and they will be looking for a demonstration that the BBC governors can effectively regulate the service. Failure to do so may well hasten the demise of the BBC governors as regulators of the corporation, with Ofcom waiting to take over.

Peter Dean

RECOMMENDED READING

Graf, P., (2004) Report of the Independent Review of BBC Online, July, Department of Culture, Media and Sport.

Cable Television – US

Instead of broadcasting over the airwaves, this technology transmits signals by coaxial cable, whose broadband capacity makes possible a far greater number of channels. It would have been possible to wire the US in the late 1940s, but the Federal Communications Commission (FCC) chose the far less expensive broadcast model that had worked so well for radio for two decades. When the FCC allocated the broadcast channels in 1952, it based its allocation on a localism principle. That is, the biggest cities in the US got the most broadcast channels, while small-town US got the least. Remarkably, after this momentous decision, some 15 per cent of the homes in the US could get no television at all.

Consider one example, where I grew up. With a mountain in between us and Philadelphia, Pennsylvania, and no local stations, we could not receive the signals. An appliance store owner who wanted to sell more TV sets put an antenna on top of a large utility pole and installed it on the top of a nearby mountain. Philadelphia television signals were received, and transported over twin lead antenna wire down to his store. Then he ran separate wires to each subscriber home. My sister and I saw these early results at friends' homes, and begged Dad and Mom for a TV set. Dad said OK as he wanted to see baseball games; Mom approved as she wanted to see her favourite from the radio, Arthur Godfrey. So on Christmas Day of 1952 there was a huge piece of new furniture in the living room with a sheet covering it. Dad had wired it – with considerable help – while we had been at school, and life changed forever. Picture and sound quality – by using coaxial cable and self-manufactured 'boosters' (amplifiers) – were perfect, actually better than our cousins', who lived in Philadelphia.

We were a test case. By 1952, about a hundred so-called community antenna television systems (CATV systems) served 50,000 subscribers nationwide. By 1962, almost 800 CATV systems were serving 850,000 subscribers. Entrepreneurial folks in towns just beyond the fringe of broadcast signals (or blocked by mountains or tall buildings) filled in the gaps so the US became a true TV nation. They followed the example of my home town, Allentown, by placing a tall antenna on top of a nearby mountain and then stringing wire into each home. Cable began to fill in the US with television because of a fundamental error made by the FCC in 1952.

In time, better technology offered improved reception but also made possible a multitude of specialised and localised services, usually weather forecasts. Then these pioneering CATV entrepreneurs began importing signals from independent stations from major cities to make their packages more attractive, so that they could raise prices and make more profits. But before remote controls the TV dial contained only thirteen clicks, so the average CATV system was but thirteen channels.

Then growth was halted in the mid-1960s by the FCC – to protect broadcast interests. The FCC asserted its jurisdiction and placed restrictions on the ability of cable systems to import distant television signals. This action had the effect of freezing the growth of cable systems. The FCC enacted regulations that limited the ability of cable operators to offer recent movies, current sporting events and syndicated Hollywood programming. The so-called freeze on cable lasted until 1972, when President Richard Nixon, who hated the broadcast networks, pushed his FCC to encourage CATV development. President Carter followed a similar policy throughout the 1970s, and with this loosening of FCC rules came Home Box Office (HBO) and then Ted Turner's WTBS – The Superstation. The former showed uncut, uncensored, ad-free movies for an extra fee; the latter made an independent station in Atlanta into a national service by sending its signals everywhere by satellite.

In 1972 Time Inc.'s new product – Home Box Office – was a radical innovation. Suddenly free, advertising-supported television had a competitor, ad-less pay TV. Folks all across the US – in rural areas, cities and suburbs – demanded that CATV simply get HBO. Suddenly CATV became a new product – cable TV. Cable demand caught fire in the mid-1970s, chiefly because of HBO and its imitators. The appeal to consumers of these pay-cable channels were movies unseen on TV in their theatrical version – in a pre-VCR age. The spur to the expansion of cable in the cities and their more well-off suburbs was the conversion of HBO into an instant national network. This change, coupled with Ted Turner's use of the then new satellite technology to make his Channel 17 independent Atlanta station a national phenomenon by offering whole days of re-runs of popular TV shows and major league sports, pioneered the growth of cable-only services to millions of happy cable subscribers. By the end of the 1970s, nearly 15 million households in the US were cable subscribers.

HBO and WTBS–The Superstation proved people would pay for TV. A rainstorm of other cable networks quickly followed, some offering pay services, some advertiser-supported programming. This alphabet soup of CNN (all news), MTV (all music), A&E (all arts), US (all re-runs), ESPN (all sports) and more than a hundred others by 2000 gave cable something to sell in the major cities and their well-off suburbs. They could offer about six to ten times what the average over-the-air viewer could receive. Cable-only programme networks had increased from twenty-eight in 1980 to seventy-four by 1989. Demand for cable-only programming fuelled rapid cable growth. From 1984 through 1992, the industry spent then $15 billion on the wiring of the US, and billions more on programme development. This was the largest private construction project since World War II.

By the late 1980s, cable was in demand everywhere in the US, and virtually every large city (and its suburbs) was wired for cable. All could get broadcast signals, but wanted more television options. Local governments got involved as they had to grant permission for cable wires to run across the common rights of way, as had electrical wires and telephone wires for decades. This local franchising established that local jurisdictions – not the FCC – would negotiate the one select cable

monopoly, but with restrictions setting aside channels for local use. This legal allocation – or franchising, in the business jargon – gave the chosen company an effective legal monopoly as with the phone or electrical service. Because of the localised nature of cable TV, the franchising authority has the principal responsibility for the regulation of the service – not the FCC as in broadcast television. This is why all systems in populated areas have set aside separate channels for use by local government, school systems and business institutions, stations for the televising of government meetings, neighbourhood stations, ethnic stations and free-speech public access stations. Satellite to home services – begun successfully in 1994 – had no such constraints. Yet the United States federal government began in the 1990s to establish some national rules. The passage of the 1996 Telecommunications Act, the first major re-write of the 1934 Communications Act, required that all cable systems 'must carry' all locally broadcast channels.

By 1990 the US was quickly becoming a cable TV nation – with two-thirds of all households attached, paying a monthly fee, and gaining more and more channels. As the twenty-first century started, only one in five households did not have cable TV, instead relying on satellite-delivered television or, in the case of the poor, settling for broadcasting. Cable fees – with non-HBO or any special services – grew to $50 a month. HBO added $10 to that figure. Other services added more so that the typical cable bill in the US neared $100 per month. Cable thus became a medium taken seriously by advertisers, and the satellite systems became saturated with niche cable networks. Advertisers could target the well off with spots on CNN and the Golf channel, target teens with MTV and sports fans with five variations of ESPN, plus a score of local sports channels. ESPN, owned by the ABC television network, played sports around the clock and, when Disney bought ABC in 1995 for $18 billion, Wall Street estimated ESPN alone was worth $5 billion.

It took little time for entrepreneurs to merge their franchises, making economies of scale. For example, one franchise needs a separate accounting department to collect the fees; five merged franchisees could still use the same one accounting department and the cost of accounting per franchise fell. These mergers usually came in clusters. So, for example, Comcast by 2004 possessed the franchises for all the systems from northern New Jersey south through Philadelphia to Washington, DC. This multiple-system operator could have the same fleet of service trucks serve Washington, DC and Baltimore, Maryland, only thirty-five miles apart. It could have one accounting department (located in Delaware for tax reasons). With lower costs, and revenues growing, profits increased dramatically. In 2004, for example, Comcast, which only East Coasters knew intimately from the regular, always increasing monthly bills, almost took over the Disney Corporation!

Advertisers embraced cable. Based on the alternative idea of targeting programming to a specific 'niche audience', the number of cable programme networks exploded. By the end of 1995, for example, there were 139 cable programming services available across the US, in addition to many regional programming networks. By the autumn of 1996, the number of national cable video networks grew to 162. By 2000, the number topped 200 and was growing as the niches became more and more targeted.

But cable seemed to stand alone. There were constant attempts to integrate it with other services – in particular to tie it to the Internet. Convergence became an ideal, but as the early twenty-first century arrived it was an ideal unfulfilled. So in a major experiment Bill Gates of Microsoft partnered with others to create WebTV. This was to merge cable – with its broadcast capability – with the Internet. But while the idea seemed promising on paper, customers seemed to use the Internet for one thing and cable TV for another. Technologically, convergence was possible but, with the necessary expansion needing to be paid for, customers voted for more and more movies and sports rather than interactivity with and through the Internet. Indeed, surveys indicated that people watched cable and played on the Net at the same time, but saw the two as wholly distinctive media with distinct uses.

This experiment – and failure by Gates – had been a blue-sky promise since CATV became cable. With the cable franchising frenzy well underway in 1980, the newly named cable industry began promising new technologies and services which were still in the research and development stage. Two-way addressable services, such as Warner Cable's Qube, were just in the demonstration stages. The Qube project sought experimental two-way communication in test market Columbus, Ohio. Everything was tried, but only sports fans voting for minor league US football games and interactive game shows seemed to gain any viewers that could regularly be measured in the thousands. Later in 1993 the newly created Time Warner tried the experiment again in Orlando, Florida, and again it failed. It was an idealist wired community dream that paying customers did not share.

More and more important was the introduction of fibre optics, and the near-infinite channel capacity. Coupled with the video compression system, the basic cable technology could offer the near mythical 500-channel universe. But investment required re-wiring and cost billions of dollars. So conversion to fibre optic – ready in the early 1990s – came slowly. Instead, customer-friendly hardware began to take centre stage in the cable industry in 1985. Alternatives to bulky and awkward converter boxes were being developed, and TV sets were made 'cable ready'. Cable operators were more worried about stealing signals. In 1986, HBO became the first programming service to scramble its signals full time. Not only did this decision to scramble signals separate HBO as a premium service provider, it meant the dawn of a new era of security, which would prohibit backyard dish owners from watching the service if they hadn't paid HBO for the programming. From a business standpoint, this was a defining moment for the protection of content and revenues. TV programming was the key to cable demand, so much so that it became common to steal the service and not pay. That – more than technical change – was at the forefront of cable corporations' minds. Wall Street and Main Street knew what people wanted – more TV, not interactive.

As such, cable TV became so popular and so widespread that by 2005 it was the way most persons in the US watched TV. Specifically, by the early years of the twenty-first century, cable television was available to more than 96 per cent of the television-viewing homes in the US with about 80 per cent of the households in the US signed up and served by over 9,000 systems. Despite the number of customers served, two companies dominate: Comcast, based in Philadelphia, Pennsylvania, had a third of all customers in the US, while Time Warner, based in New York City, had a sixth. Comcast had a presence in twenty-two of the top metropolitan areas in the US – with 80 per cent clustered so that costs were minimised.

For those who love TV – everyone save intellectuals – the cable industry has enriched the information, news, public affairs and entertainment choices of television viewers in the US. Cable television changed the US by providing grateful viewers with the greatest variety in television programming history. It's hard to remember that we once did not have twenty-four-hour music channels or twenty-four-hour sports channels or twenty-four-hour movie channels or twenty-four-hour news channels or twenty-four-hour weather channels, plus all sorts of niche channels that make the TV guide the size of a telephone book.

As the twenty-first century commenced, cable systems were slowly adding capacity and thus expansion seemed guaranteed in the future – there would be not just the average of a hundred channels, but 200 channels, and possibly more. Here the technology would not determine the future but the economics. No one knew what the viewers would pay more for. And more they seemed to be willing to pay. What had started as a $10 fee had suddenly become $50 and was climbing at a rate two or three times' inflation. TV viewers with means – not the poor – counted cable as part of their daily lives. While many never watched most of what they could get, the choices needed to be measured in the hundreds, and the world of my parents, getting cable simply to get three channels from Philadelphia, seems ancient history.

Douglas Gomery

RECOMMENDED READING

Mullen, Megan (2003), *The Rise of Cable Programming in the United States*, Austin: University of Texas Press.

Parsons, Patrick R. and Frieden Robert M., (1998), *The Cable and Satellite Television Industries*, Boston: Allyn & Bacon.

Satellite Television – US

As of 2004, satellite TV (or direct broadcasting system or DBS) could claim over 20 million satellite TV subscribers in the US. This figure seems larger than cable because it does not just count homeowners who have learned the benefits of satellite TV. Businesses, airlines, airports and even the US Congress have found that satellite TV offers a low-cost, reliable means of getting a wide variety of programming. While the cost of wiring impedes the spread of cable, the immense cost of launching and operating a fleet of satellites naturally limits the number of satellite TV providers. As such, there are currently only two significant providers in the US: DirecTV and the Dish Network. DirecTV and the Dish Network have been in business the longest, and offer the greatest selection of channels. Since its successful emergence in 1994, in the US satellite TV has sold itself as superior to cable TV, with a greater selection of channels.

Before satellite TV programming can reach its subscribers' homes, it must first begin on the ground at a satellite uplink station. DirecTV and the Dish Network operate their own satellite uplink stations. These corporations play two roles. First, video programming contains a very large amount of data; their uplink stations must, then, compress the data so that it can be easily transmitted to a satellite. Thus, DirecTV and the Dish network compress the programming they receive and then relay it back to earth, where it is received by a pizza-sized dish mounted on the customer's home. The dish then amplifies the strength of the signal and sends it to the satellite receiver in the TV, which decodes the signal and turns it back into images and sounds to be displayed on an ordinary TV set.

DirecTV and the Dish Network each operate their own fleet of satellites positioned approximately 22,300 miles above the earth in geosynchronous orbit, which means that they rotate at the same speed as the earth and so stay in the same position for use. DirecTV and the Dish Network in 2004 were operating in toto more than a dozen satellites. Both DirecTV and the Dish Network claim it is easy to install the dish and decoding apparatus. Yet this is hardly as easy as they tell you. One needs to find an optimal position, and that requires the services of an experienced professional installer. Indeed, the

most frequent complaints against satellite TV are that the dishes are moved by wind or blocked by plant growth or rain. It is not the case that you install the dish outside and it will never need adjustment. But, when it works, satellite TV does offer a greater number of possibilities than cable – in 2005. DirecTV promises 225 channels in a choice of programming packages. The Dish Network promises more. Cable delivers about half that number. Clearly there are important trade-offs between satellite TV and cable TV.

In December 2003, Rupert Murdoch purchased DirecTV for $6.8 billion. He promised better service than cable and lower cost than the Dish Network.

> We're not going into a price war with anyone. But overall, digital satellite today is getting about $54 a month per customer, and cable is averaging about $66 at the moment. People want digital offerings, but cable is just too expensive.

His purchase of DirecTV meant that his satellites could deliver TV programmes on five continents, all but dominating Britain, Italy and wide swathes of Asia and the Middle East. In the US he had a potent supplier, himself, in that he owned the 20th Century-Fox studio, Fox TV network and thirty-five TV stations, which reached more than 40 per cent of the US. Fox's National Football League broadcasts on Sunday afternoons were some of the highest-rated sports programmes in the world. His cable channels include fast-growing Fox News, which has zoomed past CNN in terms of viewer numbers, the FX general entertainment channel, and nineteen regional sports channels, which, in some markets, outdraw ESPN two to one. Indeed, his sports packages would seem to have the potential to push DirecTV to even faster growth.

In contrast, the Dish Network was a smaller, satellite TV company with no other affiliations. EchoStar, the predecessor to the Dish Network, started in 1980, after the company's chairman and CEO, Charlie Ergen, entered the satellite TV industry as a distributor of the three-metre C-band satellite TV systems. In 1987, EchoStar filed for a DBS licence with the Federal Communications Commission and slowly expanded. But without the resources of DirecTV, started by a division of the General Motors Corporation, the Dish Network has always been playing catch-up. While DirecTV, in 2004, was part of the vast worldwide Murdoch empire, the Dish Network had its headquarters in a small, suburban office building outside Denver, Colorado. It was always playing catch-up and has often been the target of takeovers.

What slowed the growth of both providers was that – until 1 January 2002 – they could not offer local broadcast signals. The Satellite Home Viewer Improvement Act mandated that,

SURVIVING CABLE AND SATELLITE TV: THE BROADCAST NETWORKS THRIVE

As the twenty-first century started, while the number of TV channels received by the average household in the US grew greater than ever before, the percentage of those channels that people were actually watching hit lows not seen in twenty years. Nielsen sample audience data revealed in 2004 by CBS Executive Vice-president for Planning and Research, David Poltrack, showed that the average household in the United States in the twenty-first century was receiving about a hundred channels but selected only fifteen for the majority of their viewing (15 per cent). That was down from 20 per cent in the year 2000 and 26 per cent from 1985, before satellite to home represented any portion of the marketplace.

TV channels received versus those viewed

	1985	2003
Channels receivable	19	102
Channels viewed	5	15
Percentage viewed	26%	15%

Source: Nielsen Media Research

Despite the growing number of channels, most people stuck with a manageable dozen or so. The four major broadcast networks – ABC, CBS, Fox and NBC – continued to enjoy vast popularity and hit status among viewers and advertisers alike. Thus, with the rise in the number of channels from cable and satellite delivery, the four major broadcast networks managed to reap disproportionate advertising price increases relative to other media, not to mention outgrowing the overall growth of the US economy.

Simply put, the traditional broadcast networks offered the best way to reach the most people at the lowest cost per thousand viewers watching. 'Advertisers have to buy more GRPs [Gross Rating Points],' said CBS's David Poltrack, referring to the need for advertisers to purchase more commercial advertising units to offset the decline in average TV ratings. Additionally, he said that an expansion in the number of advertisers, brands and services during this period exacerbated the supply-and-demand dynamics, creating 'more demand and lower supply'.

The result has been record network advertising price increases, in a period when viewers had more to watch. While those results proved that the broadcast networks remain as economically vital as ever, Poltrack said that too many executives, both on the buying and sales side of the business, tended to over-focus on the negative implications new media technologies might have on the network business model. He recounted three examples – the emergence of cable TV, the emergence of satellite TV and the emergence of the Internet – all of which have led up to potential doomsday scenarios for network TV.

Yet every prediction of the networks becoming extinct dinosaurs has been proved wrong. In 1980 HBO was going to do the networks in; then VCRs would; then cable's hundred channels would; then satellites offering 300 channels; then TiVo time-shifters. And none have made much difference. ABC, CBS, Fox and NBC remain the most recognisable TV brands, and the most profitable propositions in the television industry as the years pass by in the early twenty-first century, and history would indicate that nothing will change that. The television industry will remain a broadcasting-centric, network-dominated world, with cable and satellite servicing small audiences (about 3 per cent at most).

Douglas Gomery

once a satellite carrier exercised its discretion to provide the programming of all local television broadcast stations within that station's local market, the satellite carrier must, upon request, carry without compensation the signals of every television broadcast station located within that local market. So, as cable carries all local broadcast signals, in practice so does satellite TV.

By August 2004, their trade association, the Satellite Broadcasting and Communications Association (SBCA), could announce that the direct to home satellite industry had surpassed 23 million total subscribers. DirecTV announced that it held far more than half that total and, with Murdoch in the process of taking over, he promised to increase that lead. The growth of DBS is directly related to the flattening of the percentage of homes subscribing to cable TV, the DBS industry's seemingly overwhelming competitor in what policy-makers call the multichannel video marketplace.

According to the Television Bureau of Advertising, cable even lost approximately 867,000 households during the first seven months of 2004 – as it continually raised its prices to customers. Clearly cable had reached a plateau of potential possible customers, and Murdoch was set to take away some of its power. What he will accomplish is hard to guess. I can only note that Murdoch has been a success at all the media ventures he has entered. He did not invest nearly $7 billion to fail in this endeavour. Starting in 2005, Murdoch began an industrial experiment carrying the same risk as his Fox television network and his other worldwide ventures. He has bet on globalisation, and only the future will tell us how successful he will be with his investment.

Satellite TV will never be as reliable as cable TV, but will always be cheaper. How the consumers in the US will sort this out remains a central conundrum of the television industries as the twenty-first century passes.

Douglas Gomery

RECOMMENDED READING

Grover, Ronald and Lowry, Tom (2004), 'Rupert's World', *Business Week*, 19 January.

Parsons, Patrick R. and Frieden, Robert M. (1998), *The Cable and Satellite Television Industries*, Boston: Allyn & Bacon.

Television and Video Technology: From Analogue to Digital

Television has always taken full advantage of the technologies available to it. Indeed, from the earliest days, the limitations that technology has imposed on television have spurred further technological development. For example, the emergence of electronic scanning in the 1930s was in large part a response to the very obvious problems with the original mechanical scanning.

Today, digital technologies permeate right through television: production, archiving and, most recently, transmission and consumption. Again, all the advantages offered by digitisation are put to use. Miniaturisation means that cameras can now go to places once inaccessible; the exploitation of ever more powerful computers allows more complex special effects; and the viewer is now able to sift and sort through hundreds of channels and store hours of video on hard disk recorders.

TECHNICAL LIMITATIONS

At the outset, the quality of the television pictures was a consideration. John Logie Baird's experimental transmissions at the end of the 1920s, grudgingly permitted by the BBC, constructed an image made up of just thirty scanned lines. The image quality, by any standard, was poor but, of course, that was of little concern compared with the wonder of transmitting moving images over the radio waves. By the time regular transmissions began in 1936, Baird had developed his scanning into a 240-line system, but this had already been eclipsed by the 405-line, EMI electronic scanning camera.

This illustrates an issue that remains important today: what is an acceptable quality for television transmission and, thus, how should any competition between quality and quantity (number of channels) be balanced? A higher-quality picture would result from using more lines in the scanning, at the expense of needing a higher bandwidth of frequencies; but the limitation in the 1930s was technical, as both cameras and receiver tubes scanning technologies were working at their limit. The demand for frequencies then was nothing like it is now, with just one TV and a few radio stations. Nowadays, when high-definition television is certainly a *technical* possibility, the constraint is the lack of available spectrum.

Innovation added complexity. With the arrival of a new UK television channel, ITV, in 1955, viewers had to buy new equipment to receive the new broadcasts. But it was the birth of colour in the mid-1960s that stretched the technical capabilities of television the most. The new colour TV cameras separated all colours into their red, green and blue components, each producing its own signal, and so cameras and studios became far more complex. With colour, receivers also became more sophisticated and more expensive (as did the TV licences) – yet again viewers were required to buy new equipment to keep up with the latest developments. By now, television was also operating at a higher definition, 625 lines

John Logie Baird

rather than 405, and so yet more of the available frequencies were called upon to carry these new transmissions.

WATCH WHAT YOU LIKE WHEN YOU LIKE – VIDEO

Recording video presents far more problems than recording sound because the amount of information is far greater, and it wasn't until the 1950s that it became possible to squeeze the bandwidth of video onto tape.

Videotape offered new opportunities in making programmes. The editing possibilities (originally by splicing, but later by dub editing) were almost unlimited. When shooting TV programmes, video offered huge advantages over the celluloid it replaced. Without the need for processing, rushes could be viewed instantly and, if a shot hadn't worked, maybe it could be done again. The video camera also became more compact, and its enhanced portability had a consequent impact on news-gathering (MacGregor, 1997, pp. 178–9).

The same technology later developed into a domestic incarnation. The home video cassette recorder (VCR) has become a standard piece of household equipment. As people began to buy the VCR in growing numbers, commentators speculated about the consequences. It was assumed that people would use the recorders for time-shifting, for recording scheduled programmes and viewing at a later time. This, after all, is what the industry had used tape for, to transmit programmes some time after they had been filmed. Articles of the time talked of the end of scheduling. Slotting programmes into particular viewing periods would become meaningless as viewers would, in effect, be creating their own schedules, and their own channels (Crisell, 2002, pp. 215–17). One important consequence for commercial television would be the implications for advertising.

But it hasn't has not turned out like this. Of course, people do 'set the video' to record programmes when they're out or asleep, but 'rescheduling' an evening's viewing is not one of our aims in using the VCR. Instead, we use it for something the industry never anticipated: to substitute for scheduled programming. We go to the video rental shop or the library and borrow a film for a night (now more often on DVD rather than tape). Not for the first time have predictions about the likely consequences of a new development in TV technology proved wildly overstated.

MORE AND MORE CHANNELS

The dramatic increase in the number of channels available via satellite and cable television was a rather belated development in the UK. While cable systems have long been well established in many European countries and the US, the wide availability of high-quality UK television reception over the airwaves meant that there was a limited demand for alternatives. In comparison, the US cable industry had been driven by the relatively poor quality of terrestrial TV in many areas. Satellite television evolved as an efficient means of distributing ready-to-broadcast programming to widely dispersed cable TV companies across the US.

In the UK, the growth of satellite television (and, to an extent, cable) was assisted by a removal of any public service obligations and its acquisition of the rights to major sporting events (such as top football matches). Once the satellite is launched, of course, it offers a very cheap way of delivering almost universal coverage, and when adding another channel to the service, it immediately becomes available to all. By the early 1990s, upwards of fifty TV channels were available in the UK via satellite, compared with four terrestrial channels. What satellite cannot do, however, is restrict coverage geographically – and 'local' programming as such does not exist, though, of course, satellite can carry programmes aimed at a local audience. However, cable, as a switched system (like the telephone network) can, in principle, deliver highly specific programming. Yet the business of television is as a mass medium, and in practice the cable companies offer programming similar to the satellite broadcasters.

AND DIGITAL TELEVISION?

In some respects digital technology mainly extends most of the functions and practices within television, but in others it suggests new roles and uses.

Initially digital systems allow television to do new things without changing the basic practices and purposes of the medium. For example, digital cameras are smaller and lighter than their analogue counterparts, and thus generally more portable. Coupled with other miniaturisation techniques, they can be deployed relatively unobtrusively for the making of 'reality TV' in its many forms. They have also been widely used in undercover, investigative reporting, for example, recently to reveal racism among police recruits in *The Secret Policeman*. Combining digital cameras with portable, digital satellite phone systems, reporters were able to carry equipment and file live reports, albeit of poor quality, from the heart of the battlefield in the 2003 war on Iraq. While this may certainly be considered a remarkable technical achievement, debate continues about the value of this so-called embedded war reporting (Miller, 2004).

For viewers, digital transmission and reception of television (whether by terrestrial, satellite or cable means) simply extends television in a quantitative sense: more channels, new radio stations, more subscription choices. Typically, between five and ten times the number of channels is on offer, at varying costs. Without entering into the debate here about the

THE GREAT ANALOGUE SWITCH OFF: WHEN WILL DIGITAL TV TAKE OVER?

Governments around the world want to switch off analogue terrestrial television, and replace it entirely with digital transmission. In the US, early predictions even suggested 2006 as a possible date. In the UK, the hope is that analogue can be switched off by 2012. In the city of Berlin, it has already been switched off.

Broadcasters would be only too happy to be transmitting on one system. When analogue is switched off, there will be more room for new channels on digital terrestrial services. Transmission will be able to use higher powers, giving more reliable reception. They too then are keen for analogue broadcasting to end.

What are the prospects of it happening? Broadcasting in this respect is a victim of its own success. Around 99 per cent of UK homes have a TV set, and most have more than one. All of these will need either replacing or adapting to receive digital signals if the analogue switch off is not to render them useless ornaments. What if that hasn't happened by 2012? It would take a brave (some would say foolish) government to switch off the existing TV service (viewers are also voters, of course).

By mid-2004, around 56 per cent of UK households had digital TV receivers. However, that bald statistic needs a little unravelling: most of those homes have more than one TV, and it is likely that only one of those would be digital. Second, the initial early growth was spurred when satellite broadcaster Sky launched its digital service, charging customers almost nothing to switch. Consequently, it was able to switch its analogue satellite service off within three years of its digital launch. Since that time, while digital take-up continues to grow, the rate of growth is slowing.

What then are the broadcasters' and governments' options? Viewers need an incentive to switch. If the cost is extremely low, that incentive might not need to be too great, and maybe the prospect of new channels would be enough. But currently the cost is *not* low, particularly if more than one TV set needs adapting. The incentives promoted by digital broadcasters are principally new channels and, in some scenarios, better-quality reception.

Perhaps previous examples help to make sense of it all.

When 625-line TV launched in 1964, it promised better picture quality than the old 405-line system (it also launched with the new BBC2 channel). This proved to be less of a draw than the coming of colour three years later. In fact, it wasn't for another two decades, in 1985, that the old 405-line system could be switched off without depriving significant numbers of viewers of their television.

When ITV launched in the UK, take-up was rapid, despite the cost of the new equipment required. A new channel, offering to be bright and entertaining at a time when the BBC was criticised for being dull, was deemed worth the expense.

The growth of satellite pay-TV in the 1990s was driven mainly by sports fans; the acquisition of exclusive rights to major sporting events, removing them from terrestrial television, persuaded many to sign up.

What does this suggest? Digital TV could use some of its increased capacity for high-definition pictures (at the expense of some of its new channels). However, this is unlikely to be a big persuader based on the 625-line experience. If some of the digital channels offer new content, perceived to be better than that currently on analogue, this might persuade more to switch, as ITV did fifty years ago. However, current evidence suggests that this is not happening. Migrating popular programming to digital-only channels could work, if it was as popular as the sport which ended up on pay-TV in the 1990s. To some extent this already happens: the new series of popular programmes like *Friends* have appeared first on digital-only channels – but not exclusively. If it really were the case that you had to get digital TV to see these programmes, some might switch. However, it is unlikely that the BBC would begin to show *EastEnders only* on the digital-only BBC3.

So it is unclear what will be the main factor in stimulating further take-up – although what does seem clear is that the industry has reason enough to switch that some way will be found.

Stephen Lax

quality of some of those channels, there is no denying the variety of channels available when you can pick from hundreds. Nevertheless, as viewing figures show that even in these multi-channel homes the existing terrestrial channels remain the ones most watched, this does not suggest a substantial qualitative change in viewing habits.

However, there *are* some new and potentially more significant possibilities offered by digital broadcasting, though these are currently rather speculative. The convergence of computer technology and television, enabled by the latter's digitisation, finds its clearest expression in the personal video recorder (PVR). The PVR combines the development of high-capacity, hard disk drives with the processing power of computers to allow the recording of many hours of television, with varying degrees of automation. At one level simply extending the facilities of the humble VCR, the ability to automatically identify programmes by type or genre and then record them without further intervention is what distinguishes the PVR. This relies entirely on a new development required by digitisation, the inclusion of *metadata*.

Metadata is normally thought of as 'data about data'; in the case of television, it will be a set of data describing what a particular programme is about, its type (drama, documentary, film, etc.), when it was broadcast, perhaps presenters' or actors' names and so on. In other words, it is an electronic cataloguing system that allows simple searches to pick out any programmes about a particular topic, or starring a particular actor. Once metadata is attached to programmes, searching can take place on any platform, not just in a PVR. For instance, TV listings on the World Wide Web allow such selections, and reminders about forthcoming programmes can be sent by text message or email.

At the risk of repeating the claims made about the VCR, which turned out to be way off the mark, it is conceivable that people could exploit metadata to view television in a different way, selecting by genre or topic. This might detract from the serendipity that has been a feature of scheduled TV since its inception – the notion that you might end up watching something you never expected to simply because it follows a programme you *did* want to watch.

Metadata finds another application in archiving of programmes. Digital storage of TV programmes as part of the normal broadcasting process also allows for long-term archiving. Again, the compatibility with computer technology allows such programming to be viewed on a computer, streaming over the Internet. Here, again, the inclusion of metadata is vital – without it, the archive would be useless, like a library without a catalogue. A precedent exists in the number of radio stations with previously broadcast programmes available on their Web pages. The BBC makes almost its entire output available in this way for one week on its 'Listen Again' service. With the growing take-up of broadband Internet, there is no reason why the same service should not be extended to television programming, and the BBC has indicated a desire to do just that (Dyke, 2003).

The Internet as a distribution network for television programming presents possibilities for new forms of television. A number of activist networks have emerged from protest groups to launch news websites (such as indymedia.com), making use of precisely the relatively cheap cameras and editing systems digital technology provides (Harding, 2001). The Internet is not a perfect medium for 'broadcasting'; unlike conventional television distribution, if large numbers try to access television over the Internet, it will tend to fail, as we have seen when a major event such as the World Trade Center attack occurs. Nevertheless, as a repository for individual programmes ready for downloading or streaming, the Internet opens up new outlets for a new and different kind of television.

Digitisation, then, presents opportunities: it remains to be seen how they will be taken up.

Stephen Lax

RECOMMENDED READING

Burke, David (2000), *Spy TV: Just Who Is the Digital TV Revolution Overthrowing?*, Hove: Slab-o-concrete Publications.

Crisell, Andrew (2002), *An Introductory History of British Broadcasting*, 2nd edn, London: Routledge.

Dyke, Greg (2003), Richard Dunn Memorial Lecture, given at the Edinburgh International Television Festival, 24 August.

Harding, Thomas (2001), *The Video Activist Handbook*, 2nd edn, London: Pluto.

MacGregor, Brent (1997), *Live, Direct and Biased: Making Television News in the Satellite Age*, London: Arnold.

Miller, David (ed.) (2004), *Tell Me Lies: Propaganda and Media Distortion in the Attack on Iraq*, London: Pluto.

Winston, Brian (1998), *Media Technology and Society*, London: Routledge.

Television and DVD

The digital versatile disc (DVD) benefits from both high capacity and compact size. Its capacity (4.7GB to 17.1GB for a read-only disk) makes it suitable for video, multimedia, games and audio applications. Thus recent years have seen the rise to ubiquitous use of the DVD for the consumption of moving images. The DVD's high quality of video and audio, easy access to selected parts of the disc and its sheer ease of use, storage and transport has helped DVD to replace VHS for pre-recorded titles in less than a decade. At the end of 2004, *Screen Digest* research indicated that: 'DVD video player/recorder penetration had reached 50.5 per cent of TV households in Western Europe' (1/2005, p. 11). *Screen Digest* 8/2004 reported that the number of DVD households in Europe had reached the same level as those in North America for the first time in 2003 (both regions had around 60 million DVD households).

Players for the DVD format became commercially available in Japan in late 1996 and in the US at the beginning of 1997. In 1998 the players reached Europe and in the US total ownership reached 1 million. Digital versatile disc technology started in 1994 as two competing formats, Super Disc (SD) from Toshiba and Warner, and Multimedia CD (MMCD) from Philips/Sony. Within a year a standard format was devised (thus avoiding an expensive re-run of the VHS/Betamax war of the 1970s). In 1994 further expensive clashes were avoided by the Hollywood Committee on standards for 'movies on CD'. The movie companies came together in their time-honoured fashion of 'organised competition' as they saw DVD as a way of stimulating the video market, producing better-quality sound and pictures on a disc that, not least, costs considerably less to produce than a VHS tape. The picture quality is as at least as good as TV and the disc can carry multichannel digital sound. These consumer-friendly shiny discs have the potential to allow a consumer to choose from up to eight different dubbed languages and from thirty-two different sets of subtitles (all at the press of the remote control button). Finally, if that were not enough, DVDs support multiple aspect ratios from the 'movie' experience of 16:9 widescreen formats to the more conventional 'TV' of 4:3. In short, this is a technology perfect for the multimedia and/or home cinema world of the twenty-first century.

The inexorable rise of the DVD has been somewhat hampered by decisions made within the industry. Regional coding was the result of movie studios wanting to control the home release (both date and distributor) of movies in different countries. It is a tribute to the power of the technology that the result has not been a slowing of uptake but rather a rapid growth of 'region free' technology to circumvent this essentially counter-productive coding.

In 2002 the prospect of a next generation of DVD was offered by two formats: HD-DVD or 'Blu-ray'. This latest attempt by the industry to shoot itself in the foot brought forth the spectre of a new format war. Within a week of the DVD Forum's Steering Committee announcing their support for 'Blu-ray', the DVD Forum itself voted to approve the use of HD-DVD. The nine companies backing the so-called 'Blu-ray Disc' format (including Hitachi, LG, Philips and Sony) saw their certainty of victory hampered by a number of big players in the movie business (e.g., Disney Corp.) supporting HD and the conspicuous lack of support from DVD Forum leader (and format pioneer) Toshiba. The lower bit-rate, lower picture quality alternative has as good a chance of victory (much as VHS beat the superior Betamax).

This spat is not just about movies. Indeed, the row highlights a relationship with TV. The driving force behind the attempts to agree a new high-density standard is the emergence of high-definition TV. Over a period of time audiences will come to expect that their discs will compare favourably with their TV pictures.

For television (analogue or digital) DVD is both a threat and opportunity. The threats and opportunities are parallel with those facing the movie business (and possibly more potent). Charlotte Lund Thomsen, Director General of the International Video Forum has noted that, 'So far feature films have represented the biggest part of the European video market . . . . In 2002 the stronger performance of other genres is noticeable: animation, music, humour and other audiovisual programmes such as TV-fiction, documentaries and sport' (*Screen International*, 25/3/2003).

DVD OPPORTUNITIES

The history of new audivisual technologies teaches (via cinema's reaction to TV) that it is foolish to avoid or resist change. As the Hollywood studios quickly grasped, any new medium equals a chance to recycle your back catalogue. TV's intelligent reaction to DVD is to sell its back catalogue. For the US-based majors, cinema and TV – at least in terms of distribution – are the same media owned by the same companies and utilising similar distribution strategies in the secondary format. Thus, 20th Century-Fox's biggest TV seller, *The Simpsons*, is marketed alongside the company's blockbuster movies. The same is true of Warner Bros.'s campaign to shift millions of units of *Friends* and *Smallville*.

Dvdloc – the Internet DVD database – lists the BBC as the distributor of fifty-four titles. In TV terms this is a sizeable output (if dwarfed by movie distribution, e.g., Columbia Tristar's 969 and Universal's 777). In comparison to the BBC,

Smallville

independent TV hardly registers as programmes are mostly the product of small companies with minimal distribution structures. No doubt the new ITV (formed from Carlton and Granada in 2004) will seek to rectify this situation. It is reasonable to assume that in TV and its secondary distribution the broadcaster can benefit from a brand. Thus, in terms of TV DVDs the BBC brand has enabled the strong performance of BBC Worldwide (see Grey Box).

DVD THREATS

The rise of DVD makes home cinema a reality (VHS quality is just not good enough). Home cinema (along with games consoles) is the obvious and most attractive competitor for domestic leisure time and expenditure. The desire to buy DVDs of TV programmes was already dealt a blow when recorder hardware was launched 2001. In addition, a virtually perfect (multiple) copying technology carries with it the threat of piracy. *Screen Digest*, in August 2004, led with the story:

Piracy soars since launch of DVD

In most countries piracy is now worse than 10 years ago. The advent of the DVD as a mass market entertainment product has almost doubled the size of the worldwide video market in the past five years. However, in addition

to providing a shot in the arm for the legitimate video sector it has also proved a huge boon for the pirates. DVDs (and Video CDs) are far easier to copy and transport than videocassettes. They are also more highly valued by consumers. As a result the business of counterfeiting DVDs is several times more lucrative than pirating VHS cassettes ever was.

Bringing ease of control (hard drive recorders can remove 'unwanted' advertising) and ease of copying together could only lead to panic in (advertising-funded) content providers. Thus the Motion Picture Association of America (MPAA) – already obsessed with movie piracy – has recently turned its attention to the dangers of TV copying with the Broadcast Protection Discussion Group (BPDG): 'a working group comprised of a large number of content providers, television broadcasters, consumer electronics manufacturers, Information Technology companies, interested individuals and consumer activists'. The group was formed specifically for the purpose of evaluating the suitability of the 'Broadcast Flag' for protecting digital TV. This flag is a digital sequence embedded in a television programme which signals that the programme must be protected from unauthorised redistribution. Promotion of the 'flag' is linked to the DVD Copy Control

Friends

BBC WORLDWIDE (www.bbcworldwide.com)

BBC Worldwide's own '.com' website gives a view of 'the commercial consumer arm of the BBC' in snapshot: 'UK's number 1 exporter of TV programmes; UK's number 1 international channel operator; UK's number 2 non-terrestrial broadcaster (with Flexitech); *UK's number 1 publisher of British TV tie-in video/DVD*'. DVD is mentioned prominently in most paragraphs of Worldwide's online publicity:

> Millions of people around the world experience the BBC through BBC Worldwide's products and activities . . . Today, with the success of brands such as *Tweenies*, *Walking with Beasts*, and *Delia's How to Cook*, millions of people around the world experience the BBC through BBC Worldwide's books, videos, DVDs, magazines and television exports.

As Chief Executive Rupert Gavin reports:

> There are many reasons why BBC Worldwide continues to perform soundly during difficult times . . . . The combination of strong new product flow and a high quality back catalogue of rights provides the raw materials for

our activities in areas such as television sales, publishing, DVD and broadband.

BBC Worldwide (BBCWW) ships 26 million units per annum.

For the second year running, BBC Worldwide is able to report an exceptional performance from its video and DVD business. An exciting range of new releases coupled with strong demand for classic BBC content on DVD helped BBC Worldwide VHS and DVD UK sales grow by 19%. DVD is one of the fastest-growing new technologies of all time and BBC Worldwide has responded to this by doubling the number of DVD releases from 60 to 115 in the last year. This huge growth is expected to continue during the coming year.

Worldwide is particularly keen on the success of *The Office*: 'The biggest UK hit was The Office Series 2 which sold 142,782 DVD copies in its first week, making it the record holder for the fastest-ever selling DVD of a non-film title.' *The Office* was able to build on the success of the strong brand of the BBC's 'Comedy Portfolio'. 'BBC Worldwide is engaged in a

The Office

major drive to migrate its unparalleled back catalogue on to DVD and is working with producers and talent on providing added value material.'

The typical DVD product of BBCWW in 2005 feeds on and supports the BBC brand of a tradition of quality in comedy and as strongly in 'public service broadcasting' documentary output. Naturally, both of these strands are continually fed by new BBC product, for example, *Auschwitz* (DVD release: 14/02/05): 'written and produced by BAFTA Award winning producer Laurence Rees, and using fresh new research' and *Journey of Life* (DVD release: 31/12/05): 'How has the human race been forged by evolution, just like all the other animals, but then uniquely managed to break free from it?'

The public service values and tradition of quality – marketed with brand integrity – are underlined by the activities of the BBC's own store (www.bbcshop.com). Its best-sellers are BBCWW products from the tradition of quality: *Acorn Antiques*, *Ascent of Man* (recycling a thirty-year-old tradition),

Civilisation (even older), *Mitchell and Kenyon* (a new DVD of even older material) and the box set of historical docu-travelogues of BBC stalwart Michael Wood.

BBCWW stresses its role in 'BBC brand protection':

> the BBC is secure in the knowledge that BBC Worldwide will not undertake any activities which jeopardise BBC brand equity or standing . . . . BBC Worldwide's activities in books, magazines, DVDs and interactive software all provide additional material to help audiences deepen and broaden their appreciation of the BBC's output.

Thus Worldwide portrays itself as 'international ambassador' while feeding off and feeding into a brand which can still claim to educate, inform and entertain (though possibly not in that order) in a Griersonian manner. Their DVD output is a key pillar in this strategy.

Graham Roberts

Association (DVD CCA) licensing of CSS (Content Scramble System) to manufacturers of DVD hardware, discs and related products:

> CSS allows consumers to enjoy the benefits of digital entertainment because the motion picture industry is able to issue their films on DVD while at the same time preventing massive piracy of their copyrighted works. De-encryption destroys this protection, which is why distribution of de-encryption devices was formally prohibited in the Digital Millennium Copyright Act.

(As the MPAA claims on its website.)

The final threat may prove to be the most potent for a medium where – it is claimed – 'content is king'. As the one form of digital distribution already widely known to the viewer, the DVD is the natural medium for changes in viewing and consuming habits. It has natural advantages over computer-based distribution as it does not suffer from the audience's resistance to viewing on a 'lean-in' technology.

DVD has potential that goes beyond repackaging (movie or TV) back catalogue. It has potential to break the *habitus* that movies have to last two hours or that programming has to fit regular formats. DVD gives independent content producers (be they small movie companies or community activist groups) potential for *samizdat* (self-distribution) activity. Productions can be made on DV (and eventually HDTV). Editing can be achieved with software available at very low cost from any high street supplier or the web. Multiple copying is already possible

using domestic equipment but increasingly commercial copiers are willing to facilitate the small producer. Distribution is – as always – a problem. But DVD is easier to transport and viewable without access to mainstream TV distribution.

Thus DVD may in reality sound the death knell of TV as we have known it for fifty years. For the time-being, however, DVD remains an elegant and attractive way to recycle TV product into a secondary market almost as soon as it is broadcast (see Grey Box). The HD-DVD recorder might end that activity sooner rather than later. *Screen Digest*, 12/2004, warned: 'Increase in worldwide demand for TV based DVD recorders will mean that by 2008 DVD recorders will account for over 50 per cent of annual DVD hardware.' *Screen Digest*, 1/2005, hammered home the point: 'Television programming on DVD has cornered a significant share of the rental market, suggesting that it is broadcast television rather than cinema that is most in danger of losing audiences.'

Graham Roberts

RECOMMENDED READING

Balio, Tino (ed.) (1990), *Hollywood in the Age of Television*, London: Routledge.

Hilmes, Michele (ed.) (2003), *The Television History Book*, London: BFI.

Roberts, Graham (2004), 'Movie Making in the New Media Age', in David Gauntlett and Ross Horsley (eds), *Web Studies 2nd Edition*, London: Hodder Arnold.

Steemers, Jeanette (2004), *Selling Television*, London: BFI.

New Production Technologies: Wireless + TV = Mobile Channels

Interactive TV (iTV) is here and although, at the time of writing, the UK is the most mature iTV market, in other countries around the world interactivity through TV is being rolled out, albeit in a variety of forms. For several years audiences have been encouraged though widespread Internet connectivity and cheap computer-processing power to interact with media in a mature manner. This has created a TV landscape that now offers unique opportunities for producers to develop new content forms.

INTERACTIVE TV

By the end of 2003 in the UK over 50 per cent of the population (*Guardian*, 2003) had access to some form of digital TV. Digital TV offers a variety of types of interactivity and it seems that the audience are using these. Figures released by the main UK digital TV platforms in October 2003, gathered from telephone interviews, show that 90 per cent of all digital cable subscribers interacted at least once a month (within the Walled Garden). The figure is also high for Sky Digital, where 82 per cent of subscribers interacted, with 60 per cent pressing the 'red button' on Sky Digital on a TV programme. This constitutes a significant audience for interactive TV content.

New TV technologies that enable interactivity and digital content to be broadcast have historically not been cheap. From early pilot services, such as Qube in Ohio in the late 1970s, to modern applications for broadcasters on the UK's digital TV networks, interactivity has been expensive.

Qube was a service that was considerably ahead of its time. Using an early two-way set-top box, Qube users could push buttons during shows to vote, select movies to watch, play along with game shows, and more. The total cost to the company, Warner Cable, was high and, given the number of subscribers available, the service was eventually doomed to the economic graveyard. However, the concepts developed as a result of this early experiment remain significant (Swedlow, 2000).

Teletext was another early form of interactivity that remains in current use. It was developed during the 1970s by the BBC. It uses the vertical blanking interval (VBI) to deliver a signal with the broadcast that can be decoded and displayed on the screen as text. This allows news, entertainment and services, such as subtitling, to be displayed on screen and accessed easily

by the viewer. This service is not, however, two-way and only uses low-quality graphics. Despite the limitations, the services were, and are, extremely popular and easy to use. (Some of the limitations of the earlier implementations of Teletext have been overcome in its current digital incarnation, which offers much higher levels of viewer choice, including multiple channel windows in one screen and 'red-button' interactivity.)

The emergence of the Web in the 1990s provided the final key to unlocking interactive TV. The growth of home Internet connections made faster and cheaper modems available. Once these were put into set-top boxes, it enabled services such as Sky Digital to successfully launch two-way interactive content and to prove that viewers would want to use it.

The UK audience has benefited from this inasmuch as it has allowed many subsequent programmes to be made interactive. The Wimbledon tennis coverage and the BSkyB premiership football coverage have all allowed viewers to control what they see in new ways. On-screen interactive voting is now almost routine on British TV and there have now been several hundred interactive advertisements, offering everything from games to free call-back from sales teams to extended video footage of commercials. Alongside this has been the emergence of interactive TV gaming, which allows viewers to play simple games such as Pontoon or Space Invaders on their TV (the technology is not currently capable of supporting more advanced games).

MOBILE SERVICES

The growth of mobile phones and data services has been rapid. According to operators, mobile phone penetration is over 80 per cent in the UK. According to the Mobile Data Association, there were 20.5 billion chargeable short messaging service (SMS) text messages sent in 2003. Put another way, this is equivalent to an average of 55 million texts per day. The total number of WAP page impressions viewed in the UK during December 2003 topped 1 billion for the first time.

In order to truly grasp the scale of the growth of mobile services, it is worth noting that last year 65 million music singles were sold in the UK, compared to 75 million ringtones for mobile phones. Finally, the number of text messages sent in one day reached an all-time high on New Year's Day 2004, between midnight on 31 December and midnight on 1 January, when 111 million chargeable messages were sent.

This leads us to two conclusions: first, that viewers now have a propensity to interact with their TVs; and, second, that they have a willingness to pay for and use services via their mobile phones.

Already a mix of SMS and TV is beginning to create new forms of content. In the UK, reality shows such as *Big Brother* and *Pop Idol* have been making great use of mobile interaction, mainly via SMS text messaging. In the *Big Brother 3* series, for example, there were 5.5 million text message votes cast and 10 million text alerts sent out. This compared favourably with traditional telephone voting, which hit 12 million during this series. As mobile use grows it is likely that this trend will continue upwards.

INTERACTING WITH TV VIA MOBILE

Clearly there are many ways to make TV interactive. The creation of on-screen 'red-button' applications (as on Sky Digital) has been just one way of approaching the subject. Perhaps the most surprising development has been the emergence of the mobile phone as a way of enabling direct interactivity with television.

Historically, the easiest way of getting viewers to interact with a TV programme has been for them to use their phone and place a call to the relevant switchboard (as seen above, the number of phone voters is still higher than votes cast via other media). Consequently, for several years phone voting has been used for events such as the *Eurovision Song Contest* as a way of canvassing opinion.

The emergence of text messaging and its subsequent near ubiquity as a means of communication has seen producers use this in many recent programmes. The biggest group of users of SMS is the demographically important sixteen to thirty-five-year age group that is much sought after by advertisers. Adding SMS interaction to programmes has generated large revenues and has engaged this desirable demographic.

So what are TV producers likely to do as the technology develops? If we look at SMS, we can see it has become an embedded technology that is both widely accepted and simple to use. Economically it works. However, its very simplicity means that it can only offer a limited mode of interaction with its content. Even so, as we shall see in the case study below, there are ways for

SMS to take on new forms of interactivity, which, significantly, have the potential to create new narrative structures.

NEW FORMS

The latest generations of phones are becoming highly sophisticated pieces of technology. These are phones that use Java as their operating middleware. They have fast data connections through either General Packet Radio Service (GPRS) systems or Third Generation systems such as 3G. They are capable of transmitting colour pictures, sound and video, as well as enabling emails and web browsing. (The question of whether these devices are actually still phones alerts us to just how radically the converged world of digital media is challenging traditional assumptions about modes of media communication and attendant technologies.)

These media channels can also be used to 'push' content to the phone in the same way that on a network in the workplace, emails 'just arrive'. This radically changes the potential of the medium. One obvious implication of this is that TV producers can allow viewers to view content via their phones. They can, for example, watch goals from a soccer match on their phone if they miss the live match on TV. However, the potential goes much further in that it actually allows *synchronised* content to be sent to the phone. NHK in Japan are experimenting with digital terrestrial broadcasting via mobile. A viewer can receive long live broadcasts of extended content, such as traffic news for drivers.

These phones are also unique in that they offer localisation, which means that it is possible to determine where the phone is, to within three metres or so. This means that it would be possible for content to be tied to someone's position either contextually or in terms of narrative. Quite what media forms will develop as a result of this technology is difficult to predict. Clearly it offers advertisers some interesting opportunities. More radically, new types of interactive entertainment could emerge as huge numbers of users push and pull narrative- and location-specific content around the globe.

David Docherty

RECOMMENDED READING

Gawlinski, Mark (2003), *Interactive Television Production*, Oxford: Focal Press.

Guardian, 17 December 2003 at <media.guardian.co.uk/broadcast/story/0,7493,1108512,00.html>.

Srivastava, Hari Om (2002), *Interactive TV Technology and Markets*, Norwood, MA: Artech House.

Swedlow, T. (2000), *Interactive Enhanced Television: A Historical and Critical Perspective*, at <www.itvt.com/etvwhitepaper.html>.

TriggerTV (2004) at <www.trigger-tv.com>.

3G

TRIGGERTV

SMS is a simple technology. It is based on a system of store and forward where, as a message is sent from or to the phone, it joins a queue waiting until the network has capacity to send it on. In practice this is normally extremely fast but at unusual peak times, such as New Year's Eve, network congestion can result in lengthy delays in messages arriving.

Up to the end of 2003, most modes of mobile/TV interaction were based on either asking viewers to send SMS messages to a number in order to vote in a poll or allowing viewers to send messages that are displayed via a caption generator directly to a TV screen, supported by cheap broadcast video. In other words, interactivity offered a limited TV chat service – a *very* limited, unreliable and 'one-way' form of interaction.

Can more be extracted from mobiles in terms of direct interactivity with TV? A patented technology called 'TriggerTV' is one system that allows timed data from a wireless device (SMS messages) to be sent to a viewer in a real-time and synchronous fashion with a broadcast (TV programme). This makes the interaction two-way or, put another way, it allows a dialogue to emerge between viewer and TV by using a conversational structure to the interaction. A message is sent to the viewer and the viewer replies; a standard conversational convention.

In its simplest form, TriggerTV has been developed to effectively bypass the queuing system in the SMS services. This means that TriggerTV can send out messages in a specific time frame and guarantee delivery. In terms of content, it means that TriggerTV can be used to send questions to the phone as they are read out on a TV quiz show; in other words, the producers can talk to the viewer, in a highly personalised way, at the points at which the key events happen, which begins to create the feeling of dialogue as outlined above. The user then has the easy task of replying a, b, c or d via SMS before the next question arrives. Score messages can also be sent out and these again can be timed to the second. In this way a fully synchronised interactive experience is delivered. A viewer can play along with a game show in real-time on their mobile phone. No set-top box, no expensive digital broadcasts and not even any need for analogue TV.

TriggerTV can also be used to feed into live editorial on TV and radio. For instance, on a sports programme, viewers might join the service by sending a message containing the name of their favourite team. Once the fans are broken down into interest groups they can be polled in different ways. For instance, the two sets of fans from the day's big match might be asked the same question about the match or they might be asked different questions. Because this is real-time and synchronous, this can be done as the match is being played and the results fed back into the editorial surrounding the game.

In these ways the mobile phone is being turned into a mobile interactive channel of its own. As viewers watch a show further content can be fed to them and the replies fed back live into the broadcast. Because the mobile phone is just that, it means that content can also follow a viewer around. For example, reality shows can use it to interact directly with their audiences by reacting live to events that are happening. In this way the mobile becomes an interactive channel tied to TV.

David Docherty

RECOMMENDED READING

<www.trigger-tv.com>.

TELEVISION INFRASTRUCTURES

Television and Government Controls in the US

The television industry in the United States is a largely privatised, commercial enterprise; however, the industry does operate under a variety of government-imposed controls. The nature of these controls varies depending upon the sector of the television industry at issue (broadcast, cable, satellite). This chapter will provide an overview of the system of government oversight of the television industry in the United States, the key principles that traditionally have motivated and guided government oversight of the television industry, and some of the most significant issues around which government oversight has focused.

Government oversight of the television industry is handled primarily by the Federal Communications Commission (FCC). The FCC was created by the US Congress via the passage of the Communications Act of 1934, which established the framework for the system of media and telecommunications regulation that is employed to this day (though substantial modifications were implemented with the passage of the Telecommunications Act of 1996). Initially, the FCC's regulatory authority extended to broadcasting and wireline telephony but over the years has expanded to include cable television, wireless telephony, and satellite. Today, within the context of the television industry, the FCC's authority extends into a wide range of areas, including programme content, ownership structure and licence allocations.

The FCC is composed of five commissioners (reduced from seven in the 1980s), who are appointed by the President and confirmed by Congress. The President designates one commissioner as the chairman. Commissioners serve staggered five-year terms. No more than three commissioners can come from any one political party; thus, typically, the party controlling the White House has three members on the Commission. Often, Commission votes follow party lines, with 3:2 splits between the Republican and Democratic commissioners quite common, particularly on highly politicised issues.

Congress can become directly involved in the oversight of the television industry via the passage of legislation (which is then implemented by the FCC). Congress can also overturn FCC decisions via legislation, an option that has received significant discussion recently, within the context of the FCC's policies pertaining to media ownership. Over the years, it has not been uncommon for Congress and the FCC to disagree over the appropriate mechanisms for implementing the directives outlined in Congressional legislation, or for Congress to disagree with the initiatives undertaken independently by the FCC.

Broadcast television owes much of its regulatory structure to the radio industry. As television developed in the 1940s, the FCC essentially transferred the regulatory structure developed for radio over the previous decades to television. This system included an FCC-controlled licence allocation process, in which licences were awarded to applicants based upon criteria that were intended to diversify the range of voices with access to the airwaves (diversity being a central communications policy principle in the US) and presumed to correlate with the quality of service that the licensee would be able to provide to the community of licence – specifically, the extent to which the licensee would serve the 'public interest, convenience and necessity'. This 'public interest' standard lies at the core of government oversight of the television industry and of how broadcasters are expected to behave as licensees of the broadcast spectrum. The underlying notion is that as government-granted licensees of a scarce public resource (the broadcast spectrum), television broadcasters are obligated to demonstrate a meaningful commitment to public service, even as they seek to maximise audiences and advertising dollars.

Broadcast licensees have operated under a variety of 'public interest' obligations, such as obligations to air locally produced programming, to air certain amounts of local news and public affairs programming, and to ascertain the needs and interests of their community of licence. However, these, as well as many other, public interest obligations have been either relaxed or eliminated over the past two decades, as regulatory philosophies have changed. This is not to say that television broadcasters today are free of public interest obligations. Current public interest obligations include a requirement to provide three hours of educational children's programming per week, to provide reasonable access to broadcast facilities to political candidates, to sell political candidates advertising time at discounted rates during campaign seasons, and to refrain from broadcasting indecent or obscene programming.

It is important to emphasise that broadcast licences in the US are local in nature – that is, a broadcaster is licensed only to provide service to a localised community, as opposed to an entire state or region (there are 210 television markets in the US). This is a reflection of the long-standing localism principle in US communications policy, in which it is believed that media outlets that are owned and operated locally are more likely to provide content and services that address the needs and interests of local communities. This localism principle is particularly important given the US's large geographic size and enormous demographic and the cultural diversity that exists across different regions of the country.

However, continuing consolidation in the television industry threatens not only the principle of localism (as locally based owners become a thing of the past), but the diversity principle as well, as the number of unique owners of stations declines as large group owners (including the national broadcast networks) increase their station holdings. Regulations to prevent such ownership concentration have been significantly relaxed in recent years, under the assumption that the rise of alternative distribution technologies (DBS, the Internet, etc.) reduce the need for such regulations.

As the overseer of broadcast licensees, the FCC has the authority to levy fines against licensees, as well as to deny licence renewals and even revoke licences. Licences are rarely non-renewed or revoked, and fines (particularly in recent decades), when they are levelled against broadcasters for violating their public interest obligations, are not particularly large. Perhaps the most common example of broadcaster misconduct involves the broadcast of obscene or indecent programming. Generally, the definitions of indecency and obscenity in the US focus on sexually explicit or suggestive language and imagery; and, not surprisingly, there has been a long history of debate over what exactly constitutes indecent or obscene programming (the controversy surrounding the 2004 Super Bowl half-time show, which provoked a re-examination of television broadcast indecency regulations, provides a particularly high-profile case in point).

As the scope and intensity of enforcement of public interest obligations for broadcasters has been relaxed over the years, the licence renewal process has become increasingly streamlined, with licence renewals now taking place every eight years (as opposed to every three years), and licensees required to provide minimal information about their performance in order to obtain renewal. This process has been labelled 'postcard renewal' by critics, as virtually all of the information the Commission requires in order to renew a licence can fit on a postcard.

Unlike broadcasters, which are licensees of the federal government, cable systems operate under locally granted franchises. Thus, an organisation wishing to construct and operate a cable system must receive permission from the local government in the community it wishes to serve. In exchange for the rights to construct and operate a cable system, a cable provider will typically provide a percentage of revenues to the local government and reserve some of its channel capacity for community access. These 'public access' channels are a mechanism by which diverse local viewpoints can be expressed via the cable system (another manifestation of the diversity and localism principles), as most cable systems provide programming almost exclusively produced and distributed by national cable networks.

Because cablecasters are not licensees of the public airwaves, they do not operate under the same collection of public interest obligations as do broadcasters. Cablecasters do not operate under the same indecency and obscenity regulations, nor do they have the same requirements to present educational children's programming. From the standpoint of the typical television viewer, the difference between a broadcast and a cable channel is hardly discernible, yet the different technological infrastructures via which the programming is delivered impact the extent to which the government can exert control over the programmers – the logic being that programmers utilising cable lines are not using the public's airwaves and are therefore more protected (via the First Amendment) from government influence over their programming decisions. The irony, however, is that most households receive their broadcast television stations via their cable system, and that cable networks are, in fact, distributed to cable systems through the airwaves (via satellite). This situation has led many critics to question the logic of employing different regulatory structures for broadcast and cable programming.

Nonetheless, federal regulatory authority does extend to the cable industry. For instance, cable operators are required under federal regulation to carry all local broadcast signals that serve their market. These highly controversial 'must-carry' rules were implemented to ensure that audiences would have access via their cable subscription to their local broadcasters. The must-carry rules barely survived scrutiny by the US Supreme Court as an unacceptable imposition on the free speech rights of cablecasters. The Supreme Court's decision would have laid this issue to rest were it not for the continuing conversion to digital broadcasting. Now, broadcasters are simulcasting analogue and digital signals and seeking 'must-carry' protection for both of these programming streams. Moreover, digital broadcasting allows broadcasters to 'multicast' up to five or six separate programming streams, and broadcasters would naturally like to see all of these programme streams subject to must-carry provisions. The FCC has yet to resolve this issue, and must do so with the recognition that the original must-carry rules barely survived Supreme Court scrutiny, raising questions about the constitutionality of any expanded must-carry obligations.

Perhaps one of the most high-profile elements of cable regulation throughout the industry's history has involved the federal regulation of subscription rates. Cable rate regulation endured a tangled, torturous history before being eliminated in 1999. For the bulk of the history of cable rate regulation, regulation of rates depended upon the existence of 'effective competition', under the presumption that effective competition would discipline rates. The effective competition standard evolved many times, incorporating factors such as the number of over-the-air broadcast stations serving a cable system's market, the presence and/or penetration levels of competing cable systems (a relatively rare phenomenon in US television markets), and the presence of alternative multichannel video programming delivery systems. It is this latter factor that led to Congress's decision in the Telecommunications Act of 1996 to 'sunset' cable rate regulation as of April of 1999. The underlying assumption of this decision was that, by that point in time, sufficient competition, in the form of alternative multichannel video programming providers such as direct broadcast satellite (DBS), would have emerged as a substantial enough competitive presence to effectively discipline cable rates (to date, however, cable rates continue to rise faster than the rate of inflation).

Satellite television operates perhaps with the greatest freedom from regulatory oversight, with minimal content regulation and no history of rate regulation. Moreover, policy-makers have taken a variety of proactive measures to increase DBS's ability to compete with cable. For instance, the FCC maintains 'programme access rules' that require cable networks to sell their programming to DBS providers at reasonable rates. This requirement is particularly significant in light of the extent that ownership of cable systems and cable networks is highly vertically integrated, with the largest cable systems co-owning many of the most popular cable networks (the FCC's efforts to limit such vertical integration were overturned by the US Court of Appeals for the DC Circuit in 2001; the FCC has not challenged this decision). Many cable companies, therefore, have an incentive to withhold their networks from DBS providers in an effort to defend their cable system business. The FCC has sought to prevent such activities – and hasten DBS's development as a viable alternative to cable – by imposing these regulations that guarantee that DBS programming can function as a legitimate substitute to cable programming by carrying all of the well-established and popular cable networks.

The DBS industry received further assistance in its efforts to compete with cable when Congress passed the Satellite Home Viewer Act of 1999. This Act gave DBS providers the right to provide local broadcast television signals to their subscribers. Unlike cable systems, which are *required* to carry local broadcast signals, such carriage is *optional* for DBS providers. However, should a DBS provider choose to provide local signals to a particular market, it must provide carriage for *all* local stations.

Reflecting upon recent developments in – and the current state of – government oversight of the television industry in the United States, it is perhaps safe to say that the overarching transition that has taken place is one in which economic considerations (about competition, efficiency, consumer satisfaction, etc.) have surpassed considerations about the political and cultural role and function of the television industry in terms of the government's policy priorities. This transition is well exemplified by the diminished public interest obligations being placed on broadcasters; the increased ease with which broadcast licence renewal takes place; and the willingness to relax ownership regulations absent compelling interest of economic harm outlined in this chapter. Absent a dramatic shift in regulatory philosophy, this trend is likely to continue.

Philip M. Napoli

RECOMMENDED READING

Horwitz, R. B. (1989), *The Irony of Regulatory Reform: The Deregulation of American Telecommunications*, New York: Oxford University Press.

Krattenmaker, T. G. and Powe, L. A. (1994), *Regulating Broadcast Programming*, Cambridge, MA: MIT Press.

Napoli, P. M. (2001), *Foundations of Communications Policy: Principles and Process in the Regulation of Electronic Media*, Cresskill, NJ: Hampton Press.

Powe, L. A. (1987), *American Broadcasting and the First Amendment*, Berkeley: University of California Press.

Red Lion Broadcasting Co. v. Federal Communications Commission, 395 U.S. 367 (1969).

Slotten, H. R. (2000), *Radio and Television Regulation: Broadcast Technology in the United States, 1920–1960*, Baltimore, MD: Johns Hopkins University Press.

Streeter, T. (1996), *Selling the Air: A Critique of the Policy of Commercial Broadcasting in the United States*, Chicago, IL: University of Chicago Press.

Turner Broadcasting System v. Federal Communications Commission, 117 S. Ct. 1174 (1997).

Public Service Broadcasting in the UK

Until the 1980s, broadcasting in Europe was largely synonymous with public service broadcasting, and television was subject to regulatory regimes broadly derived from those originally developed for radio in the 1920s. There were two main reasons for the adoption of this model in the first place: scarcity of channels meant that radio broadcasting was a 'natural monopoly', and it was thought inappropriate that this should be exploited purely for private gain. Furthermore, established opinion believed that, in the wrong hands, the new medium of radio could prove dangerous, whereas in the right ones it could benefit society.

In developing as a public service, broadcasting was akin to the health and education services, although, in general, broadcasting was subject to less *direct* intervention by the state than these. In Britain the pattern was clearly set from the start. Thus, in 1923, the Sykes Committee, which was considering the future direction of the infant radio industry, argued that broadcasting is 'of great national importance as a medium for the performance of a valuable public service'; it thus concluded that: 'Such a potential power over public opinion and the life of the nation should remain with the state' (quoted in Curran and Seaton, 2003, pp. 364, 366–7). Three years later the Crawford Committee laid down that the formerly privately owned British Broadcasting Company should be licensed by the state as a 'public corporation acting as a Trustee for the national interest' (quoted in Negrine, 1994, p. 85). In 1950, passing judgment on the BBC's new television service, the Beveridge Report argued that: 'Like the work of the Universities the work of broadcasting should be regarded as a public service for a social purpose' (quoted in Curran and Seaton, 2003, p. 365), whilst in its verdict on Independent Television (ITV) in 1962 the Pilkington Report stated that: 'The concept of broadcasting has always been of a service, comprehensive in character, with the duty of a public corporation of bringing to public awareness the whole range of ... activity and expression developed in society' (quoted in ibid.).

Much more recently, the BBC has declared that: 'Broadcasting is a civic art. It is intrinsically public in ambition and effect' (BBC, 2004, p. 6). Broadcasting, it argues, like all public services, 'should aim to deliver not only value for individuals, but also value for people as citizens' (ibid., p. 29). In this vision of things, broadcasting acts as a form of social cement or social capital; it thus creates public value and so can be regarded as a public good, aiming to serve its audiences as citizens to be educated and informed as well as consumers to be

entertained. It is based on the axiom that 'everyone has a right to high quality broadcast services, regardless of income, age, sex, race, religion or where they live' (ibid., p. 7). Underlining this are three principles: universality (broadcasting should be available to everyone); equity (it should fairly reflect the needs and interests of all its different users); and accountability (it should be answerable to the public which it serves).

However, as the BBC is at pains to point out, this most emphatically does not mean that public service broadcasting should be defined as a

> narrow set of particular programme categories which the market may fail to provide, but as a broad and integrated system of programmes and services .... PSB includes soaps, drama, sport, comedy and natural history just as much (and in some cases, even more than) the traditional 'public service' categories of current affairs, arts and religion. (Ibid.)

The same crucial point is made by the new broadcasting regulator, the Office of Communications (Ofcom), when it stresses that:

> PSB values need to be reflected in a wide range of programme types, not just programming thought to be 'beneficial'; citizens' interests can be met through many programme types and indeed may be most effectively met via programming which viewers think will entertain them as well as 'make them think'. (Ofcom, 2004a, p. 75)

In Britain, state regulation has always been an arm's-length affair. In the case of the BBC, governors are appointed by the state (although traditionally on a non-party-political basis) to regulate the corporation in the public interest. And when it arrived in 1955 ITV, although commercially funded, was regulated according to public service principles by the state-appointed Independent Television Authority (ITA). This eventually became the Independent Television Commission (ITC) in 1990, which was responsible for regulating all non-BBC television. In 2003 this was folded into the new 'super-regulator' Ofcom.

Until the 1980s, it was axiomatic that any new television channel, however funded, would operate according to public service principles. But then new technology began to promise an end to spectrum scarcity. And new commercial operators, such as Murdoch in the UK and Berlusconi in Italy, started to lobby strenuously to be allowed into the television sector, and, moreover, to run television channels according to purely commercial, profit-driven principles. In the UK a Conservative government deeply hostile both to public enterprise and to liberal values attempted a degree of 'deregulation' of broadcasting, forcing what it contemptuously called the 'cosy duopoly' of the BBC and ITV to operate in a much more commercially competitive environment by relaxing the public service obligations on ITV and, crucially, allowing Murdoch to run the satellite service BSkyB with a bare minimum of such regulations. In opposition, Labour was deeply hostile to such departures from public service tradition, but in power Labour has followed the deregulatory path with quite remarkable enthusiasm, culminating in the Communications Act 2003.

Fifty per cent of households now have digital TV, and other forms of digital technology are increasingly competing for viewers' attention. The number of channels has mushroomed. BSkyB's subscription revenues now exceed the total amount raised by the BBC licence fee. Total revenues for the television industry rose by 11 per cent between 1998 and 2002, but the terrestrial channels' share of that revenue dropped from 65 to 57 per cent. Under-thirty-fours in multichannel households now devote less than half their viewing to the terrestrial channels. New forms of technology are making the viewing experience not only more personalised but also more fractured and fragmented. And eventually the analogue signal will be switched off, making the televisual environment an entirely digital one. As Ofcom itself has pointed out, the consequences of these developments for public service broadcasting are considerable:

> For the commercial channels, regulatory requirements may begin to weigh much heavier as the market becomes more competitive and advertising funding is squeezed. The licence fee may become harder to justify as fewer people watch the programmes it pays for, and over time licence fee funding may struggle to fund programmes sufficiently to satisfy viewers' expectations in a competitive market. Some of television's traditional strengths – its ability to provide a common reference point for society, or to bring people challenging content that they might not encounter elsewhere – becomes harder and harder to sustain as individuals begin to create their own schedules. (Ibid., p. 66)

Meanwhile, purely commercial operators such as Murdoch utilise every conceivable opportunity to advance the argument that broadcasting should cease altogether to be a public service and, through subscription, be turned into a private good to be sold to individual consumers.

One possible future scenario is that, in this increasingly competitive broadcasting market, the BBC will soon be the only broadcaster with sufficient non-market funding to be able to act as a public service provider. However, in such a situation, the BBC could well find itself unable to compete adequately for audiences with channels dominated by entertainment, thus making it hard to defend the continuation of the licence fee. Furthermore, with channels no longer competing with one another to provide high-quality public service programming, public service broadcasting on the BBC could well suffer a significant drop in quality, leading to a decline in audiences for such programming.

On the other hand, however, these threats, along with the creation of Ofcom and the impending renewal in 2006 of the BBC's Charter, have actually stimulated considerable debate about public service broadcasting and its future in the digital age.

Thus, for example, expanding on the idea of public service broadcasting as creating public value, the BBC (2004, p. 8) has usefully argued that it does this in four main ways:

- Democratic value – supporting civic life and national debate by providing trustworthy and impartial news and information that helps citizens to understand and engage with the world.
- Cultural and creative value – showcasing the nation's cultural achievements, breaking new cultural ground, broadening the national conversation.
- Educational value – offering formal and informal educational opportunities, and thus helping to build a society strong in knowledge and skills.
- Social and community value – enabling the UK's various communities to get a better sense of one another, thus building social cohesion through greater understanding.

Meanwhile, Ofcom (2004c, p. 27) has offered a new definition of the role of PSB:

- To inform and increase our understanding of the world, through news, information and analysis of current events and ideas.
- To reflect and strengthen our cultural identity through original programming at UK national and regional level, and through bringing audiences together for shared experiences.
- To stimulate our interest in and knowledge of the arts, science, history and other topics, through accessible programming that encourages informal learning.
- To make us aware of different cultures and alternative viewpoints through programmes that reflect the lives of other people and other communities, both within the UK and elsewhere.

It also suggests (ibid.) that public service broadcasting content can be defined by the following features:

PUBLIC SERVICE PRINCIPLES

Until the Communications Act 2003, the principles of public service broadcasting were not explicitly spelled out by the legislation governing broadcasting. Successive broadcasting acts laid down generalised public service mandates, but it was left to the BBC and the Independent Television Commission (and its predecessors) to formulate the actual principles.

However, Section 264 (pp. 234–7) of the Communications Act 2003, in laying out Ofcom's duty to ensure that the terrestrial broadcasters fulfil their public service remits, usefully encapsulates, for the first time in statutory form, the principles of public service broadcasting.

Broadcasting is defined as 'a public service for the dissemination of information and for the provision of entertainment', and the public service broadcasters are required to ensure that:

- The full diversity of cultural activity in the United Kingdom is reflected and supported in drama, comedy, music, feature films, and in programmes about the other visual and performing arts.
- Civic understanding is facilitated by fair, comprehensive

and authoritative news and current affairs coverage of the United Kingdom as a whole and the world in general.
- A wide range of sporting and other leisure interests are satisfied.
- The schedules include a suitable quantity and range of programmes of an educational nature, and of programmes dealing with science, different religions and beliefs, social issues, matters of international significance and matters of specialist interest.
- The schedules include a suitable quantity and range of high-quality and original programmes for children and young people.
- A sufficient number of programmes reflect the lives and concerns of different communities, cultural interests and traditions within the United Kingdom as a whole, and within its various constituent parts.
- An appropriate range and proportion of programmes are made outside the M25 area (in other words, outside Greater London and its environs).

Julian Petley

- High quality – well-funded and well-produced programmes.
- Original – new UK content rather than repeats or acquisitions.
- Innovative – creating new approaches rather than recycling old ones.
- Challenging – making viewers think.
- Engaging – remaining accessible and enjoyable.
- Widely available.

Ofcom argues (ibid., p. 81) that the task of PSB regulation is to:

- Support high-quality content across the PSB system.
- Ensure that the substantial amount of public funding made available to UK broadcasting is well spent.
- Underpin independence and impartiality in provision of news and current affairs.
- Secure effective and fair competition in the broadcasting market.
- Produce a common regulatory framework for all public service broadcasters.

As both the BBC and Ofcom agree, public service broadcasting must learn to live in the competitive digital broadcasting marketplace. Clearly there are dangers here, but there are considerable opportunities too. As Ofcom points out: 'Emerging digital technologies offer rich potential for the future to develop

local, regional and national services that meet citizen-consumer needs considerably more effectively than the current model of provision by the main networks' (Ofcom, 2004b, pp. 85–6). This is particularly important, given the recent significant diminution of the regional element of the ITV network.

The digital broadcasting revolution clearly offers many opportunities to build substantial public value. As the BBC puts it,

> They will include new ways to involve people in civic processes and institutions, personalised learning tools, access to previously closed archives, new ways of connecting communities, more convenient ways to watch and listen to programmes, more localised content, tailored services for minority groups. (BBC, 2004, p. 9)

However, the digital revolution has passed many people by. And many of those who do have digital channels complain that the quality and range of content has not kept up with the technology. It is also vital that the new technologies are available and affordable to all. Otherwise the 'information gap' or 'digital divide' will widen still further, in turn threatening social cohesion. This is an area in which intervention based on public service principles and ideals is clearly not only desirable but also highly necessary.

Julian Petley

RECOMMENDED READING

BBC (2004), *Building Public Value: Renewing the BBC for a Digital World*, London: BBC.

Collins, Phillip (ed.) (2002), *Culture or Anarchy?: The Future of Public Service Broadcasting*, London: Social Market Foundation.

Curran, James and Seaton, Jean (2003), *Power without Responsibility: The Press, Broadcasting and New Media in Britain*, 6th edn, London: Routledge.

Franklin, Bob (ed.) (2001), *British Television Policy: A Reader*, London: Routledge.

Ofcom (2004a), *Ofcom Review of Public Service Television Broadcasting: Phase 1 – Is Television Special?*, London: Ofcom.

Ofcom (2004b), *Ofcom Review of Public Service Television Broadcasting: Phase 2 – Meeting the Digital Challenge*, London: Ofcom.

Ofcom (2004c), *Ofcom Review of Public Service Television Broadcasting: Phase 3 – Competition for Quality*, London: Ofcom.

Television, Public Service Broadcasting, Public Interest Mandates – US

The public interest is a central term of US television regulation. Regulation and public interest are intimately linked structurally, because government regulation is justified by the public's stake in the outcome, which inevitably shapes market practice. What exactly constitutes the public or its benefit is, of course, ideologically charged and, thus, the public interest is perennially a political football. Since 'the public interest and necessity', the legal language of the Communications Act of 1934 that governs public interest requirement, has never been precisely defined in law, all practical definition occurs at the regulatory level.

In practice, the public interest is operationalised differently in different delivery services for television. Serving the public interest in broadcasting now specifically involves, for station owners, moving to digital transmission; observing a highly flexible standard for indecency (obscenity is outlawed via other rules) and some modest electoral-coverage rules; and providing three hours of educational and informational children's programming. The public interest in cable operations usually gets specific only in the terms of a contract with the locality, a contract required because cable is laid along rights of way belonging to the locality. Contracts often include the cable company's obligation to provide free 'access channels' for the public – sometimes several, including for any member of the public on

a first-come-first-served basis, for local government activities and for local board of education activities. Cable companies may also have public interest obligations in other areas of service, such as telephony and broadband Internet. Direct broadcast satellite providers by law must make available channel space for non-commercial programmes to the public on 4 per cent of total capacity. All commercial television services would argue as well, with some justification in law and history, that they serve the public interest by providing quality transmission and programmes that win audiences.

Public interest rules in the US are conditioned in several ways. First, television in the US is overwhelmingly commercial in nature. Indeed the regulatory body, the Federal Communications Commission (FCC), came into existence to allocate spectrum among competing commercial players. Its primary objective is to encourage the widest commercial application of the state-controlled resource of spectrum. There is no public service tradition as in Europe, and the notion of it strikes many as patronising, by assuming the need for an elite to direct the culture of the society. Even US public television (see Grey Box) is merely required to be non-commercial.

Second, the First Amendment, which guarantees freedom of speech and the press, became a powerful tool on the side of media providers in the 20th century. This makes regulators extremely wary of content regulation – although 'indecency', a hot-button issue in the society, is a fringe area where there has been content regulation. Broadcasters' First Amendment rights are weaker than those of newspaper editors because broadcasters are monopolists on the spectrum they use. The absence of government television domestically, unlike such geopolitically motivated efforts as the Cuba-directed TV Marti, is also a reflection of concern that government should not interfere with media. Public television is also not governmental, but a private service, with minority funding from taxpayers (see Grey Box).

Third, public interest regulation of programming at the federal or national level primarily applies to broadcasters, because broadcasters have monopoly control over dedicated slices of the spectrum, or airwaves. As monopoly users of the public property of spectrum, and as combined distributors and content providers, broadcasting stations are required to do some programming for public benefit in return. Broadcast networks have traditionally acted as proxies for station owners on some programming issues, because of their affiliation agreements and also because they have always held some stations themselves. Other elements in the television industry – networks, cablecasters, satellite programme providers and others – do not use public spectrum in the same way, and are not subject to the same requirements, although they do have some public interest obligations.

Public interest requirements are also limited by political realities. One is lack of enforcement. The Federal Communications Commission, the primary regulatory body for television, has two basic weapons: fines, which historically have been trivial and no deterrent, and the 'death penalty', or revocation of a licence. The FCC has never revoked the licence of any station for failing to fulfil public interest requirements. Another reality is the tendency of regulators to become 'captured' by the industries they regulate. This tendency is not merely one of corruption, but of familiarity. Regulators come to understand industries according to the issues faced by the largest and incumbent players. For example, in the US regulators were initially hostile to cable TV, which posed a threat to broadcasting.

In the 1960s, the public became active in communications policy for the first time. Until then, only corporate stakeholders were permitted to participate in FCC decisions. In 1963, Rev. Everett Parker of the liberal mainstream United Church of Christ, participating in civil rights efforts of the time, asked the FCC to deny licence renewal to the Mississippi TV station WLBT. The station had openly and scandalously promoted white racism. In an appeal against the FCC's refusal to recognise the church's participation, a federal appeals court granted 'standing' – the right to participate – in 1966. The FCC renewed WLBT's licence anyway. The UCC sued again and, finally, a court decision in 1969 stripped WLBT of its licence.

'Standing' brought many more public stakeholders in the door of FCC proceedings, birthing what came to be known as the 'media reform' movement, which led to the most active period so far in the FCC's definition of the public interest. In this period, many ethnic and other rights groups, including African-Americans, gays, feminists, children's advocates, and many local community interests, including religious groups, used the threat of filing a petition to deny licence renewal in order to win attention from local broadcasters and from networks. The FCC's rule book came to include guidelines (not requirements, which would have violated the First Amendment) for public interest obligations, including public affairs programming, community affairs programming and community ascertainment, which is discovering local issues and perspectives. The FCC required stations to keep log books of all programmes and to make them available to the public. It required broadcasters to air coverage of all sides of controversial subjects, to offer politicians the lowest advertising rates and to cover news of all electoral candidates. In addition, many stations and networks willingly acceded to demands from the public and community organisations, rather than face a later challenge at the FCC. Children's advocates slogged through this period with partial victories until belatedly, in 1990, the Children's Television Act finally required broadcasters to air three hours a week of children's informational/educational programming.

Technological innovation brought a sea change in regulation from 1980 on. The multichannelisation of television via cable and the satellites that vastly reduced the cost of transmitting national cable programming transformed business practices. Digitalisation and the Internet transformed business practices again in the mid-1990s, causing both panic and confusion among all major stakeholders.

In the process, public interest policy thinking moved away from two familiar arguments. One traditional argument for regulation was to manage scarce resources in the public interest. Increasingly, neo-conservative policy analysts argued, the television universe was typified more by abundance – of channels, of programmes, of viewer options – than scarcity. Even though broadcasters were still monopolists of the spectrum, they said, other television channels were reducing the need for government concern about their behaviour because other providers were entering the marketplace. Another traditional argument was the need for government to keep monopolists and oligopolists under surveillance. With new technologies, neo-conservative policy analysts argued, there need not be monopolies. Rather, regulators should promote the development of new competitors. This latter argument worked better for telephony than it did for television, where broadcasters, cablecasters and satellite providers were all both programme providers and distributors, but it profoundly affected both telecommunications and mass media regulation.

The election of Ronald Reagan as President in 1980, with his strong support in the House of Representatives in Congress and the ability to appoint heads of regulatory bodies, swept such arguments into policy-making. The FCC promptly began to shed regulations, including, crucially, stations' obligations to keep log books for the public. This greatly impeded the use of petitions to deny licence renewal, which had been the principal tool of media reform activists. Heeding the signals for regulatory relaxation, broadcast networks gradually cut back and even eliminated their departments of standards and practices, which had often cut out offensive language or daring gestures. A new cable law in 1984 declared cable a viable competitor for broadcast, further undercutting legal arguments for broadcast regulation. In 1992, consumer backlash forced a more realistic rule for measuring competition, but the notion that scarcity had ended remained.

Comprehensive reform of communications regulation was under consideration in Congress from 1979 on, precipitated by technological changes in telephony. It finally culminated in the 1996 Telecommunications Act, which articulated a new standard for the public interest. Henceforth, competition would be the standard; the public would best be served by having competitive providers.

While the Act redesigned the telecommunications landscape dramatically, it did not change the basic architecture of mass media regulation. However, it did include three large changes. First, it required broadcasters to move to a digital platform and produce at least some programmes in high-definition television – the US's on-the-cheap solution to industrial planning. To make broadcasters warm to the idea, it permitted broadcasters to hold onto their analogue spectrum until 85 per cent of viewers' homes had digital TVs. Whether they will actually have to return that spectrum even at that time is now doubted by some. Second, it substantially loosened restrictions on local and national ownership, so that large companies could get much larger. (Broadcasters argued that they needed to get bigger to compete with cable and with projected programme services from telephone companies in the digital era.) Third, the law required the FCC to revisit its regulations every two years to see whether they were still required, given the newly articulated public interest standard: competition.

The Act included no set-asides such as had been done for public broadcasting and for public channels on direct broadcast satellite. It weakened the situation of access channels, not requiring their equivalent in similar local services. The law also effectively retired competitive claims in broadcast licence renewal.

Since the 1996 Act, the public has not been well served, either under the ancient regime understanding (monopoly providers do good things for the public) or the new (competitive services give consumers choice). The FCC has loosened restrictions on ownership further still, creating media companies of unprecedented size but not expanding competition of providers. The wedding of content provision and distribution, which cripples alternative and competitive businesses, has only increased with media concentration.

The FCC has refused to provide national regulation of cable broadband Internet, which some had looked to as an alternative distributor and which now is typically provided only by the largest local monopoly cable providers. The merger of Time Warner and AOL provided a showcase for the debate over whether cable companies should control broadband or whether their broadband pipes to the home should be made available to competing companies. Eventually, because of public pressure, the new company was forced to permit selected providers to use its pipes, but other cable companies were not so required. A Congressionally mandated inquiry into proposed public interest obligations of broadcasters on their digital channels did not result in policy. The question of whether cable companies must carry broadcasters' digital channels was unresolved in the early years of the twenty-first century.

Demands to honour the public interest one way or another may precipitate new regulatory decisions. The US public has demonstrated impatience with the quality and terms of US time-based TV by declining ratings, while demonstrating an unflagging appetite for screen entertainment by increasing VCR, DVD sales, adoption of digital video recorders, and use of video on demand. Viewers have both consumed unprecedentedly violent and sexually explicit entertainment and also complained about sexually offensive broadcast entertainment. Public outrage over media concentration galvanised many to protest during 2002–3, as the FCC relaxed ownership regulations, and caused some members of Congress to propose legislation countering the FCC's decision. A rising issue is the coming change in television business with digital video recorders, which challenges time-based television generally. This shift creates new opportunities for diverse programming as well as for tighter corporate control and surveillance of viewer choices, and raises new issues around privacy.

The public interest will continue to be a term of art in the continuing conflict among stakeholders on the US television landscape. It will also be a phrase to galvanise the discontented and a rallying cry for social movements, which link their issues to media access and media control.

Patricia Aufderheide

RECOMMENDED READING

Aufderheide, Patricia (1999), *Communications Policy and the Public Interest: The Telecommunications Act of 1996*, New York: Guilford Press.

Aufderheide, Patricia (2000), *The Daily Planet: A Critic on the Capitalist Culture Beat*, Minneapolis: University of Minnesota Press.

Engelman, Ralph (1996), *Public Radio and Television in America : A Political History*, Thousand Oaks, CA: Sage.

Horwitz, Robert (1989), *The Irony of Regulatory Reform: The Deregulation of American Telecommunications*, New York: Oxford University Press.

Huber, Peter (1997), *Law and Disorder in Cyberspace: Abolish the FCC and Let Common Law Rule the Telecosm*, Oxford, New York: Oxford University Press.

Krattenmaker, Thomas and Powe, Lucas (1994), *Regulating Broadcast Programming*, Cambridge, MA, Washington, DC: MIT Press, AEI Press.

McChesney, Robert W. (1994), *Telecommunications, Mass Media, and Democracy: The Battle for Control of U.S. Broadcasting, 1928–1935*, New York: Oxford University Press.

Montgomery, Kathryn C. (1989), *Target, Prime Time: Advocacy Groups and the Struggle over Entertainment Television*, New York: Oxford University Press.

Napoli, Philip M. (2001), *Foundations of Communications Policy: Principles and Process in the Regulation of Electronic Media*, Cresskill, NJ: Hampton Press.

Ouellette, Laurie (2002), *Viewers Like You?: How Public TV Failed the People*, New York: Columbia University Press.

US PUBLIC TV

US public television is something of an afterthought in the US TV landscape, but has earned a solid reputation for quality information services. It came of age in a broadcast-only world of three networks, when it uniquely provided high-quality children's programming, upmarket entertainment viewing and educational programmes. New channels and technologies have cut into these areas. Its current challenge is how to become an essential community service in an age of informational abundance.

Public TV was nurtured at the outset not by public demand but by the Ford Foundation's strategising and the educational concerns of one FCC commissioner, Frieda Hennock, which resulted in spectrum, much of it on the UHF band, being set aside for a non-commercial service. Since TV sets at the time then could not even access UHF, no funds were allocated and the service was to be non-commercial, in most communities the spectrum went unused or used rudimentarily by a school or college. At the height of the 'Great Society' years of President Lyndon Johnson, when many social programmes were started, the Public Broadcasting Act of 1967 was passed, and it changed public TV dramatically. It allotted a small amount of federal funds to a new private company, the Corporation for Public Broadcasting, which then parcelled out the money to individual stations for basic needs.

In order to operate, the stations needed more funds, which they raised from individuals through membership drives, from corporations and foundations, from the non-profit institutions that sponsored them, and from state and local governments. Today, public television's budget is about half tax dollars (local, state and federal), one-quarter membership dollars, and about a quarter from corporations and private foundations. Public TV signals from the 357 stations reach to almost every household in the US.

Unable to produce high-budget programmes locally, the stations also needed shared programming – something the law explicitly banned CPB from doing, in fear of creating a liberal-biased 'fourth network'. Within two years, the stations had created a membership organisation, the Public Broadcasting Service (PBS), to lease programmes that they could share. Several other programme services have since also sprung up.

Although less than half the US public watches public TV in any given week, and its prime-time shows rarely attract more than 2 per cent of the viewing audience, public TV is perennially controversial. Any evidence of liberal political opinion or cultural extremism (especially lifestyle issues, such as homosexuality) becomes fodder for conservative politicians spoiling for a fight during the Congressional appropriations that are required every three years. Controversial programmes can trigger drops in membership, and they are almost never backed with corporate dollars. By 1970, three years after the 1967 Act, President Nixon was already outraged that a public affairs programme on banks' discriminatory policies towards the poor had mentioned funders of his campaign. He, like Reagan and some members of Congress since, tried to cripple or destroy the service. While none have succeeded, partly because of viewer loyalty among targeted groups, such as parents and the elderly, public TV executives have learned caution, and public affairs remains a poorly supported programme area.

Public TV has played an innovative role with pioneering technology, for example, closed captioning and satellite programme distribution. It also continues to be a nearly unique resource for expensive programmes such as educationally tested children's shows, well-researched historical documentaries and for social-issue documentaries on subjects that address inequality. It has permitted adults to complete high school using its distance learning programmes, and it has experimented creatively with interactive programming using the Internet. Public TV stations are in the vanguard of digital transition, and were among the first to produce in high definition.

Across the many and often misaligned elements of the sprawling public TV landscape, there is growing consensus that public TV must have relevance to the local community to survive, without losing the benefits of a national network identity through PBS. Stations offer many community services, including materials for childcare providers, to boost educational benefits of public TV programmes and community outreach on certain programmes. At the same time, public TV is short on research money, and the core staffs in most parts of public TV are broadcasters, not digital media planners. The changing TV landscape, with growing interactivity, digital channels, a multiplicity of viewer choices, and intense competition from commercial services, poses a serious challenge for public TV executives, at the same time that no one body within public TV acts as a co-ordinator and public TV has few champions outside its own organisations. Perhaps the greatest challenge of all is the very fact of public TV's decentralisation, a feature built into its structure at the start.

Patricia Aufderheide

Censorship Regimes and Content Parameters – UK

Censorship is clearly a form of content regulation, but in a broadcasting system run according to public service principles (q.v.), by no means all content regulation is a form of censorship. In particular, one needs to distinguish between negative and positive forms of content regulation, the former regulating content considered undesirable out of the system, the latter regulating content considered desirable into it. Or to put it slightly differently, audiences can expect to enjoy both freedom from certain kinds of content and freedom to access a wide range of diverse programming.

In a public service broadcasting system, positive forms of regulation have traditionally been used to compensate for the deficiencies of the market, requiring the production of those programmes which commercially cannot pay their way, but whose presence is thought to be important to society. Regulation has also been used to ensure that the broadcasting arena is not monopolised by particular commercial interests. In this context, the highly experienced regulator Colin Shaw (1999) has coined the useful notion of 'sustaining diversity by compulsion', arguing that:

> The blandness of much commercial broadcasting, justified by the broadcasters' obligations to advertisers and the sensitivities of the public, can be a curb on high-flying intentions with their risks of disaster. Such programmes, whose purpose is sometimes described as pushing out the envelope, require the existence of a sympathetic regime if they are to be attempted, let alone fulfilled. The substance of regulation, therefore, plays a crucial part in the evolution of a climate in which, as an essential ingredient in a responsible broadcasting service, conventional standards, whether of decency, taste, or other things, may be challenged as well as protected. (p. 152)

In Britain, broadcasting is subject to the same legal regime as that governing books, newspapers and magazines. Many would regard the laws of defamation, obscenity, official secrecy, confidence and so on as onerous enough, but, in addition, broadcasting has always been subject to successive broadcasting acts and now falls under the Communications Act 2003, while the BBC must adhere as well to the terms of the Licence Agreement which forms part of its Charter. These measures represent both positive and negative forms of regulation, but this section will concentrate on the latter.

For example, under the BBC Charter the Corporation can be forbidden to transmit 'any matter or class of matter' which the government specifies, while Section 336(5) of the Communications Act similarly states that:

> The Secretary of State may, at any time, by notice require Ofcom to direct the holders of the Broadcasting Act licences specified in the notice to refrain from including in their licensed services any matter, or description of matter, specified in the notice. (p. 296)

It was precisely the Charter and the then current Broadcasting Act which were invoked by Home Secretary Douglas Hurd in 1988 to prevent the direct broadcasting of interviews with members of certain political organisations that were active in Northern Ireland, a ban which lasted until 1994.

However, for the most part these measures have required the broadcasters and those who regulate them to draw up and enforce their own codes on matters pertaining to content, including the censorship of content deemed unacceptable. In this respect, Geoffrey Robertson and Andrew Nicol complain of 'excessive regulation in the interests of good taste and good politics' (2002, p. 769), and note in particular that recent governments' attitudes to broadcasting deregulation have been decidedly schizophrenic. In particular, under the Thatcher government, which was the first to attempt to move away from the public service model, economic and structural deregulation was accompanied by *more* stringent regulation of programme content. Thus, for example the 1988 White Paper on broadcasting, which resulted from the 1986 Peacock Committee Report and preceded the 1990 Broadcasting Act, stated that: 'As new services emerge and subscription develops, viewer choice, rather than regulatory imposition, can and should increasingly be relied upon to secure the programmes which viewers want.' It swiftly added, however, that: 'Rules will still be needed to safeguard programme standards on such matters as good taste and decency and to ensure that the unique power of the broadcast media is not abused' (Home Office, 1988, p. 5). In this vision of things, censorship was euphemistically presented as the 'consumer protection aspect of programme standards' (ibid., p. 34).

Under the Broadcasting Act 1990, broadcasting was brought under the Obscene Publications Act, although this was largely a symbolic gesture to appease television's moralistic critics (who included Mrs Thatcher), as, thanks to the broadcasters' own codes, nothing remotely obscene had ever been broadcast on British television. Up until this point, the Independent Broadcasting Authority (IBA), which regulated ITV and Channel Four, had had the power (which they indeed used) to cut or even ban programmes that they considered broke the law and/or offended against their own regulations. However, the Act abolished the IBA and replaced it with the 'light touch' Independent Television Commission (ITC); this did not have the ability to preview programmes, and thus to pre-censor them, but it did have what Robertson and Nicol call 'reprisal powers' (2002, p. 771); in other words, if broadcasters transmitted programmes that infringed the ITC Programme Code they could be fined and, in extreme cases, their licence to broadcast could be terminated. In addition the Broadcasting Standards Council was formed, whose somewhat paternalistic attitude to television can be gleaned from its first report, which described the medium as a 'guest in the home' whose conduct might acceptably become 'more relaxed and informal' as the evening wore on.

It is perhaps unsurprising, then, that Robertson and Nicol conclude:

> The 1990 Act ushered in a decade in which freedom of
> expression was bounded not by precise laws but by
> imprecise codes, drafted and interpreted by Government
> appointees on a number of bodies whose jurisdiction
> overlapped and whose decisions could not be appealed or
> attacked on their merits. (Ibid., p. 772)

At one point broadcasting was variously (and expensively) governed by the ITC, Broadcasting Complaints Commission, Broadcasting Standards Council (merged with the former in 1996 into the Broadcasting Standards Commission) and Radio Authority. No wonder, then, that disgruntled Peacock Committee member Samuel Brittan complained that:

> In putting forward the idea of a free broadcasting market
> without censorship, Peacock exposed many of the contra-
> dictions in the Thatcherite espousal of market forces. In
> principle, Mrs Thatcher and her supporters are all in
> favour of deregulation, competition and consumer choice.
> But they are also even more distrustful than traditionalist
> Tories of policies that allow people to listen to and watch
> what they like, subject only to the law of the land. They
> espouse the market system but dislike the libertarian
> value-judgements involved in its operation. (1989, p. 40)

However, a very similar attitude underlay the 2000 White Paper on communications. On the one hand, as Steven Byers, the Secretary of State for Trade and Industry, and Chris Smith, the Secretary of State for Culture, Media and Sport, put it in the Introduction to the document:

> We want to ensure the widest possible access to a choice
> of diverse communications services of the highest quality

> . . . . We want to include every section of our society in
> the benefits of these services, and to use to the full the
> opportunities now available for enhancing their diversity
> and quality. (DTI/DCMS, 2000, p. 3)

But, on the other hand, they were careful to point out that: 'We want to make sure that the right balance is struck between freedom of speech and basic standards of decency and quality' (ibid.).

The Communications Act 2003 merged all of the broadcasting regulators into the Office of Communications (Ofcom). It also required Ofcom to produce its own Broadcasting Code in the light of the broad stipulations laid down in the Act. This appeared in May 2005 and replaced the six previous codes of the Broadcasting Standards Commission, the Independent Television Commission and the Radio Authority. Ofcom regulates certain aspects of BBC programming too, but to a considerable extent the BBC regulates its own programmes in accordance with its *Producers' Guidelines* (1993), which, again, follow the Act's stipulations on content.

In many respects, the creation of Ofcom represents a welcome tidying-up operation in the area of broadcasting regulation. Those who had found its predecessors overly censorious in the field of negative content regulation welcomed the statement made on the publication of the Code that:

> As listeners and viewers exercise choice in a digital and
> multi-channel environment, it is important to allow
> broadcasters as much freedom of expression as is consis-
> tent with the law as well as the flexibility to differentiate
> between services and to enable their audiences to make
> informed choices . . . . We wanted to create a code that
> recognised the rapidly changing broadcast environment
> and increased levels of media literacy. This enables us to
> ensure that children can be protected and adults are given
> the information to make informed choices. (<www.ofcom.
> org.uk/consult/condocs/Broadcasting_code/bcstat>)

How the Code operates in practice remains, of course, to be seen. But it is clear that in the new broadcasting environment, regulation, both positive and negative, will become more a matter of self-regulation, with the regulators laying down the basic rules but intervening only to ensure that these are obeyed or to penalise offenders. In such a situation, censorship tends to transmute itself into self-censorship, something which is notoriously nebulous and difficult to pin down. At the same time, there is a distinct fear that broadcasting content could be adversely affected by commercial and competitive pressures which, by narrowing the range of programmes on offer, could act as a form of market censorship every bit as damaging to

---

THE COMMUNICATIONS ACT 2003

Section 319 of the Communications Act lays down a number of 'standards objectives' for Ofcom. These include the following:

- Persons under the age of eighteen must be protected.
- Material likely to encourage or incite the commission of crime or to lead to disorder must not be included in programming.
- Broadcast news must be presented with due impartiality and accuracy.
- Generally accepted standards must be applied to all programming so as to provide adequate protection for members of the public from harmful or offensive material.
- Advertising which may be misleading, harmful or offensive is prohibited.
- Advertising which is inserted by or on behalf of a body whose objectives are wholly or mainly of a political nature, or which is directed towards a political end, or which has a connection with an industrial dispute, is prohibited.
- Unsuitable sponsorship of programmes is prohibited.
- There must be no use of techniques (such as subliminal ones) that exploit the possibility of conveying a message to viewers or listeners, or of otherwise influencing their minds, without their being fully aware of what is occurring.

In drawing up its Programme Code, Ofcom is required by the Act to have regard to:

- The degree of harm or offence likely to be caused by the inclusion of any particular sort of material in programmes.
- The likely size and composition of the potential audience for particular programmes or particular channels.
- The likely expectation of the audience as to the nature of a programme's content and the extent to which the nature of a programme's content can be brought to the attention of potential members of the audience.
- The likelihood of people who are unaware of the nature of a programme's content being unintentionally exposed to it.
- The desirability of maintaining the independence of editorial control over programme content.
- A proper degree of responsibility being exercised with regard to religious programmes, which must avoid any abusive treatment of the religious views and beliefs of those belonging to particular religions or denominations.

Julian Petley

---

free expression as the more obvious and overt censorship of the *ancien régime*. Meanwhile, the manner in which the government treated the BBC over its coverage of the invasion of Iraq shows all too clearly that it is just as ready as its predecessors to employ bullying and intimidation as a form of political censorship.

Julian Petley

RECOMMENDED READING

BBC (1993), *Producers' Guidelines*, London: BBC.

Brittan, Samuel (1989), 'The Case for the Consumer Market', in Cento Veljanovski (ed.), *Freedom in Broadcasting*, London: Institute of Economic Affairs.

Communications Act 2003, London: TSO.

Department of Trade and Industry/Department of Culture, Media and Sport (2000), *A New Future for Communications*, London: TSO.

Home Office (1988), *Broadcasting in the '90s: Competition, Choice and Quality*, London: HMSO.

Ofcom (2005a), *The Ofcom Broadcasting Code*, London: Ofcom.

Ofcom (2005b), *Statement on the Ofcom Broadcasting Code*, London: Ofcom.

Petley, Julian (1989), 'Doublethink', IPPA Bulletin, Summer, 4–5.

Petley, Julian (2001), 'Television', in Derek Jones (ed.), *Censorship: A World Encyclopedia*, vol. 3, London: Fitzroy Dearborn.

Robertson, Geoffrey and Nicol, Andrew (2002), *Robertson and Nicol on Media Law*, 4th edn, London: Sweet and Maxwell.

Shaw, Colin (1999), *Deciding What We Watch: Taste, Decency, and Media Ethics in the UK and the USA*, Oxford: Clarendon Press.

Censorship Regimes and Content Parameters – US

When pop singer Janet Jackson's breast was exposed during a surprise half-time stunt in the broadcast of the 2004 Super Bowl, the incident set off a national and international debate over standards of taste and decency in American television. Within hours of the incident, the Federal Communications Commission – the federal agency that regulates American television – had announced a formal investigation. The FCC chairman personally telephoned the head of Viacom, CBS

Television's parent company, to chastise him for his network's affront to decency during the highly rated afternoon show. In the ensuing weeks, the momentary 'costume malfunction' had mushroomed into a much wider public controversy. Conservative advocacy groups used their websites and email newsletters to generate letter-writing campaigns and sponsor boycotts. Washington political pundits – on the left and the right – debated the issue on the Internet, in the print press and on the dozens of television talk shows and twenty-four-hour news channels that peppered the media landscape in the 500-channel era of cable and satellite TV. The FCC began slapping fines on dozens of other broadcasters, jawboning industry leaders to clean up the airwaves. The US Congress held a series of public hearings on broadcast indecency. The TV industry hastily organised a 'summit', calling together network executives, producers, advocacy groups and advertisers to address the problem. And the V-chip – which had fallen into obscurity after being mandated in all television sets a few years earlier – was dusted off and reintroduced to the American public through prominent newspaper ads and public service announcements.

The fact that this controversy erupted at the beginning of a presidential election year was no accident. 'Culture' issues were known to poll well, and to serve as an effective tactic for diverting public attention away from more complex and vexing matters such as rising unemployment, deficit spending and the continuing war in Iraq. Nor was it a coincidence that Viacom found itself in trouble over its programming at a time when both Congress and the courts were deliberating possible reversal of new TV ownership relaxation rules passed a few months earlier by the FCC.

This most recent flap over broadcast indecency is emblematic of the highly political, complicated nature of TV content control in the US. Rather than a clear-cut, transparent set of 'censorship regimes', the boundaries of acceptability in television programming have repeatedly been established, tested and redefined through the complex interplay of key institutions in American society. These have included: TV industry players – networks, producers, local stations, advertisers and global media conglomerates; government institutions – regulatory agencies, the Congress and the courts; as well as other sectors of society, such as interest groups, academic institutions, medical associations and the press. This 'negotiated struggle' over television content has also been very dynamic, strongly influenced by marketplace fluctuations, technological change, social trends and shifts in the political winds (see Cantor, 1980; Montgomery, 1989). Throughout its history, American television has experienced periods of intense controversy and political pressure followed by more placid periods of institutional stability. Industry responses to these outside

pressures have followed a predictable pattern: when thrust into the spotlight and forced to defend their practices, television executives have vowed to correct the problem, invoking the efficacy of various self-regulatory mechanisms. When the pressure has waned, many of these mechanisms have fallen into disuse, only resurfacing during later crises. In some cases, however, these institutionalised content policies have remained in place over time. All of these processes are deeply rooted in the structure of American television, its basic business model and its particular relationship to the government (Barnouw, 1975; Montgomery, 1989).

Unlike the television system in many other countries, American television is primarily a private enterprise, with government playing an indirect regulatory role. Since the 1920s, over-the-air broadcasting has been regulated as a public trustee, subject to licensing (of local stations, not networks) by the Federal Communications Commission. The FCC is barred by law from engaging in 'prior restraint' of content, which would violate the First Amendment of the US Constitution. However, the agency can develop rules designed to ensure that broadcasters serve the 'public interest, convenience and necessity'. Over the years, the FCC has issued directives in a variety of content areas (e.g., children's television, broadcast editorialising, etc.), often walking a fine line between regulatory guidance and programmatic intrusion. Because cable and satellite television are not licensed by the FCC (though they are subject to some local licensing), many of these content-related rules have not applied to them (see Bittner, 1994).

The broadcast indecency rules may come closest to being a 'censorship regime' in US television, though even with this policy the government can only act after the fact by fining the licensee for offensive content already broadcast. The FCC defines broadcast indecency as 'language or material that, in context, depicts or describes, in terms patently offensive as measured by contemporary community standards for the broadcast medium, sexual or excretory organs or activities'. With the stated aim of protecting children, the rules require that indecent content may only be broadcast between the hours of 10 pm and 6 am. 'Indecent' content, unlike 'obscene' content, is considered constitutionally protected speech; it cannot be banned, but it can be 'channelled'. Nonetheless, when the Commission fines a station, launches an investigation, or even writes a letter to a broadcaster (the latter two often referred to as 'raised eyebrow' regulation), these government actions can have a 'chilling effect' on freedom of speech in television (Heins, 2001, pp. 109–36).

Both the US Congress and the courts play important roles in influencing television content though, like the FCC, usually through indirect means. FCC decisions are sometimes appealed through the federal courts, which can overturn, support, or 'remand' them to the agency for further deliberation. In addition to passing laws to regulate the television industry, Congress has oversight over FCC actions (Bittner, 1994). One of Congress's most influential roles has been its ability to hold public hearings, which in turn can generate significant press coverage. Since the earliest days of television, Congressional hearings – on TV violence, political advertising, children's programming and a number of other issues – have spawned widespread public debate (see Rowland, 1983).

In response to public and government criticism during the 1950s, the television industry's chief lobbying body, the National Association of Broadcasters (NAB), established a 'Television Code of Good Practice', which functioned more effectively as a shield against pressure than it did as a content policy (Barnouw, 1975). Under direct pressure from Congress and the FCC, the code was amended in the 1970s to include a 'family viewing hour' during prime time, but was struck down by the US Court of Appeals after being challenged by a coalition of Hollywood creative community members (Cowan, 1978). The courts subsequently struck down the entire NAB Code because its restrictions on advertising time were considered a restraint of trade. In the ensuing years, there have been numerous (so far unsuccessful) attempts to get the industry to reinstate the Television Code (see Bittner, 1994).

Advertisers have had a particularly significant impact on the content policies of US television, though the nature of that influence has shifted over time. Throughout the years, sponsors have also been an important pressure point for organised campaigns over programme content. During television's first decade, sponsors were the most important institutional players in determining the content of American programming. In a system inherited from radio, sponsors packaged and produced programmes, which often bore the names of the product advertised. In the 1960s, the rising costs of advertising time, changes in network programming practices and government oversight of broadcasting all combined to alter the relationship between advertisers and programme content. Rather than producing and packaging programmes, advertisers began purchasing spots within a number of different programmes throughout the schedule. This change largely removed sponsors from the arena of content control, shifting that responsibility to the networks (Barnouw, 1978).

In the 1970s, organised pressure campaigns from the medical community, parents' organisations, educators and media reform groups forced television advertisers back into a more active role as arbiters of content. As social scientists presented new research to Congress documenting the harms of TV violence, NGO coalitions adapted these research tools to identify which products were advertised in the most violent programmes (Cowan, 1978; Montgomery, 1989). Threatened with

consumer boycotts, advertisers quickly developed their own mechanisms for self-protection, drawing up official policies to spell out the kinds of problematic programme content in which their ads could not appear, and commissioning pre-screening companies to flag possible problems in advance of the broadcasts. The campaigns only temporarily reduced violent content, but they left in place institutional mechanisms that advertisers have used repeatedly for routine surveillance of the programming in which their commercial messages appeared (Montgomery, 1989, pp. 101–22).

Within the television networks, the standards and practices departments have been the primary divisions responsible for both dealing with outside pressure and developing internal content policies. Their role became particularly important in the 1970s during a period of heightened pressure on the television industry. In addition to campaigns over TV violence, protests came from a variety of groups – representing African-Americans, Latinos, Asian Americans, women and gays – all demanding greater (and more positive) representation in programming. The standards and practices departments developed a number of strategies for 'managing' these 'special interest groups', negotiating with them over what were acceptable and appropriate depictions. These 'sensitivities' were internalised into the networks' unwritten content policies. After the television industry was deregulated in the 1980s, the major broadcast networks cut staff in these departments, though most were forced to build them back up during subsequent periods of pressure. Many cable networks have also found it necessary to create their own standards and practices departments (Montgomery, 1989).

By the last decade of the 20th century, the US television system had undergone dramatic changes. An already fragmented media culture exploded still further into hundreds of cable television channels, many of them pushing at the boundaries of acceptable content. The Internet and a host of accompanying digital technologies rapidly intruded into Americans' daily lives, challenging many prevailing expectations and conventions. The 1990s also witnessed the first major Congressional rewrite of the nation's telecommunications laws since the Depression era, sparking a flurry of intense political activity as industry lobbyists, politicians and interest groups competed to stake their respective claims in the new policy regime (see Aufderheide, 1999). These simultaneous tectonic shifts – in both the media and the regulatory landscapes – created particularly fertile ground for a renewal of long-standing debates over TV content.

One of the provisions of the Telecommunications Act of 1996 was a requirement that all new television sets be equipped with a 'V-chip' device to enable parents to protect their children from inappropriate or harmful programmes.

(Cable companies were already required to provide channel-blocking capability to subscribers who requested the service, but they had done little to promote its availability.) In order for the V-chip to work, television programmes would have to be rated and the rating would need to be encoded electronically. While the government could not mandate a ratings system, Congress and the White House found ways to encourage co-operation from an industry seeking to benefit from other deregulatory provisions of the Telecommunications Act. Immediately after passage of the new law, TV industry executives announced at a White House summit that they would develop a self-regulatory ratings system to be modelled on the movie ratings (see Price, 1998). When the planned new ratings system was unveiled a number of months later, however, a coalition of health, education and child advocacy groups campaigned against it, arguing that the proposed 'age-based' ratings failed to include any indication of programme content. Under public and Congressional pressure, the television industry agreed to engage in a series of negotiations with the advocacy groups, resulting in an amended ratings system that included 'content descriptors' for violence, sexual activity and offensive language.

Unlike the process for rating theatrical films, where an MPAA-appointed committee decides how to rate each film, television programmes (both broadcast and cable) are rated by networks, studios and, sometimes, individual stations. Given this decentralised labelling process, the confusing hybrid age and content labels (e.g., TV-14 DSL), and the industry's failure to promote the new system, it was no surprise that very few parents either understood or used the V-chip. But when public outcries, Congressional scrutiny and threats of further government regulation arose again, the V-chip was viewed as a useful tool for deflecting some of the pressure without significantly impacting the actual content of television programmes.

Kathryn C. Montgomery

RECOMMENDED READING

Aufderheide, Patricia (1999), *Communications Policy and the Public Interest: The Telecommunications Act of 1996*, New York: Guilford Press.

Barnouw, Erik (1975), *Tube of Plenty: The Evolution of American Television*, New York, Oxford: Oxford University Press.

Barnouw, Erik (1978), *The Sponsor: Notes on a Modern Potentate*, New York, Oxford: Oxford University Press.

Bittner, John R. (1994), *Law and Regulation of Electronic Media*, New York: Prentice-Hall.

Cantor, Muriel (1980), *Prime Time TV: Content and Control*, Beverly Hills, CA: Sage.

Cowan, Geoffrey (1978), *See No Evil*, New York: Touchstone/Simon and Schuster.

Greenberg, Bradley S. (2001), *The Alphabet Soup of Television Program Ratings*, Cresskill, NJ: Hampton Press.

Heins, Marjorie (2001), *Not in Front of the Children: 'Indecency,' Censorship, and the Innocence of Youth*, New York: Hill and Wang.

Montgomery, Kathryn C. (1989), *Target, Prime Time: Advocacy Groups and the Struggle over Entertainment Television*, New York, Oxford: Oxford University Press.

Price, Monroe E. (ed.) (1998), *The V-Chip Debate: Content Filtering from Television to the Internet*, Mahwah, NJ: Lawrence Erlbaum Associates.

Rowland, Willard (1983), *The Politics of TV Violence*, Beverly Hills, CA: Sage.

MAKING PROGRAMMES

PBS (Public Broadcasting Service)/BBC

At one level the BBC and America's public broadcasting service (PBS) are strikingly similar; both systems are not for profit, leaving the viewers, rather than the shareholders or advertisers, as the primary stakeholders. Both broadcasters embrace a set of core public values built around a shared idea of an informed citizenship underpinned by notions of education, culture and community.

PBS and the BBC, as well as other UK public broadcasters, particularly Channel Four, also often share the same programmes. The long-running drama series *Masterpiece Theatre*, which is held in great affection by the viewers and members of PBS, is the shop window for British literary classics adapted for television. Dickens, Austen and Hardy are regularly featured in *Masterpiece Theatre*, leavened by an occasional more modern piece, like Zadie Smith's *White Teeth*.

In factual genres too, PBS is quintessentially British. The US version of *Antiques Roadshow* is more often than not the most popular programme on PBS and many of their most successful science and history series have been originated in the United Kingdom. Only public affairs remains resolutely American in focus.

Both broadcasters are also firmly part of a multimedia landscape. The largest PBS licensees, like WGBH in Boston, also run regional radio stations and there is a close sibling relationship to the radio equivalent of the PBS network, National Public Radio (NPR). Increasingly too, the long-term public value of both PBS and the BBC is reflected in non-commercial, content-rich online sites.

Yet, for all these similarities the differences between the two systems are even more profound. While the BBC sits centre stage in the British public and cultural life, PBS sits on the American television margin. It's the big commercial operators – NBC, CBS, ABC and Fox – who are the dominant forces in American media, owning not only terrestrial television stations but also cable outlets and movie studios.

While BBC1 reaches nearly 25 per cent of the population and BBC2 nearly 11 per cent, PBS currently hits around 1.7 per cent, albeit of a larger population (BARB, 2004). Although even this figure puts PBS ahead of some of the well-known cable channels, like Animal Planet or the Food Network, it falls

a long way short of the critical mass audience needed to make an impact upon the wider society.

PBS was founded long after the BBC which, by the birth of PBS in 1969, had already been running for over forty years. Now PBS is a complex web of 349 non-commercial stations operated by 170 non-commercial licences with a network commissioning, distribution and engineering centre in Alexandria, Virginia. Its role is similar to the ITV Network Centre, a body apparently independent from its owners, choosing the most effective schedule from independent as well as owner-producers.

The origins of PBS sit squarely in education, which in many ways is still the core purpose of the network. The first breath of life was in 1917 when a radio broadcast from the University of Wisconsin but it was not until fifty years later that President Lyndon Johnson signed the Public Broadcasting Act and it became law.

As the author E. B. White wrote in 1966 in support of public broadcasting,

> Non-commercial TV should address itself to the idea of excellence, yet the idea of acceptability which keeps commercial TV from climbing the staircase. I think TV should be providing the visual counterpart of the literary essay, should arouse our dreams, satisfy our hunger for beauty, take us on journeys, enable us to participate in events, present great drama and must explore the sea and the sky and the woods and the hills . . . it should restate and clarify the social dilemma and the political pickle. (White, 1966)

Even today 30 per cent of PBS station licences are colleges and universities. Although the BBC plays a significant role in the formal learning through programmes for schools and colleges, its mission is primarily based upon stimulating an informed democracy via the more informal learning embodied in the range of its provisions in news and other factual genres.

Although PBS stretches into every geographical corner of the US, the service is more marginal than the BBC because it does not enjoy the universality of a licence fee. For all the millions of households tuning into PBS, the licence fee means that the BBC is owned by everyone and used by 94 per cent of the population each week. This universality enables the BBC to

PUBLIC IMPACT: THE BLUES AND THE BIG READ

As public broadcasters mark out their territory in the crowded digital landscape, they will increasingly use their impact beyond broadcast as an additional measure of their public value to viewers. In America, PBS has been trying to measure Points of Impact Beyond Broadcasting (PIBB) since the 1990s. The 2003 series The Blues was a good example.

The Blues comprised seven feature-length documentaries directed by distinguished movie directors, including Mike Figgis, Clint Eastwood and Wim Wenders. The executive producer was Martin Scorsese. Major funding came from Seattle-based company Vulcan, owned by former Microsoft founder Paul Allen. The series was presented for PBS by WGBH in Boston.

Apart from the PBS broadcast, Vulcan and WGBH created a string of initiatives to add depth and sustainability to the broadcast. An official year of The Blues, blessed by Congress, included a mobile exhibit, a series of concerts from Memphis to New York, a thirteen-part public radio series and an outreach programme to give schoolchildren a social and economic context to Blues music. This teacher's guide was aimed at high school teachers in English, Social Studies and Music and included online lesson plans. The car company Volkswagen was a major sponsor of the public events, as well as the broadcast series.

The Big Read from the BBC was aimed at widening accessibility to reading by finding Britain's best-loved book. Led by BBC2, The Big Read was supported by radio, online, edu-cational outreach and interactive services, with a public voting dimension to add audience engagement.

The Big Read, working, via the Reading Agency, with every one of Britain's 4,200 libraries, led to the lending rate of favourite titles, like Great Expectations and Jane Eyre rising tenfold. To further encourage group reading the BBC created an advice pack on how to set up a book group; 2,150 new Big Read book groups were registered. In schools a partnership between BBC Learning and the National Literary Trust developed teaching resources for each stage of the national curriculum. In total there were 45,000 downloads of these teaching resources.

Finally, commercial partners in bookselling and publishing saw the BBC's value as a business driver, with huge increases in book sales for the Top Ten titles and a free copy of the winner, The Lord of the Rings, sent to every secondary school. Paul Hoggart wrote in The Times, 'The Big Read satisfies the contradictory demands of popular accessibility, celebrating heritage and widening cultural horizons'.

The BBC believes it can act as a cultural and social catalyst; creating effective partnerships with a range of organisations, it can use its power to engage large audiences, its diversity of outlets to reach a wide social spectrum and its trusted brand for the wider public good. Apart from The Big Read, other recent examples range from the BBC World Service's AIDS campaign, broadcast in forty-three different languages, to Restoration, a campaign to restore Britain's neglected buildings.

John Willis

---

bring Britain together, to glue its constituent parts into a whole, at the moments of national mourning or joy, from the funeral of Princess Diana to the Olympic Games. Fragmented and diversely owned, PBS is a federation of licence holders with inevitable tensions between local independence and central or network control.

In return for the licence fee, BBC television and radio must provide something for everyone in its audience and as a result it offers a wider range of output than PBS, including popular soap operas like *EastEnders*, or *The Archers* on radio: a genre that would be hard to imagine in American public television.

A recent study, however, suggests that broadcasting in the UK may be a strong contributor to social capital. *EastEnders*, for example, is watched by people of all ages, social classes and unusually, compared to US television, all ethnic backgrounds, providing shared experiences between otherwise disparate groups (Brookes, 2004).

The licence fee, currently £121 a head, has also enabled the BBC to fund originated British production at a high level with a licence fee income of £2.7 billion. In contrast the operating revenue of PBS is just £181 million ($324 million), plus income raised by local stations in addition. More than that, the funding is stitched together like a patchwork quilt. In 2000, federal grants brought in 18.3 per cent but the biggest source of income was donations by individual members and their families at 23.5 per cent of the total.

The membership system, which registers about 4.5 million individuals, adds an extra dimension to the relationship of PBS to its audience. In urban centres, supporting the local PBS station is akin to being a supporting member of the local art gallery or opera company. Through regular 'pledge' drives on air and a string of off-air events, from auctions to special screenings, PBS stations create the membership base without which it would not have sufficient revenue to operate.

Although every ten years, when the BBC renegotiates its Royal Charter, there is intense political debate before the licence fee is set, the BBC can plan its investment in technology as well as develop long-term plans for services or programmes. If advertising revenue declines in the commercial sector, the BBC also enjoys a counter-cyclical role, providing secure funding for the British production community in leaner times.

The hand-to mouth funding of PBS makes long-term strategic thinking more challenging. Downturn in the wider economy soon translates into loss of revenue from individual members and corporate donors. Appropriations from government via the Corporation for Public Broadcasting (CPB) are on a two-year cycle, inhibiting planning and making PBS susceptible to political interference. Recently, CPB added more conservative members to its Board and political pressure sharpened in the run up to the 2004 election.

So while the BBC has to create a vision for its future that seizes the opportunities of digital broadcasting, its universal funding model is probably safe for the Charter period starting at the end of 2006 and currently planned to last for ten years. The BBC Charter document, *Building Public Value*, paints a picture of a more open and fluid organisation bringing global, social, cultural and democratic value to the nation in a more measurable and accountable way (BBC, 2004).

Even so, the challenges to the BBC to justify its scale and scope in a multichannel landscape are intense. PBS, however, is in a much more vulnerable position. Not only is it much less part of the national fabric of America than the BBC is in Britain, but its low level of funding makes it much harder to justify its existence on the basis of offering programmes that are distinctive from commercial operators.

Much PBS production is of a high quality but increasingly, new channels like Discovery or National Geographic have invaded traditional PBS territory. Outside of children's programmes, this lack of distinctiveness and the continuing political uncertainties make PBS vulnerable. It is not hard to imagine PBS slipping back to its origins primarily as a broadcaster of formal education.

The BBC believes its value is more important than ever,

creating a fully digital Britain is a public challenge that the BBC must help to lead. It is a Britain from which the BBC, and only the BBC, can ensure that no one is excluded. It is a Britain where investment in British talent and British voices and the widest range of quality British content will be more important – and more at risk than ever. Again only the BBC, with its unique method of funding and its unique mission, can guarantee that this investment will be made (BBC, 2004).

John Willis

Budgeting Programmes — UK

It is no longer possible, as it was twenty or so years ago, to be complacent about programme budgets and to think that what *really* counts is making a programme that gets noticed and that if this means an overspend, then so be it. When there were just three TV channels in Britain, audiences were large, producers were mainly employees and production funds flowed freely, it was much easier to play fast and free with budgets. These days, austerity is the name of the game in many areas of the industry. As the number of TV channels goes up, the financial cake is being sliced ever more thinly. For all but the most populist of programmes, that means broadcasters are asking more and more for less and less. Many programmes are now produced under commercial contracts between broadcasters and independent producers, where an overspend that dents a company's profit margin will inevitably also bang a hole in a producer's career prospects. In the freelance world, that, of course, matters. So today budgets clearly define, and set strict limits to, the creative ambitions of programme-makers. A well-designed budget can offer solutions to the unseen problems that inevitably crop up along the thorny production path from delivery to transmission. Conversely, a badly thought-through financial plan can make a nonsense of a production schedule and compromise a programme-maker's best intentions.

The first issue to be considered in preparing a budget is simple: how much is my programme or series worth to a broadcaster? The Communications Act that became law in 2003 has made public service broadcasters in Britain take a more open and transparent approach towards the funding of the TV programmes they commission from independent producers. Under the guidance of the Office of Communications (Ofcom, the regulator for the UK communications industries), the terrestrial broadcasters have introduced a clearer framework for the commissioning and funding of TV programmes. The new system makes it much easier for producers to discover both how much broadcasters will pay for different kinds of programmes (see below) – and what rights the broadcasters will get in return for their money. What they will pay generally depends on four key factors: the channel airing the show; the genre of the programme; the time slot it is aimed at; and the methodology used in its production.

As a rough-and-ready rule, the bigger the potential audience, the larger the likely budget. For example, broadcasters will obviously pay more for shows aimed at the mass audience channels BBC1 and ITV than they will for those transmitting on the niche market digital channels. Clearly some genres, like drama, have high built-in overheads and inevitably command higher prices than programmes made in other areas. For a few 'landmark' dramas each year the BBC is prepared to pay more than £900,000 an hour, although the majority of its drama slate costs the 'Beeb' between £630,000 and £700,000. Conversely, the most expensive factual and lifestyle show will only command a £300,000 budget and most of them cost much less than this.

Where a show airs in the schedule also determines its price: the most expensive shows tend to be those airing in the prime-time, mid-evening slots. The final factor concerns the methods used to realise the programme: largely studio-based discussion or quiz shows are low-cost programming: the price tag here can be as low as £10,000 an hour out of prime time. On the other hand, shows requiring a lot of foreign travel, high production values, extended production schedule or a lot of expensive archive footage will inevitably cost a lot more.

Budgeting is an art, not a science and most programme budgets are informed guess-timates of the real costs of a project. This is because, at the time of needing to prepare an estimate of the costs of a show, it is frequently not possible to know exactly what is going to be required to make the programme. Can you really say how many days filming will be required for your fifty-minute programme when you have not begun the research, do not know who is going to be interviewed or exactly where you are going to be filming? Can you know how much archive footage and how many stills you are going to need, and what the royalty clearance costs are going to be, before you've researched the archives and cut the clips into the show? Often you can't. That is the reality of most factual programmes at the commissioning stage and part of the art of budgeting is to build in enough padding to allow for the unforseen. More on this in a moment. What counts more than anything in budgeting is experience of making programmes and any producer who prepares a budget without the advice of an experienced production manager should also prepare themelves for a bruising time.

Budgeting a programme or a series can appear daunting to newcomers to the trade. Flick through a pro forma budget spreadsheet and it is easy to come away intimidated by the plethora of headings, sub-headings, categories and codes. But these pro forma sheets are designed to cover just about any spending eventuality on any kind of project and very few shows require spending in every one of the outline categories. Many programmes need far less. Every cost a production is likely to incur, from research, through filming and right through to the end of post-production, including clear-up time at the end, should be in your budget because, once a budget has been agreed with a broadcaster, there is normally no room to add anything else later on.

In essence a budget is nothing more than a glorified shopping list, one that anticipates every cost that your production is going to incur and breaks the spending down into accessible headings and categories. If this is an independent production, one of those costs is the mark-up, or production fee, your company takes for making the show. But there is one clear difference between a programme budget and the list you prepare for your weekly shop in Marks and Spencer – some spending categories are linked to others. Change an item in linked budget lines, and you force changes elsewhere in the budget. That means a small adjustment in one line can result in big damage on the bottom line of the budget. Understanding this requires a knowledge of film production processes, but even old hands can forget some of the linkages when making alterations to the scheduling assumptions on which a budget is based. If you over-shoot the amount of tape you have allowed in the budget, for example, you won't just be paying a few extra pounds for more stock. You're also likely to to have extra copying costs if your director wants to view VHS copies of the rushes before he or she prepares a film structure. All those extra tapes have then got to be 'digitised' into a form that can be edited on a computer. That's more money for the machinery and for someone to do the job. If the facility house cannot do this elsewhere, you might need to extend your edit by a day to do the job in the offline suite – paying more for your editor, your director and the offline editing kit. And there might also be transcription costs for interviews recorded on those extra tapes. So what might have started as little more than a £100 overspend in one budget line can add up to ten times as much when all the changes work their way through the budget.

Making sure you understand the linkage between budget lines is a vital skill. Another is the frequent need to rob Peter to pay Paul – which brings us back to the issue of 'padding' a budget. It is almost inevitable in the actual working out of a production that some real costs will exceed the sums you've estimated as likely costs at the start. If that exclusive interview you've been offered with the US President has got to take place on Easter Monday, then no matter what you've allowed in your budget, you'll have to swallow hard and pay premium holiday prices for your air fares. And if the International UFO Society just happens to have booked up all the cheap hotels on the island of Sao Tome for its annual convention when you're in town, you might just have to stay in the luxurious but wildy expensive Presidential Palace. You can achieve this without going over budget if you have made sure that some of your original estimates are, in fact, overestimates. Now that doesn't mean you can double the real hourly cost of a sound dubbing session, for example. Nor can you pretend that it costs £400 a day to hire a crew van when the real cost is £100. The broadcasters pay good money to their financial controllers to make sure you do not hike prices like this. But what you can do is ensure that budget lines reflect the maximum price you might have to pay for items or services, safe in the knowledge that you can then 'do deals' with suppliers to cut your costs and thereby create financial buffer zones to be called upon in a crisis. Many facilities firms, for instance, will charge only four days for a seven-day camera hire – saving you hundreds of pounds on a three-week shoot, money that can be saved up for that rainy day. You can also shop around to find a better quote for post-production, tape stock and transcription, etc. than the rates you have put in your original budget. Do this and Peter will usually have sufficient spare cash stashed away to pay Paul when the going gets tough.

Sensible budget design is all about making informed assumptions about likely costs, while also ensuring that there is sufficient room to respond to a crisis. With an experienced hand on the tiller, what might seem like a daunting task is made all that much easier.

Tony Stark

Budgeting Programmes – US

A budget is strictly a reference frame. Every producer has his or her own budgetary expenditures. They use different types of budgets and so many different budget forms one cannot issue dicta with any particular budgetary format.

And since union and contractual fees are kept secret, sadly, precise figures are hard to come by because they are considered 'trade secrets'. We can only get averages issued by trade associations or trade publications. They told us in 2004 that a typical *CSI* episode cost $1.5 million, but the exact budget numbers are never specified.

Yet the principles are well known. In short, budgets for programmes in the US fall into several loose categories.

The short budget represents a bare-bones essential production cost. A more comprehensive budget would break down costs in more detail, often laying out twenty- to thirty-page budget estimates. An all-encompassing budget accounts for everything – but is only known after the production is completed and all items are paid for.

There are as many budget 'styles' as there are budget estimators, but they specify fixed costs – which one cannot avoid

paying – and variable costs – over which the producer has some negotiating options.

In the end, starting from the script narrative, which defines the show, to the major star's compensation – and everything in between – this defines the final production budget. This is really the cost of production of the first copy. Thereafter duplication costs are small compared to the investment up front. Thus the budget needs to be seen as an accountant's tool in the preparation of the investment for the production.

But the investment is for profit maximising. Profit is defined as revenues (direct payments and/or advertising fees) minus the budgetary costs. The costs are budgeted so as to make as much profit as possible for the programme producer, but this varies by the type of programme. The key principles are as follows.

THE STAR SYSTEM

Since the rise of Mary Pickford and Charles Chaplin in the 1910s, the movie industry has shown that fans up the ante to see their favourite stars. Television simply adopted this. These workers are paid enormous fees. So, as the long-running comedy, *Friends*, on NBC ended, its five stars were being paid more than $1 million per episode. Yet that did not break the budget because the show drew the highest advertising rates ($500,000 per thirty seconds) of any show on television in the early years of the twenty-first century.

Stardom began in television with Milton Berle, Arthur Godfrey and Lucille Ball. Berle had failed on radio and in the movies, Godfrey was a minor radio star and Ball a minor Hollywood star. But with television they became household names, incorporated their own companies and could not walk down the street without fans mobbing them. Many more fans in the US – and around the world – saw them than any movie star in a theatre.

Paying stars is the defining aspect of any budget for television. This is true in all genres. The other costs pale in comparison. But stars draw viewers, whom advertisers want, and/or fans pay their cable company to access these programmes and thus the budget top heavy with stars seems odd but means vast profits.

NETWORKING

The reason hit shows with top stars can make profits is that their costs are spread across many outlets. The networks in the US have 200 or more outlet stations, and reach 99 per cent of the population. Thus if a $2 million show is spread across 200 stations, then its average cost per station is a mere $10,000.

And then with cable, satellite, DVD and the like there come what are called ancillary revenues. An episode of *I Love Lucy*

Lucille Ball

Arthur Godfrey

Milton Berle (right) in *Margin for Error* (Otto Preminger, 1943)

may have cost $100,000 in the mid-1950s but has been running over and over again since then – for more than half a century. This revenue means that, even if a show does not generate a profit in its initial run, if it becomes what is called an 'evergreen', then the revenues literally do not stop, and the show's extra revenues fifty years later are all pure profit.

UNIONS

For Hollywood shows and programmes created in major cities (principally local news), the programme staff are protected by a union – or, in nicer terms, a guild (such as the stars' Screen Actors Guild). The union negotiates a blanket minimum contract every three to five years to protect the non-stars and technicians. The unions also demand and get healthy pension and health care packages. New companies, without stars, looking to be picked up by a network, often shoot in Canada so as to avoid union requirements.

With these three principles – stars, networking and unions – we can examine the various genres of programming and see how their budgeting differs.

1. Broadcast prime time draws the most consistent audiences. Here is where the budgets per programme can run into millions of dollars. Only major media conglomerates, which own both a studio to make the show and a network to present it, can afford this investment. These are four entities: (a) Viacom, which owns CBS and Paramount production studio; (b) Disney, which owns ABC and the Disney studio; (c) General Electric, which owns NBC and Universal Studios; and (d) Fox, which owns the Fox network and the 20th Century-Fox studios.

They invest millions per year on programmes looking for that elusive hit that will generate a profit even on its first run, or perhaps generate a negative for the budget but a profit in later runs. As the twenty-first century begins, comedies and dramas of whatever genres are, by and large, budgeted and produced by these four companies, plus a few other major Hollywood entities.

2. Cable TV prime time draws far smaller audiences, and creates little in the way of new programming. It is comprised of previous broadcast programming, movie presentations and some original shows. There are many cable networks but most show non-original programming, from re-runs of older TV shows to older movies. They package these shows to target a particular audience and, if they can keep the budgets low, they can make a profit.

For example, the Discovery Network secured the rights to documentaries made by others – usually with government subsidies. Then Discovery shuffled them into attractive packages – such as Shark Week – and with low costs, even if only 2 per cent of households in the US tuned in, it could make a profit.

3. Sports crosses both broadcast and cable. Broadcast TV in the US sends out the most popular attractions, while cable takes the left-overs. Here the stars – like basketball's Michael Jordan – are created by the league, in this case the National Basketball Association (NBA). Then the NBA contracts the rights to games on a national network, regional cable network and local basis. Budgeting for television is the payment for these rights.

This is done on a three- to five-year contractual basis with the league and interested networks. Sometimes, for college sports, this is done only for a certain region, such as the Atlantic Coast Conference along the east coast of the US. Here the rights are paid to the league and then split among its members. Thus a losing team often earns as much as a winning team.

Rights can be very expensive, running into millions, even billions, of dollars for long-term contracts. Indeed, on a regular basis the top-rated programme of the season in the US is the Super Bowl (US-style football), held near the end of January each year. The rights cost millions, but so do the advertisements – usually the costliest of any TV season.

4. News is expensive to do. As discussed in Douglas Gomery's *CNN News Gathering* on pp. 90–2, a major international news organisation like CNN requires hundreds of workers. So how does a CNN keep budgets small so that its owner Time Warner can make a profit?

First, it has few stars. It highest paid star in 2004 was Larry King, the host of a talk show. King is paid well, but the guests come on for free, and the required technical support is minimal.

Second, a CNN is a non-union shop. It is run by young people who work there for a while and then are let go for cheaper, usually university-trained new, but lower paid, staff. This keeps CNN's costs very low.

In contrast, a broadcast network has stars – Dan Rather Tom Brokow and Peter Jennings as the twenty-first century started. Each was paid well in excess of $1 million per year. Fans tune in to their favourite, as studies show the news shows cover virtually the same issues. Then stars also work on so-called magazine shows, like *60 Minutes II*, so that Viacom, CBS's owner, can spread their salaries across several programmes.

At the local station level, budgets are 'average', as the station owners keep their real costs proprietary. So, for example, for a top-ten market station not owned by a network, we know that about two-thirds of employees are involved in news, accounting for half of the expenses. Other programmes shown come from affiliation with the network. To reiterate, half of the total station expense is tied to news.

Of this, there are two kinds of expenses: operating expenses and capital expenses. Operating expenses are the day-in and day-out expenses and are relative to the size of the city and market size. They include production crew and all personnel salaries, including on-air and off-air personnel. It is a function of market size: anchors are very highly paid if they are the star attraction for a top-ten station. Capital expenses include generators, news vehicles, microwave trucks, satellite trucks, news cameras, editing and technical machines, and the rest of the equipment. Capital cost is the same regardless of the market size or city size because equipment costs will be the same no matter what.

Generally, and rather unfortunately, the newsrooms tend to lose revenues when in times of national or domestic crisis or a breaking news situation, because, in times of war or crisis, newsrooms run fewer advertisements in order to use optimum time and resources to provide additional coverage. Ironically, the costs also rise in such situations in an effort to get the maximum footage; newsrooms often end up working overtime, hence adding costs. Revenues are neutral in such cases and cannot be used to cover up lost time or recover expenses. The time is gone. The revenue is gone.

5. Talk and game shows are the low-budget fare of television in the US. The star system still works; Oprah Winfrey's talk show or Bob Barker's *The Price Is Right* consistently do well in the ratings and are owned and produced by their stars. Yet, save the director and line producer, the staff is minimal and does not require a high budget. And if they prove popular, as have these two, the advertisers will line up to pay near prime-time advertising rates for shows presented during the day.

These are generally taped (as opposed to many prime-time shows and movies, which are filmed), so productions can be done in a single day. They are scripted to be evergreen, so can be played any time of the year. These – and soap operas with no major stars – are the most profitable shows on television in the US because they cost so little and produce so much in revenue. Yet even these profits do not match those that a prime-time 'high' can make – even with a multimillion-dollar budget.

Children's shows are, likewise, very profitable. At the beginning of the twenty-first century, only parents and young children had ever heard of 'Sponge Bob', whereas more recently it hits the top ten every week in cable show ratings.

In the end, programme budgets simply outline an investment in the future. What programmes will people like a year from now? (That is how long the process takes, at a minimum). This is tricky to predict, and no one – however they have tried – has come up with a formula. The budget outlines the costs, and then the revenue comes from advertising and cable or satellite customer fees. The differences equal the programme profits. And that is what matters to the major companies.

Douglas Gomery

RECOMMENDED READING

McFarland, Ruth (2002), *Bacon's TV/Cable Directory*, Chicago, IL: Bacon's Information Service.

Ottina, Theresa J. (2002), *Television Financial Report*, Washington, DC: National Association of Broadcasters.

Co-production: Television and the European Union

The term 'co-production' generally refers to a project in which two or more separate companies join forces to work on a programme or series where it is calculated that there will be tangible gains from the pooling of resources and the sharing of particular types of knowledge, talent and expertise. It is sometimes claimed, indeed, that the cross-fertilisation of different ideas and approaches can also result in certain creativity gains.

In no small number of cases, what is sometimes categorised as a co-production is essentially a co-financing arrangement in which one financially well-endowed partner agrees to put money into a co-production in exchange for acquiring special rights to the airing and distribution of the resultant programme. Thus, whilst there is frequently talk of a creative pay-off in co-production, it is mostly the case that co-productions are undertaken for economic reasons. As one observer has commented: 'There are very few TV stations, on either side of the Atlantic, which are able any longer to provide 100 per cent financing to independent producers or fully finance their own in-house production at previous levels' (Chanan, 1993, p. 37).

The striking of a co-production deal – especially for small and medium-sized companies – can be one way of keeping afloat in an ever more competitive world. This is especially true of the situation in Europe, where independent producers from the smaller countries regularly forge alliances with others. This is partly dictated by economic reasons, but governments also have an interest in ensuring the survival of some local production in a world dominated by multinational, global operators. In the context of the EU, then, co-production schemes are viewed by some as a strategy for mounting an economic and cultural defence against what is seen as an undesirable flow of imported, especially American, TV material.

Co-production also helps the strong and the powerful to reinforce their positions of strength. In this respect co-production reflects the more general trend towards greater media concentration and the domination of large media corporations. Most of the BBC's blockbuster wildlife series, such as *Life on Earth* or *The Blue Planet* are also international co-productions. The emergence of new international production partnerships has also not been without consequences for the type of programming levelled at multiple audiences. There is, namely, a distinct danger that, in striving to make the programme more accessible to such an audience, the work will have to be shaped according to an imagined internationally acceptable format. This can easily result in a bland, standardised product with which few actual audiences will be able to identify (Goldberg, 2002, p. 20).

The trend towards homogenisation in international co-productions was perhaps most clearly marked in a number of drama series stemming from the late 1980s, which sought to trade on the international success of American programmes such as *Dallas* and *Dynasty*. The Austro-German co-produced series *Black Forest Clinic* (1986) and the French-Italian-Swiss offering *Chateauvallon* (1986) both exemplified the attempt to produce Europeanised and cloned versions of American originals. Both series, not without justification, quickly attracted the pejorative epithet 'Euro-pudding' (Kilborn, 1992, pp. 112–15).

TV CO-PRODUCTION IN EUROPE

Within the European Union a number of schemes and initiatives have been introduced designed not only to make European audiovisual industries more competitive in a global media marketplace, but also aimed at increasing the level of understanding that member states have of each other (Collins, 1994). Co-production, as one of these initiatives, thus acquires a socio-cultural role as a vehicle for aiding European integration. These twin aims, the desire on the part of the EU to provide an adequate support for its audiovisual industries and the claim that such support could play a role in the wider integrationist project, have always been difficult to reconcile. In many ways the various EU schemes introduced to promote audiovisual production, including the diverse co-production support schemes, reflect the underlying difficulties of harmonising economic policy aims with those wider integrationist aspirations. The guiding principle was that special measures needed to be taken to safeguard the European media industries, to combat the perils of fragmentation and to meet the challenges of linguistic diversity.

As ever greater union was sought, so the European Commission and Parliament attempted, in a number of ways, to exercise their influence on media affairs. The objective was not only to make the European media industries more competitive, there was also a recognition that rules and laws governing broadcasting in the EU would have to be liberalised (Theiler, 1999; Collins, 1994, pp. 53–80). From the mid-1980s

Dallas

the EU introduced a number of 'Europeanising' broadcasting policies which attempted to break the mould of structures and systems which had hitherto been closely identified with the socio-cultural identities of single nation states. For instance, the 1984 Green Paper *Television without Frontiers* (TWF) (later embodied in the 1989 Directive and further amended in 1997), set out to 'co-ordinate national rules of Member States in order to remove barriers to an internal market for television broadcasting and related services in the Union'. TWF signalled a bold statement of intent to introduce what was in effect a quota system for TV programming. The TWF initiative also sought to promote the free flow of European programming between member states by specifying what constituted 'European' programme content. Likewise, it attempted to introduce regulations intended to make the participation of non-European partners in co-produced work difficult, if not impossible (Wheeler, 2003, p. 12). To these ends the Directive made provision that henceforth more than half of programmes aired in member states should be European works (see Paraschos, 1998, p. 3). The thinking was that such a move would, at a stroke, reduce Europe's reliance on imported (mostly American) programming and provide a major fillip to indigenous audiovisual industries, particularly those located in the smaller European states.

Beginning in the 1990s, the EU also began to introduce a series of support and subsidy schemes designed to bolster the European media industries. These multifaceted programmes, known respectively as MEDIA 92, MEDIA 95 and latterly MEDIA Plus, attempted to stimulate and promote audiovisual production in the EU by, among other things, subsidising training programmes devoted to skills such as scriptwriting, and by introducing support mechanisms for improved distribution of audiovisual products (including programmes to facilitate the dubbing and subtitling of film and television programmes). In spite of laudable intentions, the various EU MEDIA initiatives have only had limited success in stimulating and enhancing audiovisual production within the EU member states (Wheeler, 2003, p. 28; Venturelli, 1998, p. 210). Overcoming the problems of fragmentation and at the same time being mindful of the cultural diversity of the European nations (some of that diversity enshrined in long-established broadcasting traditions) has proved to be a greater challenge than at first imagined. Likewise, some observers have drawn attention to the difficulties of reconciling, on the one hand, the free-market desire to liberalise the broadcasting market and, on the other, the politically motivated wish to make strategic interventions in order both to preserve cultural diversity *and* to transmit certain common cultural values (see Weymouth and Lamizet, 1996, pp. 30–5).

All these initiatives to introduce more of a European dimension into Europe's broadcasting affairs have been fraught with difficulty. A particular challenge has been how to address the problem of a cultural and linguistic difference. This is perhaps most clearly exemplified in the failure of the attempt to introduce pan-European television through the Eurikon and Europa projects (ibid., p. 27; Collins, 1994, pp. 162–3).

THE BUSINESS OF CO-PRODUCTION

In spite of the reservations expressed, some of the EU-initiated subsidy schemes for most production companies regular involvement in co-production has become virtually an economic necessity. Privately negotiated co-production deals will be struck between one or more independent producers and broadcasters (see Grey Box). In addition, producers will always be looking for ways of tapping into one of the EU audiovisual support schemes, including those designed to promote co-production. A couple of examples of this follow. One MEDIA 95 initiative, MAP TV (memory, archives, programmes), provided funds to

> assist co-production of archive based creative programmes which have partners from at least three European countries and at least 51% of resources originating in EC states. MAP TV provided up to 7.5% of budget for projects which included a 20% minimum of archive footage and were, according to Commission specifications 'in keeping with the hope of bringing together the peoples of Europe in the long term; as well as with a European view of world events and culture'. (EU Commission document of 1991, cited in Collins, 1994, p. 101)

Another scheme was the Eurimages programme. Initiated in 1989 by the French and since then organised by the Council of Europe, it seeks to aid 'the co-production, distribution, broadcasting and exploitation of creative cinematographic and audiovisual works'.

Programme-making is never straightforward at the best of times, but involvement in a co-produced project introduces an additional level of complication. It certainly does not make the business of organising and progressing a project any easier. Intense networking is often required to put together funding packages and, as already suggested, it is almost always the case that co-production money comes with strings attached. Programme-makers – especially those working in non-fiction genres – are thus anxious that involvement in a co-production could mean that their independence will be compromised by the need to meet the style and format requirements of powerful broadcasters (Goldberg, 2002, p. 21).

EUTOPIA (MOSAIC FILMS, 2000)

Of all the many co-produced works to be made and screened in recent times, the documentary series *Eutopia* is certainly one of the most ambitious. The series comprises twenty half-hour programmes, each of them attempting to illuminate what it means to live in the EU and to show how much (or how little) we know of our fellow Europeans. In the words of the programme-makers:

> *Eutopia* delves inside all the countries of the EU. Working with 45 single person filmmakers, the series consist of a variety of intimate and personal stories as well as observations of shared experiences of European identity. This is a multi-lingual, multi-ethnic project, which will be accessible to the entire audience of the community. (Mosaic Films press release)

The series attempts, in particular, to reveal the diversity of the European experience, with individual programmes ranging in topic from German families buying up properties in Sweden and Portugal (*Wanderlust*) to the experience of migrants seeking political or economic refuge (*Under the Wire*).

Eutopia was conceived as a large-scale project and the production budget set at £1.4 million. It was clear from the outset that the company Mosaic Films, which, back in 1996, had come up with the original idea for the series and which had already acquired a reputation for a similar collaborative style of programme-making, would need to secure co-production finance from a number of different sources. Following an initial commitment of £500,000 from Mark Thompson, then controller of BBC2, Mosaic was then able to secure £25,000 of development finance from the EU MEDIA fund. This led to other European broadcasters showing an interest in the project. In April 1997 the Swedish channel TV4 came on board as a co-production partner and soon afterwards TV2 Denmark and YLE Finland concluded pre-sales

deals. It took a further year, however, to get the rest of the money together by agreeing co-production contracts with French, German and Dutch partners.

This necessarily abbreviated account of the production history of *Eutopia* clearly reveals one of the hazards of co-production and co-financing arrangements. Getting a funding package together can be an extremely time-consuming and energy-sapping experience. As the executive producer of the project Adam Alexander comments:

> By 1998 all partners had confirmed their intention of participating, [but] it was to take a further 9 months to get a production agreement signed. I decided, in my ignorance, to create a single document that all the investors and producers would sign. Never again. It took 20 drafts to reach agreement and a small fortune in legal expenses.

Eutopia illustrates both the pros and cons of co-production. Though nominally a co-produced work, the modus operandi employed by the small editing team back at central command, (that of editing together the huge amount of footage supplied by individual film-makers into twenty nicely structured half-hour programmes) effectively deprived the individual film-makers of having any meaningful creative input into the project. At the same time this modus operandi did ensure that a number of aspiring young European film-makers were able to get their work aired and that, on completion, the series was widely screened throughout Europe. If anything, the *Eutopia* project illustrates some of the broader political challenges of European integration. Politicians have, namely, to persuade all EU citizens/constituents that the centralising tactics employed in driving through the project are necessary aids towards achieving the harmony and integration towards which all (or most) of the involved partners aspire.

Richard Kilborn

CONCLUSION

It is against the background of some of the above-mentioned EU initiatives that the practice of co-production has to be viewed. There is a recognition among European TV programme-makers that the various forms of co-production and co-financing constitute important 'enabling devices' in their quest to secure adequate production funding for their projects. One consequence of this is that, among many other skills they have to acquire, today's generation of producers have to develop the techniques necessary to persuade commissioning editors from key European broadcasting institutions to invest money in co-

produced projects. It is to these ends that, each year at the International Documentary Film Festival in Amsterdam, there is a two-day event, the FORUM for International Co-financing of Documentaries, at which producers and programme-makers gain experience in pitching projects to experienced TV commissioning editors. They also have to develop a facility for the reversioning material, that is, producing multiple versions of a programme in accordance with the wishes of various broadcasters who have given financial support (see Kilborn and Izod, 1997, p. 180). As the following case study reveals, however, getting involved in a co-production frequently means a trade-off between being able to acquire the economic where-withal to support a programme-making project and having to confront the logistical problems associated with any collabora-tive venture – especially those of having to reconcile the diverse interests of multiple partners.

Richard Kilborn

RECOMMENDED READING

Chanan, M. (1993), 'Coping with Co-production: Prospects for Independent Documentary Co-production in Europe', *DOX (Documentary Film Quarterly)*, Winter, pp. 37–42.

Collins, R. (1994), *Broadcasting and Audio-visual Policy in the European Single Market*, London: John Libby & Company.

Goldberg, M. (2002), 'Under the Sign of Partnership', *DOX (Documentary Film Quarterly)*, no. 42, August, pp. 20–1.

Kilborn, R. (1992), *Television Soaps*, London: Batsford.

Kilborn, R. and Izod, J. (1997), *An Introduction to Television Documentary: Confronting Reality*, Manchester: Manchester University Press.

Marshall, J. (1994), 'The Right Pitch', *DOX (Documentary Film Quarterly)*, no. 4, pp. 49–50.

Paraschos, E. (1998), *Media Law and Regulation in the European Union*, Ames: Iowa State University Press.

Theiler, T. (1999), 'Viewers into Europeans? How the European Union Tried to Europeanize the Audiovisual Sector and Why It Failed', *Canadian Journal of Communication*, vol. 24, no. 4, pp. 557–87.

Venturelli, S. (1998), *Liberalizing the European Media: Politics, Regulation and the Public Sphere*, Oxford: Clarendon Press.

Weymouth, A. and Lamizet, B. (1996), *Markets & Myths: Forces for Change in the European Media*, Harlow: Addison Wesley Longman.

Wheeler, M. (2003), 'Supra-national Regulation: Television and the European Union', paper (unpublished) presented at the Media and Policy panel at the PSA conference, University of Leicester.

Discovery International: Programming

On 27 February 2004 Douglas Gomery spoke to Leanne Norton Long, who agreed to share her experience of working at Discovery Communications International (DCI). Below is an edited version of what she said.

As the twenty-first century commenced, Discovery had become one of the most famous TV brands in the US, indeed in the world. This was driven by, of all things, the presentation of documentaries – a form of TV that had almost disappeared in the US as Discovery started, with a handful of employees, in the mid-1980s. Discovery found its niche in cable TV.

There are four types of shows that DCI networks used to fill their schedules, ranging in level of completion and price: acquisitions, pre-sales, co-productions and commissions.

ACQUISITIONS

In the early days of cable programming, there was a glut of material already produced and available. Programmers and buyers would go to annual trade shows or 'markets', such as MIP Com in Monte Carlo, to shop for the upcoming year's inventory.

Meetings between independent producers, agents and buyers were conducted at fifteen-minute intervals and a typical day ran from early in the morning to late at night. After a week of intense networking, Discovery reps would return with heavy briefcases full of pitches, business cards, T-shirts, key chains, baseball hats and anything else the salespeople could think of to make themselves stand out from the masses. Cases of screen-ing tapes would later be shipped to company headquarters.

Some shows, due to popularity of subject or prior experi-ence with a particular producer, would be instant buys. This would ensure that competing networks would not get a guar-anteed ratings-grabber. Other programmes were a bit more questionable. A commitment might be made to a particular vendor that a DCI network would purchase thirteen episodes of a certain series, or efforts would be made to combine indi-vidual documentaries to create anthologies. Graphic packages could be created and tacked on later to make the separate inde-pendent films look like part of a preconceived series.

Hundreds of screening tapes were libraried by DCI in the offices outside Washington, DC. Then, weekly preview meet-ings were held where each tape would be popped into a VCR for two to three minutes. If they were good the tapes were sometimes allowed to run for as long as five to ten minutes but, with so many to go through, the panel of judges were quick to say 'pass' or 'evaluate'. If a show made it to evaluation, a department of screeners would watch the show in its entirety and fill out a computer database form, complete with key-words for searches, a thirty-word description for the listings magazine, a rating on the storyline and production technique, and flags for questionable accuracy, datedness issues and appropriateness for the target audience.

At the following week's preview meeting, the evaluators would present their reports to the programming scheduler, editing manager, network general manager and buyers. The evaluator had two to three minutes to make a case for whether or not to purchase a show. Sometimes there was pressure to buy a programme due to relationships with the vendor. Sometimes a title would lead the people who had gone to the trade show to believe it was a definite 'Yes'. By watching the show in its entirety, the evaluators were the watchdogs and insurers that what DCI was purchasing was a quality product. During the presentations, the evaluators had to put forth an argument, and sometimes even a prediction, about how a show would do in the ratings. Later they would be held accountable for their statements – lauded if they got a ratings winner at a good price, chastised if their prediction fell flat. A level of trust was built among the team as to which screener was good at a particular genre. There would be an 'animal expert', a 'culture and arts' person, a 'science guy'. Each of these individuals had strong writing and research backgrounds, and many eventually moved on to scriptwriting or programme reversioning.

The odds that an unknown, independent producer's film would make it to the air were very slim. If the producer was represented by a known vendor, the chances were better. If it was a previously successful producer, and the subject matter was perfect for a scheduling need, it was just a matter of negotiating rights and terms to the deal.

PRE-SALES

Frequently a producer would seek funding for a film before it was complete. Slick multicoloured printed proposals were sent – one, in particular, on Egypt came in a case shaped like a miniature mummy's sarcophagus. These pitches were logged into a huge tracking database and assigned to executive producers and writer/researchers to read and review. Like the evaluators, the following week, these readers had to report on their findings. Sometimes the production schedule was too elaborate and the budget too high, other times too little was known about the production company. Like panning for gold, hundreds of proposals could be read and reviewed before an evaluation panel would say, 'Yes, let's try this one.'

CO-PRODUCTION

Many times an acquisition or even a well-monitored pre-sale would be delivered by deadline but not be all that had been originally hoped for in the programme. To make it more appropriate for a particular audience, or to have that specific Discovery marque, often reversioning work had to be done – a script re-write, a re-narration, new or different music, editing out questionable scenes, and work on the pacing. All of these nuances could make a huge difference in attracting and keeping the viewer. Reversions, as they are known, proved quite economical. Despite having to rework the material, the footage could be acquired much more cheaply as an acquisition than as an original, and internal employees could put their creative hats on to add the polish.

This, then, became what was called a co-production – a hybrid between a pre-sale and a Commission. One network might put up 40 per cent of the cost and then share the show with another network that was also putting up a percentage of the price. The outside production company would also put in some money up-front and a panel of executive producers would share the responsibility of successfully shepherding the project to meet deadline, budget and editorial views.

COMMISSIONS

If the acquisitions process and pre-sales resulted in very limited inventory for a scheduled genre (for example, Science Frontiers may need a show on the exploration of Mars), a request for proposal (RFP) would be sent out. An RFP could be as elaborate as a pre-sale proposal but created internally. It could also be as simple as one sheet that stated quickly and concisely what the idea was, who the audience would be and the unique attributes of this particular project. These RFPs would then be sent to a select handful of well-trusted production companies who would submit a proposal stating their vision of what such a programme should look like, exactly how they would produce it, and a budget.

Commissions were the high-ticketed productions. Milestones were attached to the contract so that the executive producer could check the production each step of the way to ensure that the product delivered was close to what the original vision had been and the best possible to attract, entertain and educate the viewers. The ultimate goal was to secure high ratings, which result in strong ad revenue without compromising Discovery Channel's integrity and name brand.

Sometimes a well-respected producer would be sought for a pet project (such as *In the Company of Whales*) to bring a higher marque value and compete for Cable Ace Awards and now Emmys. The budget would allow for four to six 'highly promotables' – one or two per quarter, per year. These programmes were the ones that got the billboards on city buses, full-page ads in the papers and cross-promotions on all DCI networks. Branding became the name of the game as a show could lead to home video sales, to CD-Roms for schools, to premium items sold in Discovery Channel stores. The bigger budget meant a bigger gamble, and some of Discovery's most expensive and most advertised specials did not break even on the spreadsheet, but helped maintain the credibility of the network.

As the network grew and matured, more and more ideas were internally generated. Discovery Channel (and its offshoot Animal Planet) no longer take unsolicited proposals. The majority of the shows in their scheduling line-up are straight commissions. These networks need programmes that hit specific scheduling targets and internal ideas are more likely to be greenlighted. The Learning Channel (TLC), another sister channel, also fills most of its schedule with commissions but there are a very few limited spots in the

HOW THE MAJORS PROGRAMME: VIACOM'S PARAMOUNT PICTURES AND CBS

The US television majors, as of 2004, are the vertically integrated media conglomerates that own a Hollywood studio and a major television network. This means that CBS is no stand-alone network, but a division of Viacom Inc., which also owns Paramount Pictures. Thus, Viacom – by owning stations covering 40 per cent of US households, with a major network, CBS, and a production studio – can make, distribute and present shows all in-house. Viacom management, headed by owner Sumner Redstone, can produce the show through Paramount and then broadcast it on CBS. Viacom executives co-ordinate production and distribution through CBS and then presentation takes place through owned stations and affiliated CBS stations.

A great example comes with *CSI*, the top-rated show of 2004. This is a Viacom product, done through its CBS produc-

CSI

tions unit of Paramount Pictures. The project was not generated in-house, but brought to Viacom by Jerry Bruckheimer Productions, an experienced producer. *CSI* was not expected to become a hit but it did, so Viacom made space on the Paramount lot for the show, as Viacom could guarantee a programme slot on CBS.

Bruckheimer was a noted movie producer whose films, like *Top Gun* and *Flashdance*, were big hits of the 1980s. In 1996 his partner Don Simpson died, and Bruckheimer branched out into TV. Who figured, in 1999, that scientists solving crimes with chemicals, DNA and analysis of physical data montages would make up the ingredients of the number one show of 2002–3, charging well in excess of $300,000 per thirty-second advertisement and being regularly the number one-rated show on television in the US, and would spin off *CSI: Miami*, and *CSI: New York.*

The original Las Vegas version began with a script by a former tram driver from Las Vegas, Anthony Zuiker. This was his first attempt yet Zuiker created the most successful show on TV in the early twenty-first century. But without the final deal through Bruckheimer, and 'greenlighting' by Viacom, the show would never have reached the CBS airwaves.

Once CSI premiered on 6 October 2000, it grew within a season to be the top show on television. Viewers seemed to love the classic investigative process coupled with the intimate autopsies and internal (digitally animated) views of traumatised flesh, bone and inner ears. It had no stars to start with, just a new theme on the mystery narrative, a long-standing TV staple. It made William Petersen, who struggled as an actor for decades, into the 'people's choice' as TV's most popular actor.

By 2004 Viacom was distributing *CSI* around the world, as Viacom had a vast international distribution network. Each episode cost $1.5 million, and was shot in 35mm and shown in high-definition television like a mini-movie. Yet with Viacom's distribution, the show easily made a profit. This offers a classic example of programming twenty-first century-style. A show like *CSI* was a risk that Viacom could take, knowing the odds were that it would not be a hit, but that if it did become one, Viacom could franchise sequels, sell past seasons on DVD, and charge advertisers top dollar for a thirty-second ad on CBS.

Douglas Gomery

schedule in which they will entertain creative ideas from the outside.

CONCLUSION

These four types of programmes, acquisitions, pre-sales, co-productions and commissions, were the jigsaw pieces that combined to form an elaborate schedule every quarter. Programmers looked to anniversary dates (such as the landing on the moon), stunt ideas (like Shark Week) and past ratings history to choose which shows would work at which time slots. Network GMs computers would ding when the Nielsen ratings came in each day. If something did well, they tried to repeat it again with a new or slightly different twist. If something did poorly, it took a long time before they were willing to try that type of programme again. For the outside producer, it is a very difficult way to make a living. What may be hot one quarter, may not work well again. How to predict the whims of the viewing public and get the most bang for the programming buck was the name of the game.

DCI PROGRAMMING TODAY

Typically these submissions are from production companies who have had prior experience with DCI. There is a website called the Producers Portal (http://producers.discovery.com) that provides a release form which must be signed before any ideas will be reviewed.

The programmers are looking to fill a specific niche. Scheduling is king – not the show's idea. Programmers will repeat shows with the highest ratings and cull poorly performing assets out of the inventory. If a format is successful, they will try to use it in multiple ways, for example, *Wedding Stories*, *Dating Stories*, *Baby Story* and *Second Chance*.

'Destination viewing' is the concept. The programmers strive to build consistency in the schedule to build appointment viewing with their audience. The networks are committed to formatted shows or limited series that do well in the ratings, for example, *Monster Garage* for Discovery and *Trading Spaces* for TLC.

To get a programme idea greenlighted with a DCI network, a producer must do their homework. They need to know the schedule, who the network is and where it is going. They need a background that inspires confidence and a reel of past work that demonstrates their capability to pull it off. If an individual does not have those three, then he or she can go to an outside production company that already has a relationship with DCI to build their experience. It is not difficult to find out who these production companies are. Simply watch the credits roll at the end of the show. Another way to research programming strategies and get a chance to meet programme executives is by attending some of the big industry trade shows: Reel Screen,

Wild Screen, World Congress of Science are all excellent opportunities to meet with executives one on one and find out who they work with.

But even if an idea comes from a well-established production company or is originated internally, it still has many hurdles to cross before making it to broadcast. The process varies from network to network. The development and programming departments screen ideas based on whether they are good or bad, the relationship with the producer, understanding the trends and ratings, the spec time, budget and comparison of alternative topics, current inventory and shows already in the pipeline. If the idea passes this stage, the production management, business affairs and legal departments review the producer, budget details and contract issues, such as rights and obligations.

Some programmes are shared across networks, a show that works on Discovery Channel may also fit in Discovery Health's line-up. When this occurs, cost allocations have to be determined across the interested networks – including the possibility of the show going international. A show can fall through at any step of this contracting process, but if it passes it moves on to production and is ultimately aired on a DCI network.

Douglas Gomery

RECOMMENDED READING

'The Discovery Channel Looks for the Next Frontier', *Broadcasting*, 11 June 1990.

Mullen, Megan (2003), *The Rise of Cable Programming in the United States*, Austin: University of Texas Press.

Picard, Robert G. (1993), *The Cable Networks Handbook*, Riverside, CA: Carpelan.

<www.discovery.com>.

Commissioning Television Programmes

In the early days of television, programmes were made in-house by producer-broadcasters and, although an independent sector existed in parallel, it focused mainly on corporate work, commercials and contributions to the overseas market (Crisell, 2002). However, with the launch of Channel Four in 1982, things began to change. Not only did Channel Four as a publisher-broadcaster make none of its own programmes, part of its remit was to ensure that 'a substantial proportion' of them were 'supplied otherwise than by persons of either of the following descriptions, namely a TV programme contractor and a body corporate under the control of a TV programme contractor' (Broadcasting Act 1980). This legislation enabled the independent sector to flourish, introducing fresh ideas into broadcasting and encouraging economic competition (Goodwin, 1998). Its prospects further improved with the 1986 Peacock Report, which recommended that, in order to keep costs down and weaken what was seen as the restrictive practices of the trades unions within ITV, both 'the BBC and ITV should be required over a ten year period to increase to not less than 40% the proportion of programmes supplied by independent producers' (Peacock, 1986). This recommendation was made into a requirement in the 1990 Broadcasting Act, although the figure was reduced to 25 per cent. Moreover, the commissioning of programmes from independents was among the public service obligations of the commercial broadcaster, Five (then Channel 5), when it launched in 1997.

Commissioning from independent producers is a key part of the work of all the UK's public service providers, namely the BBC, ITV, Channel Four and Five. Each has procedures in place and editors whose job is to find the best commissions for their channel. Commissioning editors tend to preside over specific genres of programming, such as drama, factual, sport and so on, and the information that they require is much the same for all channels: an outline of the idea, programme strand, programme length, number of episodes, and on-screen and production talent.

Commissioning editors may solicit types of programming through tender or consider unsolicited proposals. As part of their work they attend in-house meetings to discuss slot and timetable availability, channel strategy and the creative prerequisites of programmes, and they may then invite proposals that address particular scheduling requirements. Dan Chambers, Director of Programmes, Five, confirms:

> Often we'll do an analysis of where the schedule is going and say: 'Look, we need more 9 o'clock or more 10 o'clock factual or reality'. And then we might put a tender out or we'll speak to the companies that we know have got a track record in that area and see what they come up with. (Fanthome, 2004a)

Commissioners also sift through large numbers of proposals that have been sent to the channel and shortlist those with potential. This is no mean feat. Channel Four's Documentaries Department, for example, receives about a hundred proposals a week, and the BBC Documentaries and Contemporary Factual Department gets about 250 a week. It is hard to pinpoint what will constitute a successful proposal, though surprise and distinctiveness are often key elements:

> I'm always interested in ideas that feel they'll be great television but challenging for the audience; programmes that can make us uncomfortable.

> (Tom Archer, Acting Commissioner, Documentaries and Contemporary Factual, BBC) (Fanthome, 2004i)

> I am always looking for unusual programmes that stand out and that are not derivative. The majority of shows have already been done before, and then when new twists are added it re-invents a different type of entertainment.
> (Claudia Rosencrantz, Controller of Network Entertainment, ITV) (Fanthome, 2004g)

> [I look for] a very bold two-line sell that surprises, feels fresh/distinctive, resonates with me, and I feel probably will with the rest of the audience.
> (Jo Clinton-Davis, Head of Factual Commissioning, BBC) (Fanthome, 2004h)

Having selected those proposals which will be taken to the next stage, the commissioning editor may agree a small budget in order to help the producer develop the idea further. Later on, commissioners will offer support in script development and help to vet key staff if appropriate; oversee the production to a greater or lesser degree; check the programme structure and content on several occasions during the cutting-room stage; deal with matters of legal and policy compliance; and generally provide a second set of eyes and ears at all stages of the procedure.

Although access to broadcasters seems straightforward in the sense that all proposals are considered, it is still difficult for newcomers to convince commissioners that they can deliver on their promises. Hilary Bell, Commissioning Editor for Documentaries, Channel Four, admits: 'During a pitch the most essential point that goes through your mind is: "Can I trust this person to deliver?" So those without a track record are put under a lot more scrutiny' (Fanthome, 2004d). The value of knowing what is required and of maintaining an association with the broadcaster is also recognised by independent producers. Nikki Cheetham, Managing Director of Endemol UK Productions, notes:

> Having a relationship with the people who are commissioning is very key because you get under the skin of what the channel is looking to become and what it wants to achieve. It's really important to get to understand how different channels see themselves; what audiences they are trying to appeal to; why they want to go in one direction or another. (Fanthome, 2004b)

The year 2004 was significant for the commissioning process because the policies underpinning it had been reformulated. Towards the end of 2003, and just prior to its inauguration, Ofcom set guidelines for public service broadcasters

RESTORATION

A significant commission in 2003 was *Restoration*, made for BBC Scotland by Endemol UK Productions and transmitted on BBC2. Each of the ten one-hour programmes covered a particular area of the UK and focused on three buildings in need of renovation. Viewers' votes then determined which one of the thirty buildings should be saved from the funds which were raised by the programme. Background information was provided by the main presenter, Griff Rhys Jones; two 'ruin detectives', architect Ptolemy Dean and building surveyor Marianne Suhr; and by personal witnesses and volunteer campaigners. It was enhanced by celebrity endorsements, dramatic reconstructions of the past and computer-generated images to give an impression of the renovation. Each programme also tracked a successful restoration campaign within the same geographical area and was followed on BBC4 by *Restoration Secrets*, featuring other historical gems within the region.

Restoration was conceived by Endemol UK Production's Managing Director Nikki Cheetham and developed from an earlier blueprint, *Dream Ruin*. However, early on, *Dream Ruin* encountered some fundamental problems, and in resolving them the programme underwent radical changes, emerging as *Restoration*. Cheetham took the new proposal to the BBC and it was commissioned by Jane Root, then Controller of BBC2. Root recalls:

> What was great about *Restoration* was that it used some of the techniques of entertainment in a serious way. I'm a big fan of programmes that mix different techniques. It combined entertainment techniques and a really core subject material. It also had an end result. A lot of television is just television: this actually changed something in the world. (Fanthome, 2004e)

The production of the series took more than a year and was overseen by executive producers Nikki Cheetham and Annette Clarke from Endemol, and Andrea Miller from the BBC. Cheetham confirms that *Restoration* worked with all the heritage bodies and negotiated with them for a considerable grant in the event that the winning building was in their area: 'We had to apply to the Heritage Lottery Fund for each building individually, which was very scary because we didn't hear whether we had got that grant until three weeks before we went on air!' (Fanthome, 2004c).

The scale of the project was considerable. Core group meetings, attended by up to thirty people from Endemol and the BBC, were held every three weeks, as they are for the second series, which is in production at the time of writing. Annette Clarke confirms:

> There is more communication here than any programme I've known. We talk all the time. It's a very complicated programme because there are so many elements to it – BBC education, events, marketing and so on – and I talk to my own production team and the BBC every day. (Fanthome, 2004f)

The first series was successful in terms of ratings, audience appreciation and raising revenue to restore the winning building, the Victoria Baths in Manchester. The average audience throughout the series was 2.7 million, which represented a 12.4 per cent share. A total of 2.2 million votes was registered either by telephone or interactive means, raising funding in excess of £500,000, and this was supplemented by a donation of £3 million from the Heritage Lottery. *Restoration* won the Graphic Design Award at the BAFTA Television Craft Awards, and a post-transmission survey by the BBC noted that over three-quarters of the viewers enjoyed the programme and agreed that it had heightened their awareness of restoration issues.

Christine Fanthome

with regard to their dealings with independent producers. The purpose was to clarify the framework for negotiations and to give independent production companies the maximum potential to flourish. Based on these guidelines, each broadcaster drew up a code of practice. The content varied with the obligations of the broadcaster but was subject to Ofcom's approval. Regional obligations, for example, differed from broadcaster to broadcaster in respect of both the hours of programming to be originated outside London (currently 25 per cent across all BBC channels, 33 per cent for ITV and Channel Four, and 10 per cent for Five) and the proportion of money to be devoted to it (currently 30 per cent across all BBC channels, 40 per cent for ITV, 30 per cent for Channel Four, and 10 per cent for Five). Commissioning staff need to be aware of the current qualifying categories and ensure that projects conform to them.

In March 2004, and with the aim of encouraging independent production outside London, Ofcom offered further guidance to the public service broadcasters on how they should interpret their regional production quotas. To qualify as part of the regional production quota, a programme must currently satisfy two of the following criteria: the independent production company must have a substantive production base outside the M25, which is the usual place of work for senior personnel; 70 per cent of the production budget must be spent in the UK but outside the M25; and at least 50 per cent of production staff must live outside the M25. Ofcom also clarified its definition of regional programming (it should be of particular interest to local people in the area of production) and indicated how it interpreted the broadcasters' obligations to provide a 'sufficient amount' and 'suitable range' of such programming, as required under section 287 of the 2003 Communications Act. The guidelines will be reviewed in 2005 and Huw Rossiter, Ofcom's Head of Media, confirms: 'The Communications Act requires Ofcom to have guidance in place at all times. If Ofcom felt the codes were not working, we would change the guidelines which would require the broadcasters to change their codes' (Fanthome, 2004d).

The aim of the codes of practice was to provide a framework for the negotiations between independent producer and broadcasting organisation. Previously it was the latter which in most cases kept the rights to the programmes commissioned from the producer, but the codes of practice have changed this. Now, the broadcaster evaluates the worth of the individual programme according to tariff bands corresponding to the transmission slots, and this is the starting point for the negotiations at the heart of the commissioning process. Each channel has its own budget and this will be reflected in the kinds of programming it commissions. However, the appropriate codes of practice apply to all broadcasters. If it is likely that the costs will exceed the tariff band, the commissioning broadcaster may offer, in the course of the negotiations, to contribute to the budget in exchange for extra programming rights. The terms of trade were negotiated with each broadcaster in the summer of 2004 by the Producers' Alliance for Cinema and Television (PACT), the UK trade association that represents and promotes the commercial interests of the independent sector. Ofcom had no formal or legal role in these business transactions. John McVay, Chief Executive of PACT, observes:

> The new terms of trade will result in a transfer of value from the broadcasters to the independent production sector. For the first time independent producers will retain control of their own intellectual property rights which will help the sector establish proper enterprise-led businesses capable of competing on the global stage. This is good for the independent sector and good for UK PLC. (Fanthome, 2004j)
>
> *Christine Fanthome*

RECOMMENDED READING

<www.bbc.co.uk/commissioning/structure>.
<www.channel4.com/4producers>.
<www.five.tv> (see 'Producers' Notes' under 'About Five').
<www.itv.com> (see 'Producers' Page' under 'About Us').
<www.ofcom.org.uk>.

Diversity in Broadcasting

In the multiracial, multicultural country that Britain is today, diversity in the broadcasting industry has never been more important. Why is it more important in this industry than, say, manufacturing? Because television, in particular, is the viewers' window on the world: viewers absorb its images and narratives and it shapes their view of the society in which they live.

Broadcasting at its best can enable different communities within society to have their voices and their views heard and can lead to greater understanding. At its worst, broadcasting can reinforce negative stereotypes, exacerbate tensions and lead to greater alienation. In short, broadcasting can have a powerful influence on our society, for good or ill.

For the last few years the terrestrial broadcasters have acknowledged that they do need to reflect Britain's multiracial reality and so have made greater efforts to achieve more diverse output and a more diverse workforce.

As Jim Pines writes in *Black and White in Colour* (BFI, 1992), 'The history of black people in British television can be traced back to the opening day of BBC television itself – 2 November 1936 – when the black American song and dance duo Buck and Bubbles starred in a variety show.' But it was not until the mid-1950s (with the honourable exception of the 1946 BBC production *All God's Chillun Got Wings*) that British television began to look at British life from the perspective of the black working class. The intention of John Elliot's *A Man from the Sun* (1956)

> was to highlight the contrast between what he describes as the mythical image of a cosy Britain which people were receiving as part of their colonial education, and the grotty Britain which the West Indian immigrants encountered when they first arrived in this country.

This contrasted sharply with the prevailing approach, which was that of the white British reaction to immigrants and immigration.

The 1960s were a turbulent time for black professionals in television. On the one hand, black actors began appearing in a wider variety of programmes (with Thomas Baptiste appearing in *Coronation Street* in 1963, for example) and in 1967 John Elliot and Trinidadian actor/writer Horace James wrote a six-part BBC drama serial *Rainbow City*, starring the brilliant actor and award-winning playwright Errol John.

But on the other hand, race began playing an overtly malicious role in British politics and by the 1970s, Enoch Powell's infamous racism allowed what Desmond Wilcox refers to as a screaming level of prejudice to enter society. Pines argues that the

> plethora of multicultural documentary programmes which set out to 'explain' various aspects of so-called immigrant life in Britain in fact transformed the black and Asian population into 'a problem' which these programmes set out to elucidate for a basically xenophobic white audience.

The 1970s were otherwise characterised by race-related sitcoms such as *Love Thy Neighbour*, *The Fosters* and *Mixed Blessings* – and, in 1978, *Empire Road*, which was described by Norman Beaton as the most important black soap there has been in this country. It also made history when Trinidadian director Horace Ove was brought in to direct some episodes.

Perhaps the biggest leap forward for black workers in television was in the 1980s, with the establishment of Channel Four in 1982. The channel was set up with the remit of commissioning programmes from independent companies rather than making them themselves and, though criticised for not commissioning enough black independents, it nevertheless opened up opportunities hitherto denied. New programmes included the sitcom *Desmonds*, written by St Lucian actor/writer Trix Worrell, *Black on Black*, *Eastern Eye* and *Bandung File*. In addition, Channel Four supported what became known as the 'black workshop sector' – grant-supported workshops such as Black Audio Film Collective, Ceddo, Sankofa – which brought forward new talent. Both of these actions by Channel Four had the effect of bringing to the screen productions by black media practitioners about black experiences. The new productions by black media workers led to pressure on the other broadcasters to follow suit.

Deregulation of broadcasting – with the BBC and ITV made to commission programmes by independent companies – arguably opened up further 'potential opportunities' for those outside these institutions, including the new generation of highly qualified black British media professionals emerging from the National Film and Television School and other media institutions. It certainly led to expectations, which were not met as a larger and larger proportion of commissions were hoovered up by a small number of 'independent production companies', which, by the turn of the century, were bigger than some of the ITV franchises.

The broadcasting industry, like other key institutions, also had to respond to the devastating criticism of institutional racism contained within the MacPherson Report (February 1999) into the racist murder of black teenager Stephen Lawrence. The main terrestrial broadcasters adopted targets (not quotas) for the employment of black and minority ethnic workers and formed the Cultural Diversity Network in an attempt to co-ordinate strategy. The BBC Director General Greg Dyke, a lifelong proponent of diversity, caused much media comment shortly after he assumed his short-lived term of office when he described the BBC as 'hideously white' and promised to take action.

Some progress has been made: by the end of 2003 10 per cent of the BBC's 26,000 staff were from ethnic minorities while Channel Four and London ITV franchises employ a greater proportion (though a much smaller number). However, the industry sector skills council Skillset warns against comparing audiovisual employment statistics with the 11 per cent ethnic minority national workforce. Much of the audiovisual industry is located in London and the south east, where the ethnic minority workforce is much higher – 38 per cent in London. Skillset states that the proportion of ethnic minorities in the industry would therefore be expected to be greater than the UK average. It is not: overall it runs at 6 per cent.

Trevor Phillips, chair of the Commission for Racial Equality and a veteran TV journalist and programme-maker, wrote in *Stage Screen & Radio* magazine in February 2004:

> The number of ethnic minority workers in the industry is still far too small, and black and Asian producers often struggle to get someone to give their ideas a fair hearing, let alone a commission. And when ethnic minority TV producers or film makers are given a commission, it is often because the subject matter is to do with race or an issue associated (wrongly or rightly) with ethnic minorities. There seems to be this perception that a black man, irrespective of his background, is perfectly placed to produce a documentary on gun crime. The rationale being that he's 'one of them' who 'speaks their language'. Similarly a Muslim woman, who may never have entered a Mosque in her life, is regarded as the only choice to direct a programme on Islam. Now, the black man and Muslim woman may well choose to be involved in such programmes. But far too many don't have that choice and find themselves being pigeon-holed into certain areas. I don't just want to see ethnic minority TV producers and film makers getting more commissions, I want to see them getting more mainstream commissions.

It added insult to injury when the BBC screened *The Crouches*,

Love Thy Neighbour

Desmonds

an excruciatingly bad black sitcom written by a white writer, riddled with negative stereotypes.

Phillips's view underscores the irrevocable change that is taking place in British society and culture. For the last two or three decades, the country has been slowly and painfully evolving away from the white Christian monoculture that it believed itself to be, and moving towards multiculturalism. The political establishment is still feeling its way, working out what this means, in which direction the future lies, and how integration can be implemented.

Britain has now reached a fork in the road. It could proceed as suggested by (former) Home Secretary David Blunkett, who, in calling for everyone to speak English in their own homes, appeared to believe that integration was to be achieved by subjugation of minority cultural identity. One wonders what Welsh speakers thought of that. In his demand he appears to be reflecting recent French government laws which banned outward signs of religious beliefs, such as the wearing of headscarves by Muslim women, in public institutions.

However, others (such as the broadcasting union BECTU) are now beginning to argue that there is another way forward: that integration is a two-way street, and integration and cultural diversity are complementary, not mutually exclusive. Their vision is one where minority cultures become part of the mainstream and are celebrated by all as facets of New British culture, with new public holidays, for example, to allow everyone to join in Eid al-Fitr and Diwali celebrations just as people of other faiths join in Christmas celebrations. They consciously reject policies which seek to suppress cultural identity and assert that the naissance of this New British culture is the only real solution in a liberal society. For a government, in the short term, this is the tougher road as it requires greater acceptance of equality and diversity on the part of white communities and those in positions of power and authority.

It is in this context that British television could be seen as lagging behind in this journey. Integrated casting – where the best actor gets the part irrespective of their race – is still some way off, though progress has been made in some genres. Few productions give the lead role to black actors – notable successes being, for example, *55 Degrees North* and *Hustle*. Black British broadcasting professionals are demanding to join the mainstream and the right to compete for mainstream programme commissions without being forced to put forward material on minority themes. The industry, as observed by Trevor Phillips, has yet to make this change in practice.

Broadcasters are wrestling with the dilemma of how to achieve this: on the one hand, having a multicultural programming unit does result in more commissions of ethnic minority programme-makers. But on the other, it reinforces their pigeonholing on 'minority' issues and lets all the other commissioning departments off the hook. However, the closing down of such units has been criticised by black programme-makers as they believed that it then becomes no one's responsibility.

Yet the industry could, if it so determined, play an evolutionary role in the development of New British culture and, if done well, may in the process rebuild its audiences at a time when terrestrial broadcasters are facing the threat of multichannel digital broadcasting.

Janice Turner

Trades Unions in Broadcasting

A student considering a career in the broadcasting industry might at the outset be attracted by the glamour. It doesn't look quite so glamorous, however, upon learning that, if you're not one of the lucky ones who manages to win rare in-house training or, rarer still, a real job, you might find yourself competing for a job as a runner at a production company – working for no pay at all.

It is this blatant exploitation of ordinary working people that trades unions were originally set up to resist. And though unions have been in existence for around 200 years (the first entertainment industry union being set up in 1895 at the Adelphi Theatre in London), many of the issues they have to address today remain constant, such as low pay, long working hours and health and safety.

In 1988 John McIlroy wrote in *Trade Unions in Britain Today*:

> For workers, a reasonably paid, secure job is an essential basis for a decent life. But their wages are a cost to their employers, an important item to be set against profit, and thus to be minimised and dispensed with entirely where labour is insufficiently profitable. Trade unions, therefore, take the stage in order to redress the bargaining imbalance between employer and employee and render the conflict between capital and labour a more equal one, replacing individual competition for jobs by collective organisation as a means to protect wage levels and the conditions and security of employment.

In other words, the main interests of the private owners of companies are to make the biggest profits they can, and one way to achieve this is by paying their workforce as little as possible and/or employing as few people as possible. But if the workers band together to defend their pay and working conditions, rather than leaving each worker to fight for themselves, the workforce will collectively have much more negotiating strength.

Trades unions have played a powerful role in the broadcasting industry since its inception and as the industry has gone through faster and faster change, the unions have had to develop new ways of organising the workforce to keep pace with developments.

The main unions in broadcasting are BECTU (the Broadcasting Entertainment Cinematograph and Theatre Union) for those behind the camera, backstage and in administration and box office; Equity for actors and entertainers; and the National Union of Journalists and the Musicians Union, which are self-explanatory. The unions have national agreements with key industry organisations and companies, including the BBC, ITV and employers' organisations such as PACT, which represents independent production companies. These agreements cover pay, working hours, holidays, pensions, maternity leave and other provisions. The unions also take legal action on behalf of members when necessary: BECTU wins around £1 million a year in compensation for members as a result of industrial tribunals or personal injury.

One key difference between the broadcasting industry and most other industries has been the prevalence of freelance employment. While the MU and Equity have had to deal with this challenge for decades, behind-the-camera employment was relatively stable until the establishment of Channel Four in 1982 and the explosion of independent production companies, who set up to win commissions from Channel Four (whose remit was not to make programmes itself). This destabilisation of employment quickened its pace prior to the new Broadcasting Act of 1990, when ITV companies made thousands redundant in order, they said, to build a 'war chest' of money to bid for their franchise licences. During that decade ITV and the BBC began to employ more and more freelance workers as a way of cutting costs – freelances did not have the overheads associated with permanently employed staff, such as pensions, training, maternity leave and, of course, redundancy pay when they were no longer required. Then the imposition of the 25 per cent production quota – obliging the BBC to have 25 per cent of its programmes made by independent companies – caused yet further casualisation. Today at least half the industry's workforce is freelance.

The introduction of market forces into higher education had a further destabilising impact on the industry. Media courses attracted far higher numbers of students than the less glamorous subjects and so in just a few years the industry was finding itself awash with far more qualified newcomers than could ever be accommodated. Consequently unscrupulous companies were able to take on new entrants without the necessity of paying them any wages at all.

Another big deterioration in the industry has been in the regulation of working hours. In the days of the 'closed shop', when everyone had to be a member of a union in order to work in the unionised workplaces, staff may have worked long hours but would be paid a great deal of overtime pay, first, to compensate them and, second, to discourage employers from imposing such long hours. Casualisation led to changes in contracts, including 'buy-outs' and 'all-in deals', which resulted in long hours being worked but with less and less overtime pay.

It was clear that the unions had to respond to this unfettered rampage of market forces in new ways. Central to this was a new focus on the law. BECTU looked to Europe, and particularly to the Working Time Directive. This directive set limits on the hours that could be worked and the breaks that must be taken between shifts. It also gave every worker in Europe an entitlement to three weeks' paid holiday per year.

The British government attempted to minimise the impact of the directive by defining a 'worker' as someone who had worked for a company for at least thirteen weeks. At a stroke this left British freelance workers with no paid holidays. So BECTU took the British government to the European Court and won, thus establishing in British law the rights of freelance workers to paid holidays.

This same directive was implemented by the unions as a way of trying to outlaw the worst excesses of overtime working.

The Labour government's new legislation on workers' rights gave full employment protection after just one year's service at a company. The unions used this to attack the widespread practice, especially in the BBC, of keeping thousands of staff on 'rolling' three-month or six-month contracts, which had left people working for the corporation for years without access to staff benefits such as pensions. And the unions have devoted more and more effort to lobbying the government for further changes to the law. BECTU has used the new rights on union recognition to win new agreements in the broadcasting industry. When trying to win recognition in a part of Sky, renowned for its anti-union bias, the company threatened its staff that if they voted for the union they would close that part of the company down. BECTU reacted by successfully lobbying the government, alongside the TUC, to make such threats illegal.

But over the last decade, the role of the unions has expanded beyond their core mission of fighting for better pay and working conditions for their members. The unions have gradually taken on a lead role in defending public service broadcasting against the free marketeers. This role brings the unions into direct conflict with ITV, the big independent production companies and their organisation PACT, Sky, and all those who see broadcasting primarily as a business and not as the most powerful cultural medium in society, which, as such, requires special regulation.

When ITV was established, fifteen regions were created with each regional franchise being awarded to a separate company. The driving force of ITV was its regional character, and every franchise had its own programme-making staff and studios. In recent years the most powerful ITV companies – Carlton and Granada – lobbied successfully for fundamental changes in regulations, which allowed them first to dominate network commissions, then to buy other ITV franchises and, finally, to merge into one big company, which now owns most of the ITV network. While the unions could see where this was heading, they continued to argue that ownership was not as important as preserving the regional character of ITV.

However, pressure by ITV on the regulator resulted in a weakening of requirements for programme-making in the regions and ITV has lobbied hard to be allowed to jettison its public service commitments, including ending regional news. At the same time regional programme-making studios were closed down and there is a clear aim to concentrate ITV in programme-making in London and Leeds.

BECTU opposes this not only because of the massive scale of broadcasting job losses and the associated collapse of the broadcasting industry in all affected ITV programme-making centres. The union points out that this is a time when Britain is decentralising – with a Scottish Parliament and Welsh Assembly – and yet in order to maximise profits ITV plc wishes to end programme-making in most of Britain. This would inevitably increase the London-centric focus of television and further submerge regional identities from the national vision. In addition, the absence of local news on all of British television except for BBC1 would have an adverse impact on the democratic process: local issues and local politicians will largely disappear from the radar.

The unions also point out the long-term outcome of less regional programme-making: it makes ITV more tempting for takeover by, for example, a US entertainment company.

The unions have also been leading opponents of the campaign for more independent companies' access to commissions. The unions point out that these independent companies have none of the responsibilities of the broadcasters. While the BBC recruits and extensively trains staff, the indies are characterised as crewing up freelances for each production with no continuing commitment to them.

So at the beginning of the twenty-first century the role of the unions in the broadcasting industry has grown: not only

are they working for a better working life for the industry's workforce, but they are fighting hard for a better industry and better broadcasting.

Janice Turner

The Labour Force in the US

The television industry, as the twenty-first century began, represented one of the more highly unionised in the United States. Qualified candidates are numerous for a few available jobs. The work of producing and airing programmes lends itself to odd working hours, location shoots, holidays, weekends, long working days and often short-term temporary employment. Such conditions would normally permit management to exploit employees by offering low wages, few fringe benefits and no job security to employees. Historically, unionisation in the United States began in manufacturing industries, to eliminate exploitation. But there was a long tradition in the stage of exploitation as well, and such unions as Actors' Equity provided the models for the US television industry. Its impetus in television grew out of stage, movie and radio unions, encouraged by the 1935 National Labor Relations Act. Significantly the television unions have maintained this power.

By the beginning of the twenty-first century, unions and guilds representing employees in television, bargaining with networks and production companies for minimum wage scales, pension funds and other fringe benefits, were long established. The major bargaining issues were minimum wages and residual payments for past work as new forms of distribution like VHS and DVD were introduced, as well as a way to build up a pension and gain group health care. 'Residuals' is the term used to describe royalties paid to actors, directors and writers for airing programmes originally, in subsequent replays and re-runs, and for cassette sales and rentals. As other industries eliminated pension and health care benefits, the television industry in the US has not.

The degree of unionisation in television varies considerably by geographic region. Television stations and cable systems in most of the larger media markets, like New York City, Los Angeles and Chicago, are almost totally unionised. Local television stations and cable systems in small markets, however, may not be unionised. Networks and major production companies are all unionised, whereas small independent producers tend not to be.

The term 'union' in the television industry describes labour organisations that represent technical personnel, and are referred to as 'below-the-line' unions. The term 'guild' describes labour organisations that represent creative personnel, and are referred to as 'above-the-line' unions. These designations result from their actual position on the pages of production budgets in which 'creative' and 'technical' costs are divided by a line. In a typical television show production budget, below-the-line costs are fixed, whereas above-the-line costs are flexible.

For example, the budget for a one-hour drama enters a camera operator's wages below-the-line because there is a standard wage scale in the union contract with management for camera operators shooting a one-hour drama. The salary for the show's leading actor is entered above-the-line because there is considerable disparity between a relatively unknown actor's salary and the salary of a major TV star, like William Petersen or Marg Helgenberger.

Four very large unions represent most below-the-line technical personnel in television and cable today: the National Association of Broadcast Employees and Technicians (NABET), the International Brotherhood of Electrical Workers (IBEW), the International Alliance of Theatrical and Stage Employes (sic, see below) (IATSE) and the Communication Workers of America (CWA).

The National Association of Broadcast Employees and Technicians (NABET) began as a union of radio engineers at NBC in 1933. By the beginning of the twenty-first century, NABET was the exclusive bargaining agent for below-the-line personnel at the ABC, NBC, FOX and PBS networks, as well as at many local independent television stations in large cities.

The International Brotherhood of Electrical Workers (IBEW) ranked as one of the largest unions in the US, representing workers in construction, manufacturing and utilities, in addition to below-the-line personnel at CBS, Disney, independent TV stations and some cable companies.

The International Alliance of Theatrical and Stage Employes (spelling mistake kept but known by all as simply IA) is currently organised primarily along craft lines with over 800 local chapters, each representing specialised occupations within the union's overall national membership of more than 70,000 workers. In the Los Angeles area alone, some of the occupations represented by separate local chapters are: set designers, model makers, illustrators, matte artists, costumers, make-up artists, hair stylists, film editors, film cartoonists, script supervisors, film set painters, studio electricians, stage hands and story analysts. IATSE represents almost every below-the-line occupation at the major production studios and many independent production companies that produce TV shows.

The Communication Workers of America (CWA) now represents over 700,000 men and women in both private and public sectors, including over half a million workers who were building the Information Highway. CWA members are employed in telecommunications, broadcasting, cable TV, journalism, publishing, electronics and general manufacturing, as well as airline customer service, government service, health care and education. CWA had 1,200 locals across the US and Canada, living in approximately 10,000 communities, making CWA one of the most geographically diverse US unions. CWA held over 2,000 collective bargaining agreements – spelling out wages, benefits and working conditions – with the NBC and ABC television networks, and the Canadian Broadcasting Corporation. CWA is also increasing its membership in the cable television industry, and represents below-the-line personnel in cable multiple system operators, cable networks and local cable companies.

There are many above-the-line guilds representing creative workers in television. The major guilds with the most influence are: the American Federation of Television and Radio Artists (AFTRA), the Screen Actors Guild (SAG), the Directors Guild of America (DGA) and the Writers Guild of America (East and West; that is Los Angeles and New York). Most members of these unions do not work full time or regularly, but stars give the unions (guilds in nicer parlance) their clout.

The American Federation of Television and Radio Artists (AFTRA) grew out of the American Federation of Radio Artists, founded in 1937. It added television performers and 'television' to its name in 1952. These days AFTRA represents over 70,000 performers nationally, who appear on television or cable TV programmes: announcers, news persons, sportscasters, game show MCs and talk show hosts. AFTRA has about 30,000 members in its Los Angeles area alone. Yet most television performers work other jobs to support themselves while seeking occasional temporary employment as a television, or cable gig. AFTRA divides its members into four major areas: 1) news and broadcasting; 2) entertainment programming; 3) the recording business; and 4) commercials and non-broadcast, industrial, educational media. Talent payments under AFTRA contracts grew to over $1 billion per year as the twenty-first century started. AFTRA negotiated and enforced over 400 collective bargaining agreements that guaranteed minimum (but never maximum) salaries, safe working conditions and health and retirement benefits. Indeed, AFTRA was the first industry union to establish employer-paid health and retirement plans for members and any of their dependents who qualify. The Health Fund provides comprehensive medical and hospital benefits; a dental plan; prescription drug programme; free life and accident insurance; and mental health and substance abuse programmes. The fully funded Retirement Fund is portable, so that wherever members work under an AFTRA contract, whether on a television or radio programme, a sound recording, a commercial or an industrial show, employer contributions are made on their behalf. To gain these considerable benefits, as of 1 November 2003, the initiation fee was $1,300; minimum dues for the first six months were $60.90. Thereafter, an AFTRA member's dues were calculated based on her or his earnings in AFTRA's jurisdiction during the prior year.

The Screen Actors Guild (SAG) now represents over 100,000 professional actors and performing artists working nationwide in television, as well as interactive multimedia productions, infomercials and music videos. Upon joining, SAG members are guaranteed minimum wages, standardised residual payments (for re-runs), stipulated overtime compensation and late payment penalty payments, plus health insurance and a pension plan. Again, this does not come cheap for new members who, as of 2003, paid a $1,356 one-time initiation fee – with minimum yearly dues of $50 – plus 0.93 per cent of total earnings from $1 to $200,000. SAG's sizable staff negotiated and enforced collective bargaining agreements that established minimum levels of compensation, and guaranteed benefits and working conditions. It maintained reciprocal agreements with other performer unions. A performer who was a member of the American Federation of Television and Radio Artists (AFTRA), Actors' Equity (stage performers), American Guild of Musical Artists (AGMA), Alliance of Canadian Television and Radio Artists (ACTRA) or American Guild of Variety Artists (AGVA) for at least one year and had worked as a principal performer under the jurisdiction of any of the above-named unions became instantly eligible for SAG membership. In addition, SAG maintained a relationship with the Screen Extras Guild (SEG), which represented bit performers who appear in programmes produced on film. Most celebrities and successful performers belong to both AFTRA and SAG, so they are able to perform in all three production modes: live, tape, or film.

The Directors Guild of America (DGA) was organised originally in 1936, as the Screen Directors Guild, by a group of famous film directors, including John Ford and Howard Hawks. Television directors were first admitted in 1950, and the name Directors Guild of America was adopted in 1960. By the turn into the twenty-first century, the DGA had a West chapter in Hollywood and an East chapter in New York City, and represented directors, associate directors, unit production managers, stage managers and production assistants in television, and directors, assistant directors and stage managers in film. Both chapters worked co-operatively to represent their members regardless of the location of a production or shoot. The East chapter, for example, represented most play directors, and the West chapter represents most film directors. Benefits included basic minimum wages, guaranteed residual collections and competent legal assistance in disputes with the major companies. At this time, the Directors Guild of America rep-

resented more than 12,000 members working in US cities and abroad. In 2002, the membership of the Directors Guild of America ratified a three-year collective bargaining agreement with the major Hollywood studios which were all part of vast media conglomerates. So, for example, an agreement with Paramount Pictures, also represented CBS Productions and the CBS television network – as all were owned by Viacom. Here again the famous directors joined their fellow workers and provided the clout the vast media conglomerates could not avoid.

The Writers Guild of America had two branches – WGA (East) and the WGA (West) – incorporated separately because of differing laws of incorporation in New York and California, with WGA (East) located in New York City and WGA (West) in Los Angeles. Though incorporated separately, they functioned as a single organisation that represented the interests of over 8,000 members nationally, although the WGA (East) had only half the membership of the WGA (West), and has a significant number of playwrights among its membership, whereas WGA (West) was dominated by screenwriters. In 1962, WGA also joined with sister guilds in Great Britain, Canada, Australia and New Zealand to form an international union alliance among these English-speaking nations.

These are the major unions, guaranteeing the labour force of television rights, wages, pensions and health benefits. With computers, satellites and digital technology globalising electronic communication, these unions and guilds will continue to add new occupational groups to their membership and become increasingly more international in scope. In a democratic society like the United States, viable unions remain necessary to provide a countervailing force to the big major corporations, forcing management policies and practices towards employees to be fairer and guaranteed in a way that would not be possible otherwise. Unionisation has brought about changes in the television industries in the US, resulting in very different trends from those in evidence in the late 20th century; there seems little on the horizon to diffuse the unions' power.

Douglas Gomery

RECOMMENDED READING

Bielby, William T. and Bielby, Denise D. (1989), *The 1989 Hollywood Writers' Report: Unequal Access, Unequal Pay*, Los Angeles, CA: Writers Guild of America (West).

Directors Guild of America (1991), *Constitution and Bylaws*, Los Angeles, CA: DGA.

McIlroy, John (1988), *Trade Unions in Britain Today*, Manchester: Manchester University Press.

Prindle, David F. (1988), *The Politics of Glamour: Ideology and Democracy in the Screen Actors Guild*, Madison: University of Wisconsin Press.

SELLING AND TELEVISION

Television Audience Research – UK

In the UK (a reasonably typical advanced industrialised nation) most individuals consume or use the media to a great degree in their daily lives. The following percentages represent audiences or, more accurately, one particular way of defining audiences for these particular media. Broadly similar patterns are found in other countries.

In a typical week:

94 per cent of the UK population (aged 4+) watch some TV

90 per cent of the UK population (aged 15+) listen to some radio

50 per cent of the UK population (aged 15+) read a daily national newspaper.*

THE TELEVISION AUDIENCE

The concept of 'the audience' lies at the heart of all mass communications. Yet, this key term 'audience' is rarely defined or critically examined in light of what it entails. In many ways, it is a portmanteau term that encompasses a wide range of possible meanings and definitions. For example, the audience of a single TV programme (or TV advert) could be defined in any of the following ways:

Anyone who watched any part of the programme

Anyone who watched more than half of the programme

Anyone who watched all of the programme

Anyone who could recall what the programme said

Anyone who claims to have watched the programme.

Each definition of 'audience' has different implications. For example, if the first definition shown above is used ('watched any part of a programme'), the audience size estimate so obtained is likely to be far larger than by any of the other measures. But does watching, say, five minutes of a thirty-minute programme count as 'viewing' the programme? In part, the answer to this must depend on the programme. In a

news bulletin or magazine programme, five minutes might be a single item, and so the viewing activity might well be a meaningful measure of the interaction between a viewer and the programme content (and the producers' intentions). Watching five minutes of a complex one-hour drama or a single-topic documentary, however, is unlikely to be meaningful in anywhere near the same sense, and almost certainly is not what the producers wanted from the viewer. Therefore it is possible to reach quite different conclusions about what the media do to people – or, put differently, what the people do with media – depending on how audiences are conceptualised and, in the case of audience research, operationalised in terms of the measurement or assessment techniques used.

At the same time, the television industry has its own needs for information about media audiences. Public service providers have to show that programming is reaching the people, that messages are understood and that production goals have been achieved. Linked to this is the need that regulators, such as the Office of Communications (Ofcom), have for audience information so that they can make judgments about service performance. Finally, commercial broadcasts must generate revenue through selling advertising time and sponsorship of programmes and they therefore need to know the size and make-up of both programme and channel audiences.

Resulting from these various needs for information about audiences is a set of 'standard' ways of assessing television audiences. Broadly speaking, there are three main types of audience research that are routinely used. Oversimplifying slightly, two are essentially quantitative approaches designed to give reliable statistical data about audiences – *audience measurement* and *audience reaction*. The third type of research is much more concerned about audience understanding and the creative process, and relies largely on non-quantitative methods, such as focus groups – this can be labelled as *audience insight*.

AUDIENCE MEASUREMENT

In order to assess use of any one TV set, three pieces of information are needed: the *behaviour of the viewer*, the precise *time* and the *identity of the content shown* on the television set. The system in the UK is run by BARB (Broadcasters' Audience Research Board) on behalf of UK TV broadcasting and advertising organisations. In this model, a statistically representative sample of 5,100 homes (around 11,500 viewers) of UK households has a monitoring device (a 'peoplemeter') fitted to every

---

* Based on data from BARB (Broadcasters' Audience Research Board), NRS (National Readership Survey) and RAJAR (Radio Joint Audience Research). Data for week ending 17 April 2005.

television set and video recorder in the home. Each television set also has an additional handset with a set of buttons: each person in the home has their own button on these handsets. Whenever they start to watch television, they press their button and when they stop viewing they press it again. The peoplemeter records the time, channels viewed and the identity of the viewers.

This information about sets, people and channels is collated and downloaded early each morning via telephone to the BARB processing centre, where estimates are produced for viewing behaviour over time and channel.

The peoplemeter system is by no means perfect – indeed all research methods have their limitations and weaknesses. With the peoplemeter, there are issues over the sorts of people who agree to take part and to have their home 'wired' for BARB. And, how good are these people at pressing their buttons 'properly'? Also, as it stands, the peoplemeter is not good at measuring viewing out of home – in other people's homes, or in bars, etc. This has clear implications for viewing sports channels and major sporting and cultural events, where people gather together to watch. Further, the peoplemeter is not particularly good at identifying pre-recorded DVD or videotape use. The system can recognise material recorded in the same household, but cannot cope well with other people's recordings or bought or rented material.

There is a recent development that overcomes some of these difficulties: the portable people meter or PPM. This is a device that individuals carry with them throughout the day. It's a unit about the size of a small mobile phone, or one version is like a wristwatch, which 'listens' for signals from TV sets and radio sets: these signals cannot be heard by humans, and are used to give a unique identifier signal to each TV and radio service. At the end of the day, the wearer puts the PPM into a holder which recharges it and simultaneously downloads the day's record of the signals it encountered and the times involved. (The wristwatch version is worn for a week, then a replacement watch is put on, and the old one is mailed to the processing centre.)

AUDIENCE REACTION

While knowing something about audience behaviour is undoubtedly important, broadcasters also need to know in a

representative way what viewers think about television output, and how they react to what they see. Over the years there have been a number of ways of getting such feedback. Until a few years ago, BARB ran a second service called the Audience Reaction Service for the UK television industry, which asked a large sample of viewers to rate all the programmes they watched on a simple scale from very interesting and/or enjoyable through to not at all interesting and/or enjoyable. In some cases, additional questions would be asked. This provided a simple and rapid feedback service to the broadcasters. This has been replaced by a similar service offered by research companies to individual television companies, based on a national opinion-type survey. A major problem with this type of evaluation is that, in many cases, if a programme is not liked by viewers it will quickly show up as a shrinking audience, as revealed by audience measurement.

AUDIENCE INSIGHT

While audience reaction measures are generally on the wane, there has been a dramatic rise over the years of qualitative research, which is designed to look in depth, and at short notice, into specific issues. The aim is to get the feel of what people think, and how they express these thoughts. In this type of approach the key 'data' are quotes from people, not questionnaire results from surveys or charts from BARB's meter data. The most characteristic approach to this style of research is the focus group. Focus groups are widely used for television concept-testing and programme 'fine-tuning'. The BBC, for example, undertook a major and extensive series of focus groups drawn from different regions and social groupings across the UK when developing its first popular soap (which became *EastEnders*): one of the early key issues was 'Where should a new soap be set?' Options included a range of major British cities: the least problematic alternative in terms of local and regional rivalries turned out to be London.

A group of people – six to eight is a general norm – are recruited and brought together in a suitable location (often private houses), together with a trained moderator. The moderator's task is to lead the group into discussion of the issues under research. The benefits of groups are the richness of discussion and conceptualisation that can be obtained, far outstripping the abilities of quantitative surveys to concisely summarise people's feelings and thoughts. Importantly, focus groups can be, and are, widely misused in practice: the discussion of a few groups are taken by some to have the same weight of evidence as a full-scale national sample survey. Groups are widely used, though, as a means of establishing the 'boundaries' of opinions and fledgling TV and radio programme concepts often die at the focus-group stage.

THE BARB PEOPLEMETER

At the simplest level, averaging the data collected from the peoplemeter allows audience behaviour to be estimated on a second-by-second basis across the day. However, the data are normally used in a more aggregated form. The table below, for example, shows summary information for March and April 2005 in terms of how long the average person spent viewing television each week.

The data collected by BARB are available for analysis for the BARB subscribers: the BBC, the ITV companies, Channel Four, S4C and Five, the satellite and digital channel providers and the advertising agencies. The typical analyses done tend to be commercially confidential and not available for publication. However, typical questions that can be answered using BARB data include:

- How many episodes of a series did people watch? (*Almost everyone misses one or more episodes of a series*)
- When do people change channels? (*Mainly during breaks or between programmes, but also when a more favoured programme is on, or when looking for something 'better'*)
- Is a new series of an established programme performing better or worse than the old? (*BARB data used to compare audience size and 'loyalty' – number of episodes watched – of old and new series audiences*).

As well as the continuous record of viewing behaviour collected every second of the day over long periods of time, BARB has detailed information about the characteristics of everyone aged over four in each of its sample households (including age, gender, social status). BARB has also recently begun to collect information about the panellists' more general lifestyles – for example: personal interests, cinema-going, ownership of various goods, newspaper and radio use. The data collected in this manner can be analysed in many different ways. For example:

- drivers of 4x4 vehicles spend 29.8 hours per week watching TV, compared with only 22.9 hours for sports car drivers
- half of working adults get home between 5pm and 7pm.

BARB also has to cope with change. The rise of the personal video recorder (such as TiVo, Sky+) means that the amount of 'live' viewing of programmes is likely to reduce as people reschedule content to fit their lives. The BARB system can now detect and analyse the viewing of time-shifted content for inclusion in its ratings. BARB is also developing ways of tracking the use of the growing range of interactive services available with digital TV. While still in development, this service has shown that there were some 6 million people using interactive TV services in January 2005: around 16 per cent of people with multichannel TV available, or 11 per cent of all TV viewers.

Michael Svennevig

Hours of viewing and share of audience, including video time-shift

4 weeks, ending 1 May 2005

	Average weekly viewing per person		*Share of total viewing*	
	April (hrs:mins)	March (hrs:mins)	April (%)	March (%)
All/any TV	25:21	26:212	100.0	100.0
BBC1 (incl. Breakfast News)	6:00	6:27	23.7	24.5
BBC2	2:27	2:33	9.7	9.7
Total BBC1/BBC2	8:27	9:01	33.3	34.2
ITV (incl. GMTV)	5:26	5:54	21.4	22.4
Channel Four/S4C	2:27	2:23	9.7	9.0
five	1:43	1:40	6.8	6.3
Total/any comm. terr. TV	9:36	9:57	37.9	37.7
Other viewing	7:18	7:24	28.8	28.1

Note: 'Other viewing' is cable, satellite and digital terrestrial TV (Freeview/Top-up TV).

Source: BARB Newsletter, no. 6, March 2005.

RESEARCH FOR THE FUTURE

The approaches and solutions discussed above have been developed in a relatively 'fixed' media environment. Things are changing fast, though. The main development that is causing change is the Internet. Thanks to massively increased channel capacity and lowered access costs made available through broadband (via cable, broadcast or radio transmission) the Internet has now become a major influence on people's time use.

These increases in capacity and accessibility allow people to use the Internet to access radio and TV material (including other countries' services), for downloading of archive materials, linking to or setting up of webcam and video blog sites, and for buying access to a rapidly expanding range of paid-for 'TV-like' services and feature film downloads. A sign of these times is the recent decision by the BBC to offer what it terms 'podcasts': pre-packaged materials designed for iPod and MP3 users and downloadable from the BBC's website. Equally, if the amount of time spent by Internet users with, say, the CNN website could be added to the time spent accessing the channel via digital TV as measured by BARB, then CNN might be seen in a different light in the UK media environment. While there are well-established measurement systems for Internet use (for example, Nielsen NetRatings), these tend simply to measure traffic and time patterns – measuring volume rather than offering insight.

All of these developments throw major difficulties into the path of 'traditional' audience research – in particular in the measurement of the 'audience/users' of any one piece of content, which can readily be delivered to the audience in many different ways and used at different times. Yet, without this element in one form or another, the funding of content production becomes problematic; without some relative measurement of a user base, it is difficult to see how TV-style production can continue unchanged. At the same time, it is clear that people continue to value TV as a medium precisely because it is *not* the Internet in the sense that it is pre-produced for specific purposes, and designed to deliver ready-made benefits to the audience.

Michael Svennevig

RECOMMENDED READING

<www.barb.co.uk>.
<www.nielsen-netratings.com>.
<www.nrs.co.uk>.
<www.rajar.co.uk>.

Market Research – US

Market research firms like A. C. Nielsen sell measurement – the measurement of audiences. In the US, a handful of these organisations generate audience estimates for radio, television and Internet. These 'ratings' are both a commodity that is bought and sold in the marketplace, and the common currency used by trading partners to estimate the value of transactions (Beville, 1988; Webster, Phalen and Lichty, 2000). In fact, ratings shape the information system that supports econ-

omic exchange in electronic media markets; and the system persists because buyers and sellers accept it, flaws and all.

The present chapter reviews the history of electronic media measurement techniques in the United States, and summarises the major technological and methodological challenges the audience research industry faces today.

THE DEVELOPMENT OF DATA COLLECTION METHODS

This selective review is taken from the more detailed histories found in Banks (1981), Beville (1988) and Webster, Phalen and Lichty (2000). In 1930, Archibald Crossley began collecting radio listening information by calling households and asking them to identify the programmes they had heard during the previous few hours. Crossley's audience estimates were plagued by sampling error because too few homes had telephones – the sample was unrepresentative. Additionally, respondents sometimes had trouble remembering what they had heard on the radio, or they simply named their favourite programmes whether they had listened to them that day or not.

In 1934, Montgomery Clark and Claude Hooper began collecting audience information through telephone coincidental surveys. This method reduced respondent error due to memory lapses or reporting false information, because researchers asked only what individuals were listening to at the time of the call. But the sample was still limited to households with telephones, which eliminated a great number of potential radio listeners.

Sydney Roslow entered the field with an in-person survey. Not only did this method eliminate the sampling problem associated with telephone surveys, it offered the possibility of reaching different demographic groups. Roslow's firm, The PULSE of New York, is credited with changing urban radio stations by reporting the musical preferences of previously unrecognised minority audiences. However, in-person interviewing was time-consuming and costly. It was impractical and inefficient as the basis for national audience ratings.

In the 1930s, consumer market research giant A. C. Nielsen turned its sights to electronic media. The firm used a new technology, the audimeter, which was connected to radio sets to record when they were in use and the channels to which they were tuned. The new data collection method, called 'passive' because it required no action on the part of respondents, addressed aspects of both sampling and respondent error. Its major drawback was that it could only report general information about the household. Nielsen couldn't tell whether the whole family was listening or whether someone forgot to turn the radio off and left it playing to an empty room.

James Seiler believed that the best way to collect demographic information was to ask respondents to record everything they heard on the radio in a diary. This method had the advantage of reflecting actual listener behaviour. And, unlike the passive meter, it also gave insight into the programme choices made by specific individuals. Diaries soon became a standard technique in both radio and television.

When radio became a personal rather than group listening experience, diaries were used to collect audience data for all local market radio stations. In local television, Nielsen used the diary in medium and small markets, and the diary plus the passive meter in larger markets. Network ratings were calculated by combining diary and passive meter information from the national Nielsen sample. This dual method incorporated the strengths and weaknesses of both data collection techniques. Most notable among the limitations was the failure of individuals to complete diaries and mail them back to Nielsen. This non-response error has been a major concern in both television and radio.

In the 1980s, British research firm AGB attempted to launch its television audience research service in the US. AGB's peoplemeter promised to combine the advantages of passive meters and diaries, and eliminate many of the problems associated with the combined meter/diary data collection technique. Advertising agencies and media organisations met with AGB to discuss this new information product, and a few committed monetary resources for its development. But what the media industry really wanted was to use the threat of competition to force Nielsen to improve its own methodology. American media were not likely to abandon Nielsen altogether, nor were they likely to support two information services in the long term (Phalen, 1996).

Nielsen introduced its own peoplemeter in 1987, launching a nationwide service to compete with AGB. Even though researchers saw many problems with this new meter, the industry quickly adopted it as the national standard for television measurement. The large media companies renewed their subscriptions to Nielsen, and AGB was forced out of the market due to lack of financial support. SRI met a similar fate when it tried to compete with Nielsen by introducing its SMART technology in the late 1990s.

Nielsen's peoplemeter generated controversy. Early results showed an overall decline in television usage across the US, especially among certain demographic groups. Young males, for example, were largely absent from the ratings, and their 'disappearance' raised red flags among researchers. Over time, Nielsen has tried to address this problem, and others like it, by offering additional incentives to individuals most likely to decline participation and by expanding the overall sample size. They have also, under pressure from the industry, watched samples closely in order to compensate for shortfalls.

Another concern is the susceptibility of the peoplemeter to misuse, whether intentional or unintentional. Because the meter requires action on the part of the viewer, respondents experience 'button fatigue', leading them to be less diligent about signing in and out of the audience. Nielsen's response has been to rotate samples more frequently. Other sample-related complaints have carried over from the previous diary/meter system, such as the lack of data for television usage in college dorms, sports bars and hotels.

The unprecedented growth of the Internet has made measurement of online audiences a top priority for marketers. Although research on Internet usage patterns began in the 1980s, traditional audience research firms did not enter the market in a stable way until much later. One explanation is that the expertise needed to collect Internet data differed from that required to measure broadcast audiences. Among the first companies to collect Web information were Media Metrix and NetRatings; both had expertise in computer technology. As their businesses grew, they hired researchers from the broadcast industry. These firms asked respondents to install tracking software on their computers that would record all websites visited, noting the time and duration of each visit. Mountains of raw data were returned each month. This created the first major problem with Internet measurement, which was how to make the seemingly endless data useful to potential advertisers. To solve it, these organisations mimicked the information system used for television and radio, reporting statistics analogous to broadcasting's ratings and shares.

Corporate consolidation has become the norm in audience research, as it has throughout the media industries. Coincidental with the development of the Web as an advertiser-supported medium, Nielsen purchased NetRatings. In turn, Nielsen became part of the international media research company VNU. Today, Internet audience information is provided by two major competitors: Nielsen NetRatings and comScore Networks, which acquired the Audience Measurement Service of Media Metrix.

IMPROVING THE MEASUREMENT SYSTEM

Media organisations and advertisers often pressure audience research firms to improve sample designs and data collection methodologies. However, it can't be assumed that those who purchase and use audience data have doggedly pursued every opportunity for innovation. Each improvement in data collection technology has an economic cost, which may or may not outweigh the economic benefits of more accurate information. Aside from the obvious monetary costs of improving an information system, changes might require the development of new skill sets by the professionals who analyse the data. The new system might also yield vastly different numbers for programmes and/or channels, which would make historical trend data obsolete (Phalen, 1996). Costs such as these may not be immediately apparent to the market observer, but they affect the degree to which market participants actively seek improvements in the ratings system.

The ratings industry is facing several major challenges in the new media environment. First, the current methods of data collection that comprise the information system are still heavily dependent on the diligence of respondents. Industry participants would prefer a system that is entirely passive, yet still yields demographic information. Second, the consumer technologies used today are not technologies for which the current information system was developed. Personal video recorders (PVRs) and video on demand (VOD), for example, give viewers the power to decide when to watch programmes, and whether or not to view commercials. Not only is the current research system predicated on the assumption that everyone has access to programmes at the same time, but the data collection methods are inadequate to track individual programmes on a universal scale. While it is technologically possible to do this, the implementation depends on the willingness of media organisations to pay the price.

Nielsen and Arbitron have been working on ways to bring research up to speed with changes in the media industries. As noted earlier, Nielsen uses diaries and meters to measure local television audiences. The company is attempting to change this by replacing passive meters with peoplemeters in the largest television markets. The peoplemeter would provide continuous data, thereby reducing the industry's reliance on sweeps months (the four months when Nielsen measures all local audiences). It would also allow Nielsen to expand the national sample size to 10,000 homes by incorporating the local peoplemeters into the total. But this attempt is being met with resistance on the part of media companies, who fear that the new technology will drastically alter the balance of power in the marketplace.

Nielsen is also working with PVR providers to develop a way to measure audiences for individual programmes, whether they are watched in real-time or recorded and played back at a later date. Devices such as TiVo could potentially track and aggregate viewing data from every household that uses it. However, privacy concerns are a major deterrent – unless people agree to participate, researchers cannot monitor their viewing. The same is true for services like VOD, which could be supported by advertising if researchers could measure its audience.

Arbitron has faced the challenge by developing a personal people meter (PPM) that travels with the respondent and records signals they are exposed to during the day. This PPM works by tracking an inaudible audio signal that radio and television outlets put on their programmes. Critics argue that it will pick up signals that the respondent never even noticed. Another criticism is the potential for fatigue – how long will respondents wear the pager-like device before getting tired of it? Arbitron has tested its PPM in Philadelphia, and is planning tests in other US cities (Chunovic, 2003).

CONCLUSIONS

As long as advertising supports electronic media audiences, television, radio and Internet will depend on the market for audience measurement. But current media options are stretching the capabilities of audience research organisations. As consumer technologies advance, audience measurement techniques must advance with them if they are to keep pace with changing patterns of media usage. When all efforts to enhance the existing system are exhausted, we will see substantial changes in the way audiences are measured. The traditional channel-based system will be replaced by a technology that monitors individual programmes, regardless of how they are delivered to the audience. The research potential of PVR technology and digital set-top boxes may be incorporated into the information system, but only if privacy issues can be resolved. In any case, the information system of the future will be less reliant on the memory of respondents and more dependent on passive technology for data collection.

Patricia Phalen

RECOMMENDED READING

Banks, M. J. (1981), 'History of Broadcast Audience Research in the United States, 1920–1980 with an Emphasis on the Rating Services', unpublished doctoral dissertation, University of Tennessee, Knoxville.

Beville, Hugh M. (1988), *Audience Ratings: Radio, Television, Cable*, revised student edn, Hillsdale, NJ: Lawrence Erlbaum Associates.

Chunovic, L. (2003), 'When Audiences Intersect; Philly Portable People Meter Test Helps Advertisers Make Cross-media Buys', (electronic version), *Television Week*, no. 18.

Phalen, Patricia F. (1996), 'Information and Markets and the Market for Information: An Analysis of the Market for Television Audiences', unpublished doctoral dissertation, Evanston, IL: Northwestern University.

Webster, James G., Phalen, Patricia F. and Lichty, Lawrence W. (2000), *Ratings Analysis: The Theory and Practice of Audience Research*, 2nd edn, Mahwah, NJ: Lawrence Erlbaum Associates.

Scheduling Television Programmes

Scheduling turns commissioning and channel strategies into reality. (Fanthome, 2004c)

Scheduling is nothing other than editing on an Olympian scale. (Ellis, 2002, p. 131)

Scheduling is part science, part art and part sheer luck. (Docherty, 1995, p. 122)

The construction of a schedule is an exercise in planning that calls for knowledge of the programmes it involves and an awareness of the moods and predilections of today's audiences. Schedulers must be able to analyse audience data, find the right slots for programmes and programmes for the right slots, locate 'new' audiences, ensure that viewers are able to navigate the schedule with relative ease. Increasingly, they create complementary schedules across a range of channels that meet viewers' preferences and deter them from switching over to the competition.

The art of scheduling has become more important and complex as competition for viewers has intensified. In the early days of television, there were few outside constraints on the BBC's scheduling decisions: viewers were offered a diet of programmes that was designed to be not just entertaining but culturally and morally uplifting. However, when ITV began in 1955, the viewers preferred its greater emphasis on entertainment and, as a result of declining ratings, the BBC was forced to rethink its strategies. In what is often referred to as the 'golden age' of television, both the BBC and ITV produced a diverse range of output, adopting a head-to-head scheduling strategy on some occasions, when viewers had to choose between similar programmes, and a complementary strategy on others, when viewers could choose between different genres. Decisions as to when to transmit a programme were based on the assumed preferences and traditions of the nation as a whole. Although the element of competition at this time should not be underestimated, the broadcasters' differing sources of funding, together with the absence of other rivals, meant that each could survive comfortably with an audience share of about 50 per cent. ITV battled to maximise its advertising revenue and the BBC strove to justify its licence fee, but neither was fighting for survival.

However, the contemporary situation is different. New technology, the influences of globalisation and an increase in market forces have resulted in the introduction of numerous new satellite, digital and cable channels, which are in turn creating a fragmentation of the national audience. The scheduling and marketing of each channel's output have thus assumed paramount importance not only for commercial broadcasters but for the BBC. David Bergg, Director of Programme Strategy for ITV1 and ITV2, observes: 'Scheduling these days is a euphemism for running a business: every slot has a target audience and any programme that under-delivers impacts on potential profitability' (Fanthome, 2004a).

The BBC's scheduling strategy is not subject to the same commercial imperatives and is therefore somewhat different. Sandy Maeer confirms:

> The channels are not purely competitive – as a portfolio we can take risks and show programmes that would not be commissioned in the commercial marketplace. The individual channel needs are balanced with the needs of the portfolio – the aim is to optimise viewers' choice by making the whole range of programming available across the family of BBC channels.

However, scheduling has changed from being 'offer-led' – in which the schedulers assembled a schedule out of programmes that were offered to them by the producers – to being 'demand-led' – in which the schedulers seek to anticipate the viewers' preferences by starting with the schedule and then demanding programmes from the producers in order to fill it. As John Ellis notes, 'The schedule . . . drives the planning of output. It used to put programmes in order. Now, in the American phrase, it 'orders programmes' from the producers' (Ellis, 2000, p. 143). This sentiment is echoed by David Bergg, who reflects: 'You can't schedule against two hundred channels. It's more about *commissioning* in today's multichannelled era.'

Nevertheless, the ordering of programmes remains important and, as the art of scheduling has developed, an annual cycle has emerged, along with a jargon to describe it. The key points in the year are Week 36, which marks the launch of the autumn schedule, and Week 1, which marks the launch of the winter schedule. David Bergg affirms that he classifies the ITV schedules by genre, and builds them as details of programming become available. In the case of films and sporting fixtures this may be as far ahead as three years before transmission, whereas drama and comedy programming is confirmed approximately eighteen months in advance, and entertainment and factual programming about nine months before transmission. Once the key points are mapped out and the 'tent poles' (major ratings winners) are established, the rest of the schedule can be constructed around them. Unsurprisingly, great secrecy surrounds the schedules until the first details are released just over a week before transmission, and the confirmed outline goes to press on the Wednesday afternoon before the week of their commencement. Until this final deadline, it is normal practice to create what Bergg terms 'smokescreens and machinations' in order to mislead the opposition.

Of even greater importance than knowing the competition is knowing, or attempting to know, the TV audiences. Whereas in the early days viewers could be treated as a homogeneous mass, an abundance of channels has caused significant fragmentation. Consequently, today's audience is best perceived as a series of overlapping niche groups. But 'knowing' the audience is an inexact science and while schedulers can find out how many people watch certain programmes, what the demographic breakdown of the audience is at any time, and how domestic and lifestyle routine tend to affect viewers' choices, it is not always clear *why* individuals watch particular programmes or why the same individuals watch particular groupings of programmes. Broadcasters are devoting more time and money to qualitative audience research and piloting in order to be able to predict audience behaviour and translate this information into better commissioning and scheduling strategies.

Scheduling jargon is interesting since it reflects the increasing sophistication of the craft. Initially, schedulers focused on 'inheritance' (the ratings legacy of the preceding programme), 'pre-echo' (viewers turning on early in order to catch the start of their appointment-to-view) and on 'hammocking' a weaker programme between two stronger ones in order for it to benefit from the adjacent ratings. Then, as now, schedules hinged on 'bankers' (programmes that were sure to command a good audience), while including slots for 'sleepers' (programmes that might take a while to become established). However, 'flow' has become less important as audiences channel hop and certain 'junctions', such as the nine o'clock evening slot, which is common to many terrestrial, satellite and digital channels, are times of considerable audience movement.

Recently, as channels have multiplied and it has been more important for viewers to be able to navigate the schedule, the terms 'stripping' (running a show at the same time on consecutive days) and 'stranding' (rotating a show with others of the same type within the same time slot) have gained prominence. 'Themed' or 'formatted' blocks, which comprise programmes from a variety of genres on a similar topic and were first popularised by Channel Four, are now commonplace, and one of the latest buzzwords, which has coincided with the introduction of digital TV, is 'streaming', in which viewers can watch 'off-air' developments, generally of reality shows, for up to twenty-four hours a day.

TV scheduling is in a time of transition. Not only has the

proliferation of channels made it impossible for schedulers to respond to all their competitors but the changes to the UK regulatory structure, which stem from an awareness that increased competition calls for 'lightening the load of content regulation' (Ofcom, 2004, p. 18), applied since December 2004, are likely to have pervasive effects.

Ofcom's responsibilities in terms of the schedules are twofold. First, it regulates all broadcasting services that are licensed from the UK. It must enforce standards of impartiality and the avoidance of offence and harm, and ensure that broadcasters respect the 'watershed' by not transmitting before a certain time material that is unsuitable for children. The UK terrestrial channels have a nine o'clock watershed, whereas for channels that are both premium and subscription, such as Sky Movies and ZeeTV, it is set at eight o'clock. Approximately 500 licensees are regulated by Ofcom, including ITV, Channel Four, Five, numerous satellite, cable and digital terrestrial channels, and the BBC (in terms of the watershed and other standards issues, though not impartiality and accuracy). Second, Ofcom checks that the quotas of specific programming as outlined in the individual licences for the UK terrestrial channels are met; for example, the number of hours devoted to certain genres (news, current affairs and regional programmes), original productions for the channel in question and independent productions. However, other aspects of the delivery of 'public service' broadcasting changed in 2004. The commercial PSB channels (ITV1, Channel Four and Five) set their own policies for the year, and assess their own performances with reference to Ofcom guidelines. Quotas for certain programming, such as religion, documentary, education, arts and children's, are no longer mandatory. However, any broadcaster who wishes to alter the public service content of a channel first needs to gain Ofcom's approval. The legislation underpinning this is Clause 267 of the 2003 Communications Act, which applies to all 'proposals for significant change' (Communications Act, 2003). Steve Perkins, Ofcom's Manager for TV Programming, observes:

> The Communications Act aimed to make certain core areas of PSB delivery – like news, current affairs and original production – absolutely bankable. In other areas, it gave more responsibility back to the PSB channels themselves. The next key step for Ofcom will be the outcome of its PSB Review, at the end of 2004, which will set a prospectus for the future development of PSB.
> (Fanthome, 2004b)

While only time will tell whether the shape and content of television schedules has been transformed as a result of changes in 2004, it is clear from the new legislation that the *mechanism* to

NEWS AT WHEN? SCHEDULING THE LATE EVENING NEWS

For many years, the main news bulletins of both the BBC and ITV occupied what appeared to be permanent slots in the evening schedules. BBC1's *Nine O'Clock News* had been there since 1970 and ITV's *News at Ten* since 1967. Both were extremely important to their respective channels in embodying professionalism, prestige and integrity and symbolising the identity of the organisation.

However, the equilibrium was disturbed in March 1999 when ITV moved its main half-hour evening news programme to 6.30 and the shorter twenty-minute bulletin from 5.40 to eleven o'clock. In its former slot, *News at Ten* had often interrupted movies, forcing viewers to wait until approximately 10.40pm for the last part of a film they had begun to watch at 8.30 or 9 pm. This clearly created problems and, indeed, the situation was exploited by Channel 5 in its 1997 poster campaign. Promoting its own nine o'clock movie, it used slogans such as 'Mrs Doubtfire without the drag' and – next to a poster of Tom Hanks with an Oscar – 'He never thanked Trevor McDonald.'

In October 2000, the BBC moved its *Nine O'Clock News* back an hour to ten o'clock. Sandy Maeer, Controller for Scheduling, Planning and Presentation, recalls that it was considered 'a better slot editorially', as it enabled 'better news coverage in general, such as Parliamentary votes, the business markets and breaking stories in America, while also 'allowing us to play strong dramas and factual pieces of sixty minutes in the post-watershed slot' (Fanthome, 2004c). Similarly, Peter Sissons, the news anchor, declared at the launch: 'I used to

News at Ten

work on *News at Ten* and we were always aware that the time gave us an advantage over the BBC. Now *we'll* [my italics] have that advantage' (BBC, 2000).

However, by this time, rapidly declining numbers for ITV's new eleven o'clock programme had prompted concern at the ITC (which had agreed to the original changes). The consequence was that the twenty-minute late-evening programme was placed in the former *News at Ten* slot for, on average, three weeknights per week, with later bulletins on other weeknights. This began in January 2001 and led to newspaper articles and debate about what became known as the 'news at when?' debacle. Not surprisingly, the lack of a fixed nightly slot for the news also damaged audience figures, and in January 2004 ITV moved the news to 10.30pm five days a week. Justifying the move, David Mannion, Editor-in-Chief of ITV News, stated: 'We've done a lot of work on the audience. At 10.30pm, it's skewed towards men, slightly upmarket, older. We're adding sport every night, making it a slightly more upscale product, a bit more foreign news and business news (Brown, 2004).' Time will tell whether the slot works in commercial terms, and this will depend not only on ratings for the news itself but, primarily, on whether, as a result of more space in the schedule, the programmes before it can succeed in increasing advertising revenue across prime time.

Christine Fanthome

Nine O'Clock News

bring about change is in place, allowing broadcasters, in collaboration with Ofcom, to respond rapidly to developments within the television market. In such an environment, the skills of the scheduler will be crucial.

Christine Fanthome

RECOMMENDED READING

Docherty, David, (then Head of BBC Television Planning and Strategy) (1995), 'Confessions of a Justified Scheduler', in Anthea Millward Hargreave (ed.) (1995), *The Scheduling Game*, London: John Libbey & Co., p. 122.

Ellis, John (2002), *Seeing Things*, London and New York: I. B. Taurus.

CNN News Gathering: The Process

On 20 September 2003, Douglas Gomery spoke to Bu Zhong, who agreed to share his experience working at CNN. Below is an edited version of what he said.

As the twenty-first century began, CNN had forty-one news bureaus on six continents and roughly 850 worldwide affiliates. CNN's reach extended to over thirty television, radio and interactive networks, which at CNN's Atlanta headquarters, are collectively called 'platforms': (1) cable news networks; (2) radio networks; (3) private networks (such as the airport channel); and (4) websites.

So how does CNN go about creating a newscast? At its most basic level, CNN news creation can be broken into two main processes. First, news gathering is the process of gathering news from the field and bringing together and verifying news. Second, production is the process of scripting, editing and posting the news, essentially putting the individual stories or packages, and the whole newscast together for the four outlets.

CNN's world headquarters in Atlanta co-ordinates all news gathering. The news gathering 'desks', or teams of assignment editors, work together to find compelling stories, accurate information and good pictures for all of CNN's news platforms.

CNN's 'news product' starts at a 'Superdesk' in Atlanta. Physically, it's a group of workstations combined in the middle of the CNN newsroom. The Superdesk is the management hub of the CNN newsroom. Representatives from each of CNN's networks – CNN International, CNNfn, Newsource, CNN en Español, CNNRadio, the National Desk and the International Desk – have a seat at the Superdesk. An ongoing dialogue throughout the day and evening enables the network representatives at the Superdesk to share information and co-ordinate coverage.

The desks are staffed 24/7. For example, during the week between the hours of daytime and prime time, up to twenty-five National Desk staffers are at the desk at one time. The National Desk distributes alerts about breaking news and important incoming satellite feeds to all networks and newsrooms.

All newsrooms in Atlanta (CNN, CNN International and CNN en Español), along with designated offices located throughout CNN Center and CNN bureaus in Washington, DC, and New York City, have 'squawk boxes' to keep everyone abreast of the all-call announcements from the main CNN newsroom.

The Bureau Desk is the arm of the National Desk that controls coverage by all CNN news gatherers at CNN Center in Atlanta. This includes coverage by the four beats – Medical, Science and Technology, Entertainment and Political – as well as coverage by all of CNN's US bureaus – which consist of physical locations where phones and television production equipment are kept, and all of the news gathering staff, including photographers, editors, producers and reporters. A 'bureau chief' manages the bureau and its staff. Bureaus vary greatly in size. For example, CNN Chicago bureau consists of a handful of people, while hundreds make up the Washington, DC, bureau. Some bureaus have speciality areas. For example, Los Angeles's speciality is entertainment and Miami's is hurricanes.

An Affiliate Desk is the arm of the National Desk whose mission is to obtain and co-ordinate incoming news from more than 600 CNN affiliate stations in the US and Canada. The Affiliate Desk also works in co-ordination with Newsource to provide custom services for these affiliates, such as moving videos and content between affiliate stations. Those who work the Affiliate Desk serve particular geographic regions of the US and Canada. About 80 per cent of the top-ten domestic news stories each year are broken to CNN by its affiliates. Dozens of produced news packages are provided to CNN daily by its affiliates. Many are hard news stories (for example, 'Suspected Rapist Arraigned in Houston'; 'Hurricane Isabel Kills 17 in North Carolina and Virginia'), and some are lighter fare, or 'kickers' ('Baby Giraffe Born at Detroit Zoo'; 'Volunteers in Anchorage Answer Letters to Santa').

A Futures Desk is the arm of the National Desk whose role is to work closely with domestic news gathering and other CNN networks and services to oversee the planning of upcoming stories. CNN plans stories the next day, the next week and in the long term. Bureaus propose stories to the Futures Desk. The ideas are discussed in daily meetings to determine which story proposals to accept, modify or reject. CNN use the futures process to plan its coverage of major upcoming news events like political conventions and elections and the impending death of a major celebrity from a long-term illness. Such major news stories are the subject of intense long-term futures planning regarding which to develop.

But CNN gets its news from another key source called CNN Newsource, comprising more than 685 local news-producing affiliates, including broadcast TV stations and local/regional cable news channels throughout the US and Canada. In return for access to CNN-produced material and the services listed below, CNN Newsource affiliates provide CNN with coverage of local news taking place in their respective markets and are an integral part of CNN's news gathering operations. Affiliates can take their viewers live to the scene of breaking news faster than ever. CNN Newsource has over ten correspondents who provide customised and generic live shots for partner stations. Often, CNN Newsource correspondents shoot multiple stand-ups, customising them for each affiliate.

CNN Atlanta co-ordinates Newsource feeds (national, regional news and sports), live events and breaking news, archive footage, re-feeds and exclusive products, CNN Marketsource (live from the New York Stock Exchange), Newsource Washington, DC, daily news from Entertainment Weekly (offering two daily entertainment news feeds) and sends out CNN's fleet of SNG trucks.

The International Desk is responsible for all news gathering outside the US and Canada. It directs the news gathering of nearly three dozen international bureaus and dozens of correspondents. This desk is the international counterpart to the National Desk. An 'Internal Desk' arranges travel and mobilisation of dozens of international correspondents and production staff, to report and fact-check news from overseas. As needed, the Internal Desk calls dozens of stringers – experienced freelance international reporters who file stories for CNN, but are not employees – into action. CNN uses stringers when news breaks in a region of the world where CNN does not have a presence or where the story is so big that complete coverage of all the news requires dispatches and news gathering from multiple locations. Here reporters and editors must be multilingual.

Then all this news material is packaged by editors and producers based in Atlanta, who gather, document, edit, distribute and manage raw and produced digital media for CNN, CNNI, CNN Headline News and all the other CNN products. To understand the work done at 'Media Ops', as it is called in-house, Bu Zhong used the example of the Photo Pool, which is a team of photographers and sound technicians for field crews. They gather raw source material and cover live events for the news group. This relatively small group of technical experts is often supplemented with media editors.

This Feeds Department serves as the gathering and distribution hub for all raw media for the CNN news group from around the world. Feeds gathers the raw news from all the sources noted above, plus other news agencies such as the Canadian Broadcast Company, Independent Television News, Reuters Television and Associated Press Television Network, plus a score of others. The ultimate goal is to gather the news material in-house and distribute it to the appropriate CNN departments for use in the production process.

Within Feeds, editors work with the National and International Desks and the Satellites Department to co-ordinate the recording of all incoming news material – in both analogue and digital formats. Everything is recorded to digital to be viewed by anyone within the CNN news group using a typical computer and the MediaSource browser. They are draft-quality recordings that the news staff use to plan stories and make requests of the editorial staff to 'dice and splice' the raw material into an airable story.

Feeds co-ordinates digital recording onto a system that produces high-quality digital recordings used only by the CNN news group. (That's because the hardware and software needed to view and manipulate these recordings is available only in news editing bays.) With this high-quality digital footage, news professionals do not need to edit from videotape. It creates airable stories from the digital recordings.

Feeds make notes about every major point of action in the recording. As an example, let's assume a media co-ordinator is documenting the recording of a fan jumping on-stage to kiss a singer at a major concert. The media co-ordinator might document the date and time (to the second) of: the fan jumping on-stage, the singer's surprise, the security guards running on-stage, the fan kissing the singer, the security guards grabbing the fan and the singer joking about it afterward. From this documentation, the production staff can quickly choose the exact clips desired for air. All this is archived on digital servers.

Then tape producers and media editors in Media Operations transform the raw media elements into show elements. Tape producers submit requests to the video supervisors, who co-ordinate all incoming requests for show elements and co-ordinate assignments to network media editors.

Tape producers also create documentation, choose soundbites from various sources and co-ordinate the activities between the news show teams and the Media Operations edit pool. Tape producers manage the production process for edited material, which ultimately leads to the creation of the finished show elements (called packages).

Editors transform raw footage recorded in the Feeds Department into produced show elements for the various CNN networks. They edit elements on both. Less and less is done on tape, which is called analogue or linear format. When editing analogue elements, media editors have to start at the beginning of the tape and work to the end. They can't make major changes within the edited material without losing video quality. The future is digital or non-linear format. When editing digital elements, media editors can make major changes and duplicate the edited material easily, without losing quality. When finished, all control rooms can access the edited element simultaneously.

In the end, facts and videos are turned into polished stories. There are many ways to produce a newscast. For videotaped stories, a producer, reporter and editor work together to edit the footage. They may shorten or lengthen the story to fit within time constraints, add tape from the CNN library or affiliates, add graphics and text and so on. For stories anchors will share with viewers, writers develop scripts. These writers might be anchors, other journalists or copy editors. Next, the editors select the footage to accompany the script and hone the script.

CNN often has to create many versions of a script based on input from reporters and producers before it is in the final working form. The script is then passed to the 'Row' for approval. The 'Row' is a group of senior producers who approve scripts before they are aired. They may view the rough cut of the story as well. Standards and Practices teams carefully review or 'vet' scripts and footage for important issues that can affect CNN's desired image as a news organisation, for example, balanced reporting, and Legal teams deal with defamation, privacy or copyright concerns.

Once a story has been developed and approved, its fate is in the hands of a producer who is responsible for the format of the overall newscast – deciding which stories will be put on the air, the order of the stories and how much time will be spent on each report. Under a producer, to do actual newscast, a director finally puts the whole news show together in the control room.

Here, many screens show the videotapes that will be used during the newscast. A production manager makes sure all equipment is available and in place. This includes cameras, sound equipment, lighting and headsets. The cameras inside the CNN studio are very expensive, so expensive no one is allowed to touch them. They have been put on robots and are operated only by remote control.

Only then, after all this, do we – the viewers – get to see CNN!

Douglas Gomery

RECOMMENDED READING

Flournoy, Don M. and Robert K. Stewart (1997), *CNN: Making News in the Global Market*, Luton: University of Luton Press.

Friedland, Lewis A. (1993), *Covering the World: International Television News Services*, New York: The Brookings Institution.

Kung-Shankleman, Lucy (2000), *Inside the BBC and CNN: Managing Media Organizations*, London: Routledge.

Robinson, Piers (2002), *The CNN Effect: The Myth of News Media, Foreign Policy and Intervention*, London: Routledge.

<www.cnn.com>.

Selling Advertising Time – UK

It often comes as a shock to students of the media when it's suggested to them for the first time that, in the world of commercial television, programmes exist not to entertain their viewers, nor even to allow their makers to exercise their creativity, but simply to deliver audiences to advertisers. In practice, however, this view of content is taken as a truism among advertising agencies, and among those who work in the television business. Selling TV time to advertisers generates the revenues that pay for the operation, fund the programmes and provide profit for the company. It's not an optional extra or icing on the cake: it's the core business.

The advertising industry can be seen as consisting of two parts: making the adverts, and putting them in front of the audience. While the first of these – the planning and creative aspects, coming up with 'the big idea' of the campaign, the copywriting and art direction that goes into producing the ads – is what most people think of when advertising is mentioned, in fact, only 8 per cent of those who work in advertising are 'creatives', and only 20 per cent of the clients' money is spent on this work. The other 80 per cent is swallowed up in buying the media in which the ad will be shown. And that 80 per cent adds up to a considerable sum: the Institute of Practitioners in Advertising reports that UK advertising delivered £4,320 million in revenue to commercial TV companies in 2001.

When commercial advertising began in the UK in the 1950s, advertising agencies were generally what is known as 'full service agencies' (FSAs). Clients turned to them to handle all aspects of advertising their product, and the agencies provided the full range of services: planning the advertising campaign; making the ads; and buying the space (on billboards, in newspapers or magazines, or on the sides of buses, for instance) or time (in the cinema, on radio or on TV) in which the ad would be shown. As advertising developed as an industry in the late 1970s, new agencies were often set up as small 'creative shops': in other words, they would do the planning and develop the ads, but the media buying was left to a range of specialist 'media shops'. These were sometimes independent companies, but could equally be the in-house media departments of full service agencies who would also handle the media for creative companies external to their own organisation. Over the years, the debate between the virtues of FSAs and independent creative and media agencies has swung with the success of the sector and the fashions of the day, and with the same agencies evolving through different organisational arrangements according to the needs of the time.

But whether the media buyer is working in-house or for an independent, buying time on TV is a specialist business and he or she needs well-developed skills in a range of areas. These include thoroughly understanding the market, knowing the channels and their profile, and being able to negotiate the best possible deal with the media owner.

TV time is sold in terms of the cost per thousand impressions or impacts: each impression is when one pair of eyes sees the ad. So, two impacts can be two different people seeing the same ad at the same time, or the same person seeing the ad twice on two different occasions. Controversy still rages about how many times an advert needs to be seen to be effective – that is, to have the desired effect on the audience. Usually, of course, that intended outcome is to make you buy the product; but sometimes, as in the case of public health advertising, it can be to encourage you to adopt new behaviours, such as reducing the amount of alcohol you drink. In general, around eight to twelve impacts are thought to produce greatest effectiveness: but much more research is needed, and, of course, many other factors (price, in-store promotion, word of mouth, relevance of product to consumer's needs, opportunity to buy, even the weather) are also implicated in the decision to 'buy'.

However, the picture is a bit more complicated than this. It's all very well having your advert seen by lots of pairs of eyes: but if you are selling skin cream for middle-aged women, it's unlikely your sales will improve if your ads are shown only to men watching one of the cable sports channels. Both media owners and media buyers need to be very aware of the most recent viewer figures and profiles for each programme and each channel, so that they can match the audience for the programme with that sought for the advertising. TV rating points (TVRs) are used in the industry jargon to signify the number of 'valued' or relevant impressions that will be delivered for each pound of media money spent: and there is a thriving audience research industry which exists to provide the data on which these are calculated.

Most TV channels sell their advertising time, either directly or as part of the sales operation of their parent company, in packages that promise to deliver an agreed number of impressions, or TVRs, over a set period. The company then takes responsibility for scheduling the ads, taking account of any regulatory restrictions, such as not showing ads for alcohol in the middle of children's programmes. Such packages generally offer good value for money, and are very well suited to 'drip' campaigns, which are designed to maintain customer awareness of, say, established, low-value products – fast-moving consumer goods such as washing powder and supermarket brands.

For the launch of a new product, however, the advertiser will usually opt for a 'burst' campaign, showing the ad with much greater frequency over a shorter period of time in the hope of increasing the viewers' awareness of the message and winning better brand recognition.

In either case, the media buyer can negotiate to secure particular positions for their adverts: first and last in the advert break is thought to be advantageous, especially the latter as viewers are thought to be more receptive to the advertising message when their attention is focused for the return of their programme, and because the advertiser gets the bonus of a few seconds of freeze frame before the programme starts again. Last in break in an episode of *Coronation Street* was often held to be the most desirable spot in these terms, since it could be depended upon to deliver a large, mixed audience with great regularity: but the advent of sponsorship means that this advantage now goes to the sponsor, if there is one.

Sponsorship was viewed with some trepidation when it first appeared on British TV, but it has not proved as attractive to advertisers as many anticipated. It seems to work best where there is a clear and simple relationship between the product and the programme, as in the case of Bailey's Irish Cream and *Sex and the City* for Channel Four. In other cases, especially when the sponsorship hasn't run for long enough to become established, or the programme has had a short season, recall by viewers has proven it to be less effective.

From time to time, a campaign will be bought on a 'spot by spot' basis, with every screening of the advert being individually selected. This is only justifiable for a campaign where the creative content of the ad gains some of its effect from the context in which it's viewed. It's an expensive way of buying TV time, often because the ad has been designed to fit a particular event, such as a major football match, for which demand is high. Media owners publish rate cards which show a range of prices for each spot, and they will sell each spot at one of the prices on that scale. Rate cards can be found in BRAD (British Rates and Data): but it's a matter of professional pride among buyers that they negotiate a discount against rate card. One factor which makes the buyer's task harder here is the practice known as 'pre-empting'. Buyers bid for a spot at the point on the scale which they think will secure it: but if another buyer then comes along and bids at a higher level, the spot goes to them. The original buyer is given the option of bidding again further up the scale, or relinquishing the spot entirely. This doesn't happen when the campaign is buying a package, of course: but important spots in major events can command very high prices and be sold several times over before the ad is aired, changing hands up to a few hours before the slot is shown.

A media buyer's role can be very stressful, and indeed a buyer's performance will be monitored regularly in comparison with his or her peers, in terms of the value of the deals they

Sex and the City

have managed to deliver. The further the buyer can make the budget stretch, in terms of achieving the best positions or numbers of showings of the ads, the more likely the campaign will be to succeed: and the happier the clients, the more likely they and their creative agencies are to bring repeat business to the media company.

It would seem that all the power in this relationship lies in the hands of the media owner: but, of course, the proliferation of media outlets in recent times means that the buyer has much more choice than ever before. Cable and satellite have provided a range of television channels undreamed of even twenty years ago, and can often deliver specific audience profiles more reliably – and therefore more cheaply in terms of cost per TVR – than the more general terrestrial TV channels: but the proportion of time most people spend watching television, as opposed to working with home computers or on other leisure activities, is declining year on year. Moreover, the range of advertising media, apart from television, available to advertisers seems to be expanding too, with the resurgence of cinema, the growth of the Internet, and the proliferation of novel outdoor developments, such as bus stops which can give

the smell of the new perfume or coffee as well as showing it on video.

One of the recent challenges facing TV advertising revenues is the advent of the personal video recorder (PVR). Systems such as Sky+ and TiVo allow viewers to watch their favourite programmes without having to sit through the ads, or having their viewing interrupted by fast-forwarding through them. Some in the advertising industry saw this as presaging 'the death of the thirty-second ad': and indeed recent research by the media consultants Starcom confirmed that viewers with a PVR watch 30 per cent fewer ads than those with conventional digital television. However, the take-up of PVRs has been slower than anticipated, with only around three-quarters of a million homes using the technology to date. It was also found that PVR owners' awareness of advertising didn't fall in proportion with their drop in exposure, but by only 17 per cent – less than had been anticipated, and a figure which suggests that these audiences are still browsing and viewing ads, but are more in control when they do so.

In seeking to combat threats to their revenues, whether from competitors or media-savvy audiences, TV companies are clearly looking for other ways to raise money: for instance, Ofcom recently stated that it would be looking to relax its rules on product placement on British TV.

Yet it's clear that audiences are still engaged with TV advertising: for instance, there was a record number of complaints to the Advertising Standards Authority about girls speaking with their mouths full in a recent ad; and compilations of UK and international adverts become programmes in their own right. Selling advertising time may well be the life-blood of commercial TV for some time to come.

Philip and Sheila Lodge

RECOMMENDED READING

Broadbent, Simon (1970), *Spending Advertising Money*, London: London Business Books.
Broadbent, Simon (1989), *The Advertising Budget: The Advertiser's Guide to Budget Determination*, Henley-on-Thames: IPA/NTC Publications.
Campaign is published weekly by Haymarket Magazines, and is the most widely read of the advertising industry trade press. It covers media issues regularly.
<www.brandrepublic.com/magazines/campaign> is a useful website for links to media matters.

The authors would like to thank Ruth Berry of The Media Shop (Scotland) Ltd and Sara Robertson of the Scottish IPA for their help in the preparation of this chapter.

Selling Advertising Time – US

Advertising – selling time – is what brings in the most dollars to television in the US. Without advertising base, television would not exist in its current form in the US.

There are, then, three forms of advertising for television. This is defined by the geographical scope reached – national, regional and local. (Regional is called spot advertising.) So an advertiser designs a plan, and buying time on television is an option in the company's plan.

National advertising is done via networks which reach the whole of the US television audience. This is slightly less than 100 per cent of the US population. So this is the most expensive, but very useful and relatively cheap (cost to reach person) for vast corporations selling automobiles, beer, financial services and, today, even prescription drugs. 'Soaps' were thus named because, with the innovation of the mechanical washing machine, laundry soap was sold to nearly all people in the US and so Proctor and Gamble, a major soap maker, became the leading advertiser on television.

When a station connects to a network, it instantly converts from a local to part of a regional advertising medium. For advertisers of distributed products, network advertising has significant advantages: (1) advertisers, in a single transaction, can place messages on more than 200 stations of known quality, strategically located to cover the entire country; (2) advertisers can have centralised control over commercial messages, plus assurance that ads will be broadcast within the chosen times and programmes; (3) advertisers benefit from the network's sophisticated audience research; (4) networks provide convenient, centralised billing for commercial time costs.

Major corporations want to reach as many people as they can in their national advertising. In the spring before the TV season (September–May) begins they thus line up to up the ante for what they believe will be the most watched programmes, based upon history and pitches by the networks. This is called the up-front market and it can total into the billions of dollars spent even before the programme airs. Usually, the networks provide a guaranteed minimum audience, and if this is not met run the advertisements for free until the size of promised audience is reached.

This is why ratings were invented. The advertiser needed to know what she or he was buying. That is, the attention of the audience. Since this has been impossible to quantify, advertisers have settled for proxies of the demographics and size of the audience. For example, extensive research has shown – at least to Madison Avenue's satisfaction – that females in coupled households make the buying decisions; thus most products are targeted at females aged between eighteen and forty-nine. They are young enough to change to new brands, and not yet settled in their buying habits (the upper age cut-off).

Yet, of course, this does not apply to all products. Beer companies, led by the dominant seller Anheuser Busch, target males and thus their thirty-second spots are set during sporting events. Usually, the Super Bowl of US football is sold out with male-oriented products – at more than $1 million per thirty seconds – long before the game – usually held during the final week of January, six or more months after the up-front market is conducted.

But special events are easy to sell. It is the prime-time and other shows that are harder. National advertisers want as much reach to the right kind of buyers as possible and shows are categorised by the number and demographic shape of the audience. *I Love Lucy* was a long-time female favourite and so, throughout its long television run, CBS never had any trouble finding advertisers for the programme.

But sometimes advertisers want certain audiences – principally the well off. This is why there is so much golf on television. Golf matches and tournaments are hardly televised beauty, with little action and lots of narration. But they are watched by small audiences of well-off males who purchase expensive cars and the like. There is no use advertising $100,000 automobiles to persons who make the average household income in the US, $40,000 at the start of the twenty-first century.

But some product-makers only want to sell in a particular region, perhaps a swimming product which it only makes sense to advertise in warm weather areas of the US. Then agents cobble together what are called spot advertisements, to be aired only in selected regions. All stations have representatives – as do cable operators – in New York who do these kinds of deals. Often these ads are found at the top and bottom of the hour, when the network feed ceases for a minute and two thirty-second spot advertisements are inserted. Thus, while it seems that all persons in the US watch the same programming all the time everywhere, this is not the case for advertising.

Spot arrangements enable companies to put together individual stations with any combination of coverage areas, station types and programme vehicles, as desired – or they can place their ads simultaneously on several interconnected cable systems. Spot advertisers can choose from several programme vehicles – spots within or between network programmes, or in local or syndicated programmes. National spots thus enable advertisers to capitalise on audience interest in local programmes, something the network advertiser cannot do.

Finally, local companies also wish to advertise. This is

I Love Lucy

expensive and can only be done by companies with vast sales. Typical is an auto dealer selling in the millions of dollars. Television stations sell these ads for the same places on the presentation as spot advertisements. Cable lives on local advertisements, even down to a single restaurant. But even the biggest cable network rarely draws audiences of the sizes that broadcast networks do, so they are willing to sell local time – again usually at the top and bottom of the hour. Watch CNN and see the restaurant down the street tell you what its menu is.

These are usually sold by salesmen (and, increasingly, saleswomen) who work for the local station or cable operator. They bring in revenues that – if good – can make the difference between large and very large profits. And while stations are known to their audiences for their programmes, they are managed, more than probably, by former successful members of the sales staff. All TV stations, even network affiliates, and cable networks can offer local advertising media, covering single markets, although their individual coverage areas vary a great deal in the number of possible people who can be reached. Local advertisers consist chiefly of fast-food restaurants, auto dealers, department stores, banks, food stores and movie theatres. When such local firms act as retail outlets for nationally distributed products, the cost of local advertising may be shared by the local retailer (an appliance dealer, for

example) and the national manufacturer (such as a maker of automobiles). This type of cost sharing is known as co-operative advertising – or simply 'co-op' – in the business.

Commercial time has value for advertisers only in terms of the audiences it represents. Audiences constantly change in size and vary widely in demographic composition. As a result, so does the value of time to the advertiser. Most large advertisers make their electronic media buys based on ratings – the statistical measurement of audiences exposed to a product's commercials. In particular, they order spot schedules designed to achieve a predetermined number of gross rating points – that is, to reach a specific number of viewers – or target rating points, to reach audience subgroups, such as teens or women eighteen to forty-nine years of age.

No standard formula for using all these variables to set appropriate broadcast rates exists. However, market forces – including laws of supply and demand – eventually tend to bring prices into line. The industry uses cost per thousand (CPM) as the main test for comparing advertising prices. CPM represents the cost of reaching 1,000 (represented by the Roman numeral 'M') households or target groups, such as men or teens or women aged eighteen to thirty-four. CPM is calculated by dividing the cost of a commercial by the number of homes (in thousands) that it reached. Prime-time advertisers typically pay a household CPM of less than $10 depending on the composition of that audience. Since well-off households are the best for advertisers as they have the most money to spend, their CPM will be higher than for poor households.

CPM helps in comparing one medium with another, one TV outlet with another, and even one programme with another. Occasionally, stations and networks make sales 'on the come', predicting and, in some cases, even guaranteeing a specific CPM and audience rating in advance. Advertisers whose commercials don't reach the promised audience level usually receive additional commercial time at no cost; only rarely does a broadcaster give a refund. They use time as currency. These are called make-goods.

Prices paid thus vary and these key variables include:

1. Time classes. Typically, television divides its time into specific day-parts, and even subclasses of day-parts, with different prices for each. Prime time means what it says: that these evening hours are prime for the largest audiences.

2. Spot position. For an assured place in the schedule, advertisers pay the premium rate charged for fixed-position spots. Less expensive run-of-schedule (ROS) advertisements may be scheduled by a television operation anywhere within the time period designated in the sales contract. Some advertisers desire to rotate spots, both hor-

izontally (over different days) and vertically (through different time periods) to gain the benefit of varying exposures for their pitches.

3. Pre-emptibility. Television charges less for pre-emptible spots, which they can cancel if a higher-paying customer who wants those commercial positions comes along. Advertisers do not, of course, pay for a pre-empted spot. Often, when a pre-emption does occur, the station, network, or television operation representative will try to get the pre-empted advertiser to accept a spot at another time.

4. Package plans. Television offers at a discount a variety of packages, which may include several spots scheduled at various times and on various days, or may, for example, include ads across several cable networks at the same time. This is called 'road blocking' and means that, even if one switches to another channel, one finds the same ad.

5. Special placements. Spots associated with particular programmes – sporting events, for example – often earn a higher rate. Television charges a premium for commercials within local newscasts for local advertisers, particularly just before a weather forecast, because it is known that these, are more than likely to be seen, as the weather news is always the most watched part of the news broadcast.

A television entity may list more than a hundred different prices for spots, using a device known as a rate grid. For example, it might list twenty different time periods or programme rifles down the left side of its grid. Across the top it might list six different rate levels, numbered I through VI. This arrangement would create 120 cells or boxes into which specific prices can be entered. But it all comes down to negotiations as the television entity seeks to maximise its revenues, and the quoted price is rarely the actual price paid.

What the television industry wants is money. So when you see one of the *Greatest Hits of Patsy Cline* advertisements, consider the fact that they are per-inquiry (PI) deals, favoured primarily by mail-order firms. These commit the advertiser to pay nothing up-front but only later, based upon the number of enquiries – or the number of items sold – in direct response to PI commercials. This means that the television operation could not sell the time in the normal fashion and had to settle for a PI. Among the most successful PI promotion items has been music. All the 108 songs Patsy Cline recorded in her short career are available through traditional means, but a PI ad is meant to tempt the viewer into an impulse call.

As an advertising medium, television has unrivalled access to all family members under the changing circumstances of daily living. Year after year, day after day, millions watch television. Its reach is unparalleled.

Douglas Gomery

RECOMMENDED READING

Capo, Joe (2003), *The Future of Advertising*, New York: McGraw Hill.

Levine, Robert (2003), *The Power of Persuasion*, New York: Wiley.

Selling TV Formats

In recent years, the selling or licensing of formats – the basic concept and production elements that shape a programme – has become an increasingly central practice in the production and distribution of television worldwide. This is largely due to the global proliferation of reality television and the model provided by those European companies who helped spur it on. Although there are some instances where a format is sold domestically, most often the transaction is international and occurs after the programme has proven itself in its country of origin. Formats help producers predict costs and decrease uncertainty regarding a show's potential popularity (Magder, 2004). In this way format sales may resemble international syndication. However, unlike the already-produced programmes available for syndication, formats can be adapted to local interests, tastes and norms. They can also be produced by local production companies, use local talent and contribute to the local economy. This is a significant advantage in an environment where US domination of the global market of media products has led to concerns about cultural imperialism and has resulted in the institution of programme import restrictions in a number of countries.

Selling formats is by no means a new practice in the business of television. Since the early 1950s, US companies have been selling the format rights of existing programmes overseas. One of the most successful of these early companies, Goodson-Todman, made most of their money from quiz and game shows such as *What's My Line?* and *Beat the Clock*, because they quickly figured out that those were some of the easiest formats to reproduce, and therefore to sell. They would continue doing so up until the late 1970s. The BBC television service has been purchasing formats from US companies since its very early years and a number of US television's most memorable programmes – *All in the Family* and *Three's Company* to name two – have been British programmes remade into American fare. Yet this has hardly been a culturally equitable exchange. The foreign distribution of game show, talk and tabloid formats, in particular, have been extremely lucrative for US companies. However, those same companies have been more reluctant to purchase foreign media products (besides British sitcoms), since they had long convinced themselves that many of them would not appeal to US audiences. This all changed, though, in 2000 with the success of *Who Wants to Be a Millionaire?* (Celador, UK) and *Survivor* (Castaway, UK) – reality programmes that were developed overseas and became huge hits on prime-time network television. Suddenly, US broadcast and cable networks began trolling the foreign market for similar inexpensive and proven programmes and the flow of media products from the US to the rest of the world seemed to be going in reverse.

Not surprisingly, many of the reality programmes imported to the US in the early 2000s have been British products. BBC Worldwide sold formats for prime-time network shows such as *The Weakest Link* and *Dog Eat Dog*, while FremantleMedia provided *American Idol* and Granada, *I'm a Celebrity . . . Get Me Out of Here!* Programmes developed by RDF Media and BBC Worldwide also populated cable television, with The Learning Channel (TLC) being the biggest buyer of their programmes (*Faking It*, *What Not to Wear*, among others). Yet it is the Dutch company Endemol, the creator of such shows as *Big Brother*, *Fear Factor* and *Changing Rooms*, that is perhaps *the* model for the successful format pro-

duction company in the age of reality television. With a library of over 500 programmes and joint holdings and subsidiaries in over twenty countries, the company's strategy has been to create formats that have the potential to become truly international brands. These shows have been expected to generate multiplatform content and opportunities for integrated advertising strategies. As part of its programme package, Endemol provides local production companies with detailed production playbooks (often called 'format bibles'), marketing guides, and a production consultant, thereby ensuring brand continuity while simultaneously encouraging the inclusion of local cultural flavour (Magder, 2004). While this strategy has worked fine for many of their programmes, there have been programmes that were not well matched to certain markets and, as a result, have been met with criticism or disdain. This is more likely to occur the further a programme travels from the European or American site of its creation. *Big Brother Africa*, which premiered in the summer of 2003, was one such programme. The show was given a nationalist bent as contestants from twelve different African countries were pitted against each other to compete for $100,000 dollars (the GDP of some

American Idol

Big Brother South Africa

small African countries). The show was widely criticised for being pornographic, for not being African enough, and for depending on national stereotypes. In 2004, Endemol's show *Star Academy* got strong ratings when it was broadcast from Lebanon to large sections of the Middle East, but the all-Arab version of *Big Brother* was cancelled after only two weeks by the Saudi-owned channel MBC after an on-air kiss on the cheek between a man and a woman caused 1,000 people to take to the streets of Bahrain protesting what they considered to be the show's indecency.

Believing that a programme can be evacuated of its cultural particulars and then refilled with new ones once it arrives on foreign shores, production companies such as Endemol often assume that the basics of reality programming maintain a universal appeal. They also seem to believe that they are not imperialist texts because local production companies are the ones making the programmes and gearing them to local audiences. What is often forgotten is that the fundamental social, economic and aesthetic functions of a television genre itself remain intact. It is in these moments that the global popularity of reality television is helping to uncover the cultural complexities that arise from the movement of textual and stylistic elements across national borders. As the following quote from a review of *Big Brother Africa* by a Zambian journalist reveals, just because a production company may paint a house in national colours and cast locals as cultural types, the basic format itself is not value-free or devoid of the culture of the programme's creator:

> Look at how the contestants behave, their mannerisms, their idiosyncrasies. Look at the food they are made to eat. Look at the utensils they use to cook the food. Look at the drinks they drink. . . . All I am saying is that *Big Brother Africa* would make much more sense to me (and to other Africans, I hope) if it had a semblance of things that are African. (Djokotoe, 2003)

Besides concerns surrounding the cultural translatability

and impact of programmes like *Big Brother*, issues of piracy have also confronted the format market as of late. Since reality programmes are often based on a rather basic concept, some broadcasters have developed programmes that use a concept similar to that of other top-rated shows in other markets, without paying licensing fees. For example, RDF Media has looked into taking legal action against the producers of three reality shows – Germany's *Wife Swap*, Austria's *Family Swap* and Hungary's *Mother Switch* – that they believe copied their *Wife Swap* format without permission. Many in the industry have accused the Germans of being the worst offenders, airing knock-offs of everything from RTL's *How Clean Is Your House?* to *Pop Idol* and *Who Wants to Be a Millionaire?*. In fact, thirteen separate claims of copyright infringement have been brought against German producers, yet all have been dismissed.

Besides loss of revenue, the creators of formats are concerned that these copycats dilute, or perhaps even damage, their original brand. The problem is that the copyright laws are murky when it comes to game and reality programmes, because it is difficult to copyright or trademark a concept. This is particularly true when many of the details of the programme – such as title, rules, catchphrases, mise en scène – can be easily rearranged or changed. In response to what many in the industry see as a mounting problem, members of the industry formed the Format Recognition and Protection Association (FRAPA) in 2000 to study format protection, to encourage 'good behaviour' in the marketplace, and to mediate copyright disputes between their members, who include many of the major players in the format business. David Lyle, the chairman of the association's steering committee, describes FRAPA's role in the industry on the association's website:

> Under the present legal framework the business is generally run as a series of gentlemen's agreements. Sadly, many people don't act like gentlemen. Or, more precisely, they act like upstanding, law abiding gentlemen most of the time, but find the pressure of competition forces them to behave badly just this once. Against the background of international lawlessness, FRAPA has in its own way fought for protection of the intellectual property of its members. (www.frapa.org)

While the association doesn't have any real teeth in terms of what it can enforce, it does put social and professional pressure on its members and attempts to establish standards of practice and ethics. It does that by not only mediating disputes, but also by publishing a guide for format sales and protection, establishing a 'constitution', and by creating awards (such as the 'Most Innovative Format of the Year Award'), that celebrate and reward, perhaps more than anything else, strong branding. The need for and development of FRAPA speaks to the shifting meaning and use of television formats in a period of increasing competition and at a time when the industry's assumptions and traditional business practices are being challenged. But, the discussion of formats and copyright also brings up interesting questions regarding what originality and authenticity mean in the production of television texts, as well as which factors belong to a genre as a whole and which to a specific programme. More than any other television genre, the global popularity and staying power of reality television has demonstrated the potential revenue that can be generated from licensing the basic elements of programmes – elements that can be easily reproduced and repackaged. It has also uncovered the cultural complexities that arise during the movement of textual elements across national borders.

Susan Murray

RECOMMENDED READING

Djokotoe, Edem (2003), 'Soul to Soul – the *Big Brother* Controversy', *The Post* (Zambia), July 4.

Magder, Ted (2004), 'The End of TV 101: Reality Programmes, Formats and the New Business of Television', in Susan Murray and Laurie Ouellette (eds), *Reality TV: Remaking Television Culture*, New York: New York University Press, pp. 137–56.

Moran, Albert (2003), *Copycat TV: Globalisation, Program Formats and Cultural Identity*, Luton: University of Luton Press.

The World Market: TV Audiences

The introduction of television into a community seems to have one common effect: it creates an audience far more extended than solely that of the owners. Examples are countless and can be found all over the world. Philip Kitley even cites the habit of his Indonesian host of putting his television set on the veranda in order to watch TV with his neighbours as the very reason for his future research on television. This example dates back to 1969. Thirty years later, watching television is still a collective event in *L'Afrique Noir*. For example, in Ghana, a mere 12 per cent of the population in Ghana owns a television (of these, 2 per cent own a television that does not work), whereas 34 per cent of the population claims to watch television: 18 per cent at their friends' and 6 per cent in public spaces. In Nigeria only 38 per cent of the population owns a television, while 95 per cent of the population claims to

watch television. So the majority of the Nigerians don't watch television at home. Owning a television creates certain obligations; people can expect visits from gapers, whether they like it or not. In China, an eleven-year-old girl told researcher James Lull that when almost no one had a colour television, her parents rarely turned their colour television on, to protect themselves from the hoards of people who would come to watch.

For many people, their daily schedule changes as a result of the introduction of television. A Chinese professor, for example, slept in his office for years; at home his wife and child watching television distracted him. Even the social status of the TV owner can be affected. The clearest examples of this can be found in research conducted in small communities where television has started to emerge. A study conducted in two mountain villages in India showed that the simple fact that the women also watched TV had consequences for the division of labour between men and women. In order to be on time to watch TV, women would leave the land up to two and a half hours earlier to prepare dinner. Sometimes men would even have to take over typical women's chores, such as fetching water. The same study showed that owning a television set resulted in yet another division of social groups and the related opportunity for owners to increase their financial prosperity. Dependency on rich landowners, who rarely shared their knowledge, has diminished as a result of educational television programmes about new agricultural techniques. At the same time, an 'information underclass' emerges, consisting of people who do not have access to a television. This results in an increased marginalisation for this group and its position in society.

We can deduct two general points of interest from this example: the first has to do with simply owning a television and the consequences this has; the second has to do with the content of programmes that reach the audience. Content, in particular, has determined a lot of the discussions concerning the medium of television. From this such topics arise as the independence of the media, the question of what our children are watching, issues surrounding the quality of the programmes and so on. The actual underlying assumption has always been that the image is so powerful that the unsuspecting viewer should be protected from it. From the introduction of parental guidance codes to a 'No Television Day' in Korea, they have all come to life as a result of the idea that television can generate negative influences on the viewer.

These fears are usually based on presumption and rarely on empirical facts. The television ratings, the most widely gathered source of information about viewers, does not say a lot about the way the information is interpreted, or about the impact a programme has on the viewer. As a study on Turkish migrants shows, the fear that the Turks isolate themselves by watching Turkish television, expressed in the German media, in particular, is not justified. Turks do not isolate themselves in a reassuring dream world; on the contrary, watching Turkish programmes confronts them with painful questions and makes them think about their identity and the way it is constructed. Research conducted in Brazil on the telenovelas showed that (as expected) they offer possibilities for women and workers to emancipate, while at the same time it appears that social class determines how women interpret the series. Working-class women have more in common with working-class *men* than with *women* from another social class. In other words, as soon as the viewers are asked how they attribute meaning to a programme, the results can be quite surprising. But in daily television practice most of the time, viewing ratings are far more important than viewer interpretations.

And even if a government strives to take into account the needs of the viewers, they can end up ignoring them. The Netherlands is a special case here. The Dutch government wanted a broadcasting system that would offer every Dutch citizen the chance to recognise his/her own religious or ideological beliefs. This idea represents a long-standing tradition. In the 1930s, most of the Dutch newspapers only had subscriptions and almost all were linked to a political or religious faction. This ideological and religious division could be found again in the distribution of radio broadcasting time. Television broadcasting time was also assigned to the so-called different 'pillars'. In 1951 this led to the distribution of broadcasting time among the following broadcasters: KRO (Catholic), NCRV (Protestant), VPRO (Liberal Protestant), AVRO (general), VARA (working class). In 1966 the broadcasting system expanded with the addition of the TROS. They were the most commercial and general of the broadcasters. The Evangelical broadcasting corporation (EO) joined in 1970, followed by Veronica in 1975. Veronica was also more general, and was aimed at the youth market. Up to this day, this division has largely remained the same. Only Veronica retreated from the system in 1995. In 1998, however, BNN, aimed at the youth, filled up the gap.

The Dutch government set itself up as a guardian of quality and pluriformity. To encourage quality, a broadcaster has to comply with a so-called *programmavoorschrift*, a programme regulation. To guarantee pluriformity, all of the broadcasting corporations had their own task and target group, which they focused on. They were to complement each other, ensuring that the pluriformity would be maintained. The amount of broadcast time they were given depended on the number of members they had. The different broadcasters alternately filled the single channel with programmes aimed at their members. So the government had created a unique system that assumed

a segmented viewing public, which was offered programmes that fitted their religious and ideological background. However, it soon appeared that the viewer would not let his viewing choice be limited to programmes that were thought to be suitable for him. Already in 1958, a random questionnaire of television buyers showed that, among families that watched television, one in ten people watched nearly all the programmes. Among the women aged thirty and above, the figures show that as many as one in five watched everything. Ten years later researchers once again reached the conclusion that the 'pillarisation' of the viewers was not as thorough as first thought. Although viewers were selected by membership with a broadcast union, it appeared that the majority showed no preference, neither positive nor negative, for a certain broadcasting corporation. For most of the people, it was the appeal of the individual programmes rather than the ideals of the corporation that determined whether or not they would watch a programme. The viewing patterns of the public did not result in a change in the broadcasting policy. The corporations remained broadcast unions and it was the number of members that legitimised their existence.

In 1989, the Netherlands saw the emergence of a dual establishment. A commercial network RTL-Veronique (this became RTL4 in 1990) appeared beside the public broadcasting system. It managed to escape this system by broadcasting from Luxembourg. By doing this, it was officially not under Dutch law, which meant, for example, that it didn't need a broadcast licence and that it could transmit as many advertisements as it liked. Although not under Dutch law, it broadcast programmes in Dutch for the Dutch market. Well-known presenters were bought off other stations and a new, daily soap appeared on the screen: *Goede tijden, slechte tijden* (*Good Times, Bad Times*). One year after the initial shock, the public broadcasters appeared to have lost almost 25 per cent of their viewers. And with the appearance of three more commercial broadcasters (RTL5 in 1993, SBS6 and VOO in 1995), this increased to 37 per cent in 1995. Without fully realising it, the public broadcasters had changed from fighting a battle for the members, to a battle for the viewers.

In order to turn the tide, the government decided, in 1992, to divide public broadcasting in a new way among the three Dutch channels. This didn't attract more viewers and channel co-ordinators were introduced in 2000. They had to ensure that every channel had its own identity. This placed the public broadcasters in a very difficult position. They had to contribute to this unity (and gather as many viewers as possible) and at the same time they had to preserve their identity. Public broadcasters tried to tackle this problem, on the one hand, by use of very general slogans, supposed to illuminate what they stood for and with what on the channel the viewer could identify. So the TROS promotes itself as 'the largest family in the Netherlands', the KRO states it's 'the feeling that counts', the NCRV states 'Respect, Trust, Love and Decency', the AVRO says it's 'the programmes that count', BNN is 'bold' and the VPRO is 'like nothing else'. On the other hand, they try to hold on to their members by organising special activities for them. These vary from a trip to Friesland to follow the *Elfstedentocht* (a legendary ice-skating journey passing through eleven towns in Friesland, north of Holland) (VPRO) to a cruise with performances by famous Dutch artists (TROS), a visit to the police academy (AVRO-tribune 'Safe together'), attending programme recordings, or discounts for films sponsored by the company. However, despite all these efforts, the market shares for the public broadcasters are still decreasing. In 2003 it was only 34.4 per cent. The numbers of members are decreasing too and it is becoming increasingly difficult to recruit volunteers for administrative functions in the regional councils of the broadcast companies. Even the youth-oriented, popular station BNN recruited a sponsor who would pay the membership for new members so that they met the requirements of 150,000 members.

The Dutch public broadcasters have ended up doing the splits. They have the almost impossible task of emphasising individuality while at the same time radiating unity. The system that wanted to do justice to the viewer unintentionally led to one-sided attention for pluriformity and quality of that which was offered, and is now only focusing on market shares.

The Dutch case illustrates the growing pressure on public broadcasting in general caused by emerging competing suppliers. Everywhere commercial broadcasters, special interests channels, satellite TV and Internet TV have increased the range of programme choices enormously. And we might expect them to expand even more in the future. This abundance of choices seems to haunt public TV broadcasters all over the world for various reasons, such as money (how can we defend our budget with decreasing viewers?), propaganda (how can we engage them with our messages?) and moral values (how can we fight the wicked programmes?). But in the end, these concerns all show that the supposedly emancipated TV viewer is still regarded as a passive receiver and not as he should be regarded: an active subject who attributes meaning to what he sees.

Clara Pafort-Overduin

RECOMMENDED READING

Parks, Lisa, Shanti Kumar and Kumar, Shanta (eds) (2003), *Planet TV: A Global Television Reader*, New York: New York University Press.
Wang, Georgette, Goonasekera, Anura and Servaes, Jan (eds) (2000), *The New Communications Landscape: Demystifying Media Globalization*, London, New York: Routledge.
Wijfjes, Huub (ed.) (1994), *Omroep in Nederland. Vijfenzeventig jaar medium en maatschappij, 1914–1994*, Zwolle: Waanders Uitgevers.

TELEVISION CULTURE

The Simpsons

An animated half-hour, *The Simpsons* premiered 17 December 1989 and soon became the new Fox television network's first top-rated, prime-time series. Children loved it, but so did their parents, even TV critics, even academics. By June of 1990, Bart and his animated family were on the covers of *Newsweek* and *Rolling Stone*, and a new era in network television, Fox-style, had commenced. It became so ingrained in the popular culture that Montgomery Burns was voted the most hated boss in the US – despite the fact that he was a drawing, voiced by Harry Shearer.

The Simpsons was created by Matt Groening, known for his experimental 'Life in Hell' comic strips, in conjunction with TV veteran James L. Brooks, whose credits included hits such as *The Mary Tyler Moore Show, Taxi, Lou Grant* and *Rhoda*.

The animated Simpson family includes father Homer (voice of Dan Castellaneta), mother Marge (voice of Julie Kanver), daughters Lisa (voice of Yeardley Smith) and the baby Maggie (sucking sounds made by Groening himself) and son Bart (voice of Nancy Cartwright). They are no middle-class success story, but truly a representative, a dysfunctional US family.

Homer Simpson is a slob, lazy as the day is long. His idea of a good time is to lie on the couch, watch TV and drink beer all day. Still, his blue-haired, long-suffering spouse Marge loves him, although continually frustrated by his lack of manners and lack of initiative.

But the central characters were hellion Bart and ideal Lisa. Bart is a clever fourth grader, who gets into any and all types of trouble, from apprenticing as a Mafia Don (a 'Dinky Don') to playing every prank in educational history.

Surely only daughter Lisa can be called a success story, a role model. Indeed Lisa is arguably the best role model for a young woman ever on television. She is thoughtful and studious; she is melancholy and existential. She is a natural researcher and a born idealist. She suffers her family and consoles herself by going off into the corner and wailing the blues on her sax.

Youngest Maggie was just another in the list of minor characters, from Bart and Lisa's school's tense, highly strung Principal Seymour Skinner to Marge's chain-smoking, sarcastic, MacGyver-loving sisters, Selma and Patty; Wayland Smithers, Montgomery Burns' ever present sycophant; Barney, ever drunk at Moe's neighbourhood bar; Grandpa Simpson at the rest home, complete with 'where people go to die' sign out front; and so on – in excess of a hundred regulars.

The narrative joy regularly came as the self-reflexive send-ups of motion pictures and other television series passed by at the speed of lightning. *The Simpsons* had its version of *Citizen Kane*, in which evil nuclear plant owner Montgomery Burns takes on the tyrannical megalomaniac traits of Hearst/Kane. 'Itchy and Scratchy', a cat and mouse duo that takes *Tom and Jerry* to extremes of super-sadistic violence, is both Bart and Lisa's favourite programme. *The Simpsons* is surely the most self-reflexive television programme ever produced. And one of its greatest.

Douglas Gomery

The Simpsons

Celebrity, Television and The Tabloids

Television celebrity is one of the most familiar yet arguably least researched aspects of the television industry. Historically, according to Braudy (1986), fame in Western cultures prior to modernity was largely derived from either public office or heroic achievements. Modern celebrity, however, is usually associated with the rise of the mass media in the 20th century and its creation, circulation and promotion of well-known individuals (Gamson, 1994; Marshall, 1997). We can attribute much of the rise of mediated celebrity culture to the extraordinary post-World War II rise in television viewing as an everyday social activity, where performers were brought into the living room with an immediacy and presence not felt with radio or cinema. Yet, despite the narration of popular histories of television through its recognisable figures, until recently television celebrity has garnered little academic attention. Initial work, drawing from models on film stardom, argued that television produced 'personalities' rather than stars, and that television celebrity was of a lesser order to that garnered on the movie screen (Langer, 1981; Ellis, 1982). This was in part due to theorising of film spectatorship that emphasised the 'distance' of glamorous film stars and the significance of the filmic apparatus, in contrast to the seeming accessibility of television celebrity and the 'distracted' viewer of the television experience (Dyer, 1979). Such accounts are now the subject of substantial revision and television is recognised as a key site for examination of celebrity culture. A major television celebrity, such as Oprah Winfrey, arguably functions with a similar 'aura' to that of a Hollywood film star. The distinction between Oprah and a Hollywood star such as Nicole Kidman, or a pop star such as Madonna, now appears to be less to do with the technology through which they appear, and more down to the kind of performances they enact (Tolson, 1996; Lury, 1996).

The intimacy that accompanies television viewing allows a particular, seemingly intimate relationship with celebrities. This has been termed a 'para-social' interaction (Horton and Wohl, 1956). It is para-social in that it reproduces the effect of a relationship between celebrity and audience despite being a predominantly one-way flow of communication (audiences rarely get to meet celebrities). Audience recognition, accumulated by viewing the performer across previous roles and appearances, increases the performer's value in television's celebrity economy. For example, in British television the celebrity image of performer David Jason is one inflected through his various long-running performances, notably 'Del Boy' Trotter in *Only Fools and Horses* (1981–2003) and Inspector Frost in *Touch of Frost* (1992–). These all feed into and anchor the recognisable persona of 'David Jason', television celebrity and highly-paid performer. The 'poaching' of television celebrities from one channel to another is often due to their status as popular, recognisable performers, and seen as a way of attempting to guarantee initial audience and reviewer interest in a new programme. For instance, the high-value transfers from the BBC to Channel Four by British daytime television presenters, Richard and Judy, or the poaching of Ross Kemp (who played a long-running character in the popular soap opera *EastEnders*) from BBC to ITV, were predicated not just upon their talent but, as importantly, on the brand value of these performers. Celebrity brand value can

also fall – sometimes dramatically when a public scandal is involved – as in the case of the British light entertainer Michael Barrymore. Barrymore, a hugely popular television entertainer during the 1980s and 1990s, was involved in a legal case after the death of a party-goer at his house. This damaged his reputation, and led to him being dropped by television companies, who wished to avoid being associated with his new image.

TABLOIDS, TABLOIDISATION AND CELEBRITY

The term 'tabloid' refers to the popular newspaper press, usually produced in a smaller-sized format to the broadsheets. In the UK and US this tends to be associated with popular, mainstream newspapers and sensationalist, human-interest and celebrity-driven stories (sometimes termed 'soft' news). In Britain the tabloids are by far the most popular daily newspapers, with market-leader *The Sun* at about 3.8 million circulation and the *Daily Mirror* at about 2.5 million, compared to broadsheet newspapers such as *The Times* (approximately 1 million copies) and the *Guardian* (under half a million) (Allan, 2004, p. 102). The tabloid press in the UK is considerably different from that in the US in that it forms the vast majority of the newspaper market, whereas American tabloids such as the *National Enquirer* and the *Weekly World News* function as entertaining weeklies rather than daily news providers.

There is a substantial literature on news values that discusses the selection of the 'news agenda' (see ibid., pp. 55–9). Much of this suggests that the activities of celebrities have become increasingly central to news reporting overall (Turner, 2004). More negative accounts of popular journalism see the 'celebritisation' of the news press as a debasement of news values and point to the interrelated economics of the press and celebrity industries. This has been connected to an argument over the 'tabloidisation' of news, a term often used pejoratively to argue that journalistic standards have been compromised by the rise of celebrity-driven news formats (for a discussion, see Dahlgren and Sparks, 1992; Sparks and Tulloch, 2000). A key proponent of this argument has been Franklin (1997), who uses the terms 'infotainment' and 'newszak' to describe what he regards as a realignment of journalism with the marketplace, and 'soft' news values. An opposing view is offered by Fiske (1992), who suggests that tabloid readers are more sophisticated and produce 'sceptical laughter' (p. 49). Fiske claims this knowing scepticism is itself a political position, rejecting existing power relations through a negotiated engagement with the news agenda. However, Bird (1992) in a study of US tabloid readers, reveals that, despite readers enjoying the entertainment aspects of the paper, only a small minority articulated an ironic or knowing reading position. These debates can only be sketched here. However, it can be noted that, while celebrity journalism has expanded, it has yet to have been conclusively demonstrated that news coverage has declined. Instead, it might be argued that there has been an increase in the quantity of news provided generally, through the inclusion of numerous celebrity-driven supplements such as magazines and arts review sections, alongside traditional 'hard' news.

TELEVISION CELEBRITY AS A TABLOID COMMODITY

Television celebrities have a proven audience with readers and are a key means through which tabloid circulation can be increased. In Britain, the performers in the major television soap operas, *Coronation Street* (ITV) and *EastEnders* (BBC), are regularly featured in the tabloid papers. For instance, the tabloid campaign conducted in 1998 by the *Sun* to 'Free Deidre Rachid', a long-running fictional character in *Coronation Street* who faced imprisonment for fraud, demonstrates the way in which television celebrity can be leveraged by popular journalism and then fed back to achieve both a greater circulation for the paper and increased viewing figures for the programme. For both *Coronation Street*, a programme transmitted by a commercial broadcaster funded by advertising, and for the *Sun*, increased audiences lead to greater potential revenue. Cross-ownership of the press encourages these synergistic links, as in the case of the British mid-market tabloid, the *Daily Express*, which can offer exclusive stories from *OK!*, a celebrity gossip magazine also owned by Richard Desmond.

Contemporary celebrity is therefore a cross-media and intertextual phenomenon. The tabloid press has been a key driving force behind the prominence and visibility of journalism concerned with celebrity. Examining the relationship between the two is also useful in revealing shifting issues of cultural value. As distinctly 'low' cultural forms are given 'highbrow' coverage, celebrity itself has become an object of fascination for increasingly self-reflexive television programming. For example, the former editor of the *Mirror*, Piers Morgan, recently hosted a British television interview series entitled *Tabloid Tales* (2004), where he and celebrity guests such as Victoria Beckham (former Spice Girl and wife of footballer David Beckham) discussed the relationship between celebrity and the tabloid news media. Celebrities, then, are also visible across different performance sites (game shows, interviews, dramas) and this makes overarching claims about celebrity in a particular medium difficult. Famous television chefs such as Gordon Ramsay and Jamie Oliver perform in different ways to reality television stars. Interviewers and newscasters such as Jeremy Paxman or Dan Rather work in a

different kind of celebrity sphere to Ricki Lake. Yet they are all television celebrities. The differences between celebrities therefore matters as well as the glare of public recognition that unites them (Connell, 1992).

Modern celebrity can, through the global reach of the mass media, even engage a global audience almost instantaneously. An extraordinary example of the power of televised celebrity was seen at the *Live 8* concerts held in July 2005 as part of a 'Make Poverty History' campaign, fronted by rock stars and campaigners Bob Geldof, Bono and Midge Ure to coincide with the G8 political summit and the twentieth anniversary of the original *Live Aid* concerts. The concerts were broadcast live across the globe, viewed by an estimated 3 billion people, and starred a wide range of music, television and film celebrities. The spectacle of Hollywood star Will Smith creating a live 'shout-out' from the concert in Philadelphia that was relayed by each of the other countries, or pop star Madonna eulogising about British television comedian, Ricky Gervais, demonstrates how celebrities, linked by television and live satellite link, can be used to create and anchor a global media event. *Live 8* became a television mega-event, developing such a momentum that it temporarily dominated the news agenda (termed by Whannel a 'vortex of publicity' (2002, p. 206)). For instance, on 29 June 2005 the cover of Scotland's biggest-selling tabloid, the *Daily Record*, was headlined 'The G9' and contained a picture of Bob Geldof, with a story about how he and rock star Bono had been invited to a meeting at the G8 political summit (and implying they were also leaders of people).

What, then, can we conclude from the varied nature of television's celebrity economy? First, that, without falling into crude distinctions about serious and entertainment genres, or high and low culture, there is a need to investigate television performers in more detail and their intertextual flow through different media. Recent audience research (Hill, 2005) has considered how audiences interact with reality television, and further work is necessary to investigate why and how audiences enjoy watching a wide range of celebrities on television. Second, as well as addressing the symbolic currency of celebrity, there is a need to consider how celebrity functions in the television and publicity industries. How is celebrity manufactured? What kinds of controls allow access to television celebrity, and to what extent can celebrities control the circulation of their own representations? As increasingly varied and nuanced accounts of different kinds of television celebrity emerge, we will be able to begin to examine the social and political implications of television's celebrity culture.

Philip Drake

CELEBRITY AND REALITY TELEVISION

Over the last decade, what has become known as 'reality television' has been one of the most visible sites of television celebrity. Characters like Maureen from *Driving School* (1997) and Jade Goody from the third British series of *Big Brother* (2002) are presented as examples of 'ordinary' people being made into celebrities. This process has been seen in two ways. It can be viewed first as a 'corruption' of fame, where individuals become famous through appearing on a particular show, adopted by some of the broadsheet news press. The second discourse, one favoured by television executives, is that reality television represents the 'democratisation' of fame, whereby 'ordinary people' not usually seen on television can become celebrities (for a critique, see Couldry, 2000). Su Holmes notes the 'dynamic *appeal* of the relationship between ordinary people and celebrity culture' as an important factor in the rise of reality television (2004a, p. 113). Either way, the 'personalisation' of docusoap and reality television, as Dovey (2000) notes, has encouraged a relatively new and widespread television discourse based on the *accessibility* of fame, seen most clearly in reality television shows structured around the search for a star, such as *Pop Idol* (2001–) and *Fame Academy* (2002–). One of the most significant exponents of this discourse has been the internationally franchised reality television series *Big Brother* (1999–). In this programme, chosen members of the public are placed in a house under twenty-four-hour surveillance and compete to win the votes of the viewers and claim a prize. In the British version, currently in its sixth incarnation, the coverage given by the tabloid press to each series has been crucial to its success during the transmission, and then afterwards, where newspapers compete for 'exclusives' with the contestants. Jade Goody, a bubbly and outgoing twenty-one-year-old 'house-mate' from the third series of the programme and a regular tabloid feature, became famous initially through a vitriolic press campaign to vote her out of the *Big Brother* house, then through her notorious and comical misunderstandings broadcast on the programme (once asking 'Rio de Janeiro? Isn't that a person?'). Not all reality celebrities maintain public interest, and previous *Big Brother* contestants have often joined the lower ranks of celebrity before slipping from the public gaze. However others, like Jade, manage to maintain and even enhance their profile in the media, often through scandal and relationship drama played out in celebrity magazines such as *Heat*. For instance, in 2004, Abi Titmuss, a former nurse inadvertently made famous through a scandal involving an ex-television-presenter boyfriend, a pornographic

video that was circulated illicitly on the Internet and an appearance on a reality television show, had become one of the most highly paid reality television celebrities in the British media.

In the late 1990s, reality television programmes began to be adapted for existing celebrity performers (Holmes, 2004b). *Celebrity Big Brother* (2001–), a shortened version of the show, saw a number of well-known television celebrities enter the house to compete for money for a nominated charity. Here viewing fascination lay in seeing the performers caught 'off-guard' by the cameras, potentially revealing something of their 'authentic' selves. Other programmes, still based around twenty-four-hour surveillance, have placed celebrities in the jungle (*I'm a Celebrity . . . Get Me Out of Here!* (2002–)), going through detoxification (*Celebrity Detox* (2003)), on a farm (*The Farm* (2004–)), cooking (*Hell's Kitchen* (UK, 2004–), and sunbathing and canoodling on an island (*Celebrity Love Island* (2005)). As these shows multiply, so individuals in earlier programmes are recycled and

Pop Idol

presented as celebrities in their own right, with one example even entirely based around ex-reality television celebrities (*Back to Reality* (2003)). An increasing self-consciousness, complete with knowing references to the fame-constructing process (with contestants openly discussing how they will be received by the press at the end of the show) has diluted the reality effect that such shows once had. It remains to be seen if the interwoven relationship between celebrity and reality television can be sustained, and how new programming configured around television's mediation of celebrity might emerge.

Philip Drake

RECOMMENDED READING

Allan, Stuart (2004), *News Culture*, 2nd edn, Maidenhead: Open University Press.

Bird, S. Elizabeth (1992), *For Enquiring Minds: A Cultural Study of Supermarket Tabloids*, Knoxsville: University of Tennessee Press.

Braudy, Leo (1986), *The Frenzy of Renown: Fame and Its History*, Oxford: Oxford University Press.

Connell, Ian (1992), 'Personalities in the Popular Media', in Peter Dahlgren and Colin Sparks (eds), *Journalism and Popular Culture*, London: Sage.

Couldry, Nick (2000), *The Place of Media Power: Pilgrims and Witnesses of the Media Age*, London, Routledge.

Dahlgren, Peter and Sparks, Colin (1992) (eds), *Journalism and Popular Culture*, London: Sage.

Dovey, Jon (2000), *Freakshow: First Person Media and Factual Television*, London: Pluto.

Dyer, Richard (1979), [rev. edn 1998], *Stars*, London: BFI.

Ellis, John (1982), *Visible Fictions: Cinema, Television, Video*, London: Routledge.

Fiske, John (1992), 'Popularity and the Politics of Information', in Peter Dahlgren and Colin Sparks (eds), *Journalism and Popular Culture*, London: Sage.

Franklin, Bob (1997), *Newszak and News Media*, London: Arnold.

Gamson, Joshua (1994), *Claims to Fame: Celebrity in Contemporary America*, Berkely: University of California Press.

Hill, Annette (2005), *Reality Television: Audiences and Popular Factual Television*, Abingdon: Routledge.

Holmes, Su (2004a), ' "All You've Got to Worry about Is the Task, Having a Cup of Tea, and Doing a Bit of Sunbathing": Approaching Narratives of Celebrity in *Big Brother*', in Su Holmes and Deborah Jermyn (eds), *Understanding Reality TV*, London: Routledge, pp. 111–35.

Holmes, Su (2004b), ' "Reality Goes Pop!": Reality TV, Popular Music and Narratives of Stardom in *Pop Idol* (UK)', *Television and New Media*, vol. 5, no. 2, pp. 123–48.

Horton, Donald and Wohl, Richard (1956), 'Mass Communications and Parasocial Interaction', *Psychiatry*, no. 19.

Langer, John (1981), 'Television's Personality System', *Media, Culture and Society*, vol. 3, no. 4, pp. 351–65.

Lury, Karen (1996), 'Television Performance: Being, Acting and "Corpsing" ', *New Formations*, no. 26, pp. 114–27.

Marshall, P. David (1997), *Celebrity and Power: Fame in Contemporary Culture*, Minnesota: University of Minnesota Press.

Sparks, Colin and Tulloch, John (eds) (2000), *Tabloid Tales: Global Debates over Media Standards*, Lanham, MD: Rowan and Littlefield.

Tolson, Andrew (1996), *Mediations: Text and Discourse*, London: Arnold.

Turner, Graeme (2004), *Understanding Celebrity*, London: Sage.

Whannel, Garry (2002), *Media Sports Stars*, London: Routledge.

Television as Spectacle

There are a number of interrelated ways to consider the concept of 'spectacle' in the context of television. The first is the way in which the industry works to create breathtaking moments or experiences in television programming through the presentation of entertainment specials. The second involves television's excessive or sensational coverage of particular news events that are highly graphic, lurid and/or startling. The third relates to a more theoretical understanding of the term spectacle that speaks to a consumer society enthralled, almost to the point of distraction, with media images.

Television specials, usually one-off programme presentations, are conceptualised as event programming, meant to attract a mass audience. This can involve the use of stars and live broadcasts (such as the Oscars), sports events (like the Super Bowl), telethons, variety, theatrical or concert formats, or the presentation of a fictional narrative that carries with it social and/or historical significance, top-quality talent and an extensive marketing campaign. In the 1950s, Sylvester 'Pat' Weaver was the first programmer to focus on what he called 'spectaculars' in order to attract a wider audience as well as to associate NBC with prestigious (and expensive) programming. Such shows were usually big-budget, star-studded, network-produced, once-only events that were anywhere from one to three hours in length. The genre varied from musical revues and Broadway plays (*Peter Pan* starring Mary Martin, for example) to non-fiction programmes, such as a tour of India with former ambassador Chester Bowles. Weaver considered spectaculars investments in the future of NBC, as they were rarely profitable from an advertising sales point of view, but were most often critical and public relation successes. In 1956, television critic Jack Gould described them as 'thoroughly commendable and sometimes brilliant illustrations of the fact that, when they want to, the broadcasters are entitled to hold up their heads proudly' (Gould, 2002, p. 233). Spectaculars also seemed to bring back the novelty of the medium, as they were meant to impress and inspire viewers with not only television's potential for aesthetic and narrative quality, but also with its ability to create the sense of a programme as a shared national experience.

One of the most extraordinary spectaculars of the period was *Light's Diamond Jubilee*, a two-hour tribute to Thomas Edison that aired on all four networks and was produced by Hollywood heavyweight David O. Selznick. The programme was conceived as a celebration of the seventy-fifth anniversary of the light bulb and combined, among other things, documentary footage, a talk by President Dwight Eisenhower and musical numbers and sketches featuring Hollywood stars. A consortium of the most powerful electrical manufacturers and utility companies paid the $1million cost of the programme, envisioning it as an opportunity to improve the public image of their industry by connecting it with ideas of nation, power and science for the social good (Anderson, 1994, p. 79). In doing this on such a grand scale and by disrupting the normal programming schedule, the sponsors and the networks created a moment that was intended to feel historical, or at least monumental, to the television viewer. As Christopher Anderson points out, 'spectaculars were the networks' attempt to create media events' (ibid., p. 83). Daniel Dayan and Elihu Katz describe media events as programmes that 'cancel all other programs, bringing television's clock to a stop, and while they are on the air, they cannot themselves be interrupted . . . . [They bring] social activity to a standstill. For a while, [they occupy] society's center' (1987, p. 182).

The idea of media event as spectacle, rather than simply a spectacular, is a useful one as it allows the term to refer to a range of genres and formats. In the current television environment, media spectacles are often thought of as news-related or based on real-life events and involve a more generalised notion of excess in presentation. When the term is used to describe such moments, it implies a combination of a number of the following qualities: immediacy, focus on the image, massive output, the sensational, repetition, crisis, urgency and a sense of connectedness for the audience. The story itself is usually exceptional in some way, either in its scope, its national or global ramifications, or in the extent to which it evokes drama or sensationalism. Examples of media spectacles of this type include the four-day coverage of JFK's assassination in 1963, television's obsessive focus on the O. J. Simpson case in the 1990s and the more recent images of war sent from Iraq. The coverage of the attack on the World Trade Center in 2001 is, perhaps, the definitive example of television's excessive presentation of an exceptional event. To grasp the full meaning of television's employment of spectacle, one only has to think back to the news footage shown repeatedly in the days and weeks following the attacks. The startling images of the moments of the planes' impact, the trail of smoke against the surrounding New York skyline, the towers' collapse, the resulting massive cloud of dust, debris and smoke, and the various shots of people running in terror or collapsing in grief and fear. Certainly, these real-life moments are vivid, moving and meaningful in their own right, but it was in their initial capture and then continuous replay that the images of this event became so enlarged, so inscribed and so impossibly poignant. In the coverage of September 11th, which some have described as this century's first global spectacle, we can see how, through the use of spectacle, television can help foster a sense of disaster (and, later a sense of nationalism) writ large.

Whenever media theorists write about televised spectacles, they almost inevitably refer to the work of Guy Debord. In his 1967 book, Debord describes a mediated capitalist society wherein spectacles of consumption have become the centre of social life, hypnotising and eventually depoliticising their spectators. His concept of spectacle is a fairly generalised one that encompasses a mode of production and a socio-political state. As Debord writes, 'The spectacle is not a collection of images, but a social relation among people, mediated by images' (1995, p. 4). Douglas Kellner, expanding upon and refining Debord's concept, identifies specific locations and sources of spectacle and shows how they work to display a nation's most gripping social anxieties, fantasies and conflicts. He also argues that increasing competition in the global consumer market has only intensified the production of spectacle in all media forms (2003). Both Kellner and Debord observed changes in the quantity and quality of media output during the times in which they were writing. It would appear that the global expansion of markets, together with the development of new technologies and the growing power of media conglomerates, has had the effect of amplifying the power and impact of media spectacles over time. The introduction of new technologies, which create special effects, change the composition and quality of the image, link multimedia platforms and allow for more immediate or extensive coverage, has raised the stakes exponentially for the presentation of media events on television.

While living in such a crowded media environment as our own, it is difficult to imagine how post-war spectaculars could ever have played a similar industrial and cultural role to that of the spectacles we see on television today. They don't seem to boast the vividness, the jarring content, or the larger-than-life narrative contained in our current media events. Yet, their connection can be found in the manner in which they were used to display television's distinguishing characteristics, technical prowess and aesthetic innovations. Perhaps more than anything else, television spectacles have always revealed the medium's unique ability to gather vast numbers of viewers together to experience an event as it unfolds and to make them feel as though the whole world is watching with them.

Susan Murray

RECOMMENDED READING

Anderson, Christopher (1994), *Hollywood TV: The Studio System in the Fifties*, Austin: University of Texas Press.

Dayan, Daniel and Katz, Elihu (1987), 'Performing Media Events', in James Curran, Anthony Smith and Pauline Wingate (eds), *Impacts and Influences: Essays on Media Power in the Twentieth Century*, London: Methuen, pp. 174–97.

Dayan, Daniel and Katz, Elihu (1994), *Media Events: The Live Broadcasting of History*, Cambridge, MA: Harvard University Press.

Debord, Guy (1995), *The Society of the Spectacle*, New York: Zone Books.

Gould, Lewis L. (ed.) (2002), *Watching Television Come of Age: New York Times Reviews by Jack Gould*, Austin: University of Texas Press.

Kellner, Douglas (2003), *Media Spectacle*, New York: Routledge.

KENNEDY – A NEW TV IN THE US

If there was one day that changed television's place in life in the US, it was 22 November 1963, when John F. Kennedy's death united a nation in front of television sets. For the baby-boom generation no one ever forgot where they were that afternoon.

Air Force One's arrival at Love Field was broadcast live but they signed off ten minutes before the motorcade got started. Their equipment remained at the airport to cover Air Force One's departure later on in the afternoon.

Minutes after the motorcade got underway, New York newsrooms erupted as the first bulletin was sent over the wire: 'Three shots were fired at President Kennedy's motorcade today in Dallas.' Within thirty minutes CBS, NBC and ABC had halted all regular programming. Without any warning or preparation, the most massive broadcast coverage of any event in history had begun.

People watched and learned how well their government could transfer power.

But there was nothing to show. As a result, church services, panel discussions and memorial concerts helped fill air-time on Friday. Abraham Zapruder, a spectator, had taken 8mm home movies, but *Life* magazine outbid the networks for the dulling seven seconds. For twenty-five years we would only see still images.

On Saturday, Kennedy's body lay in the East Room of the White House – while it was raining outside. Throughout the day, reporters in raincoats accompanied by TV cameras covered with plastic followed notable mourners as they arrived to pay their last respects. Former presidents Truman and Eisenhower, and even the Russian ambassador, came to view the coffin.

Sunday morning saw the most violent image. All of the networks planned on live coverage of suspect Lee Harvey Oswald's move from city to county jail in the late morning on Sunday. ABC was stationed at the county jail awaiting his arrival; CBS and NBC were ready to broadcast from the basement of the city jail. As the elevator door opened and Oswald stepped out, he walked past police and reporters – then a man came from the bottom right-hand corner of the screen, charged towards Oswald and shot him!

It was only seen on NBC. Later CBS aired a videotape, and then played it again . . . and again . . . even in slow motion. ABC aired the reactions of people on the streets to the news.

News crews began to investigate his murderer, Jack Ruby, a nightclub owner. After a few hours, interviews with people who knew Ruby were aired.

On the Monday, for the funeral procession, TV cameramen were told to wear formal suits. Eighteen months after the first *Telstar* broadcasts christened the age of international television, viewers in twenty-five countries saw portions of President Kennedy's funeral rites as they occurred. As the coffin reached Arlington Cemetery, fifty fighter jets, one for each state, flew overhead with Air Force One behind them. One NBC camera with a telephoto lens provided close-ups.

Closure had been achieved. LBJ was president. On Tuesday, 26 November 1963, at 7 am, entertainment and commercials were back on television screens.

Douglas Gomery

Interactive Television

The first type of interactive television was developed in the early 1970s, when the use of remote control technology, meant that the viewer could switch channels more easily. The next phase of interactivity arrived with the digital services, which enable viewers to choose from a variety of offerings within the same channel. Early definitions of interactivity reflected this: 'Interactive broadcast television, TV-i, involves the direct manipulation by the viewer of the content or form of an ongoing programme' (Frenette and Caron, 1995). This amounts to more opportunity to select, but not to interact in the sense of making a personal intervention in the product offered on screen. Hence BBCi, for example, was devised to televise Wimbledon for cable and satellite viewers in such a way that they could keep themselves informed of the situation throughout the tournament by selecting from an on-screen menu of results and alternative matches on other courts. Such events are infrequent and the service is often unused. Educational uses, whereby a question-and-answer approach is taken, have continued to grow.

Today, interactivity has reached the stage where the events on the television screen can be a direct result of the viewer's actions. The PlayStation 2 has, for example, given rise to the Eye-Toy, a camera placed on top of the television that enables the players to make gestures in front of the camera which are transformed into actions on screen. Thus the cartoon boxer can be knocked out by quick punches from the gamer. In this case the viewer is literally interacting with the on-screen events and acting within the fictional diegetic world shown. What all these phases have in common is the increasing ability for viewers to determine their own viewing experiences rather than remaining mere passive recipients of the broadcast. Currently, however, the producers have determined the forms of interactivity that are available.

Interactive television is an example of a process of 'mass customisation', which the post-industrial era has ushered in. The product is still distributed to a mass market but it is offered at the point of consumption in a manner which can be chosen by the consumer to increase its appeal. As the demand for more and more kinds of interactivity increases, it may be the case that the broadcasters struggle to maintain their control of the broadcast. Streaming (the process of creating and broadcasting digital content which can be moved easily from one channel or medium to another) threatens to disengage the product from its producer's control if interactivity becomes even more sophisticated. Shaadionline is a company which offers to webcast family weddings to India using streaming and to allow viewers to interact by conversing over the Web while

the webcast is shown. Already, the BBC laments the fact that it cannot track interactive viewers' watching habits easily. Advertisers who might help to offset the cost of such extensive programming cannot be guaranteed the mass audience they require. Standard interactive television is expensive to produce and can only reach those homes which have access to cable or BSkyB satellite services and can enjoy the full interactive experience. Viewers using digital Freeview boxes, for example, are largely restricted to interacting by texting the programme-makers in response to polls presented on-screen. The BBC currently have problems in designing content that will reach all the viewers at a reasonable cost. They partly attribute this to the availability of broadband Internet services. BSkyB currently enables over 4 million viewers to enjoy interactive television throughout the day.

From the point of view of political economy, what will determine the future of interactive television is the cost of reaching a mass audience with the kinds of interactivity that mean that one product can be tailored to satisfy vastly different tastes. Digital viewing also holds out the prospect of a much quicker and more accurate way of discovering the nation's taste and acting on this information.

The major question at this moment is whether interactive television or Internet access with television included will dominate. It has been suggested that interactive television with the opportunity to include Web browsing and email might breach the 'digital divide', since the vast majority of homes could afford television sets and Microsoft, for example, has been aiming to provide integrated services. However, as Steve Curran says, 'bet on Web/TV not TV/Web' (2003, p. 173). The Web arrived and the interactive elements of television were superseded. As Bill Gates says in *The Road Ahead*, 'Almost overnight, the Interactive Television Gold Rush all but died, and the Internet Gold Rush was born' (1996, p. 260). The TiVo form of interactive television, which enables digital television recording onto a hard disk and can be slowed down if someone calls, has now found competitors. Now products, such as Gigapocket for the Sony range, can also provide this facility on the 'Media Centre' PCs. The convergence of computers and television looks likely to lead to a battle for the main domestic viewing experience.

Although television is available to most homes, producers of television content cannot currently finance continual interactive offerings on a scale that pays. Advertisers would like 'walled gardens' where their own products are offered in a sector which they can safely anticipate. Further, the degree of user choice would appear to be crucial and the PC can offer greatly enhanced interactivity. At the moment there are 40 million homes with a computer in the United States and Curran notes that 27 per cent of American viewers report watching TV and surfing the net at the same time. Microsoft first enabled the introduction of television tuners in Windows 98 and now they are working on 'cross-over links', which will enable broadcasters to take viewers from a segment of a television programme to related Web content at the click of a button. It may only be a matter of time before Web access and television are consistently offered in the same package with all the interactivity that Web browsing provides. As Nick Garnham says, however, the attempt to launch a combined television and telephone foundered because the audience didn't want to do both at the same time and this might also occur with shopping on television (2000, p. 72). Path dependency theory also suggests that the initial purchase of equipment may compel viewers to continue to purchase one or the other to avoid wasting money.

The makers of interactive television could respond to competition by exploiting the potential of their contracted dramatic offerings to attract viewers. Janet Murray, for example, suggests that a future type of television drama like *NYPD Blue* might feature the possibility of looking inside the lockers of the characters while they are on-screen and discovering more about their lives and backstory. Alternatively, 'mobile viewers' may choose to explore far more than a classic narrative format (Murray, 1998, p. 259). Murray even speculates that the viewer may one day be able to assume a character role and participate in the drama. Swann (2000) describes the possibility of viewers pausing *Ally McBeal* to shop for goods shown in the programme. As Curran says, the best examples of interactive television are those designed as interactive products rather than normal programmes offering interactivity as an additional feature (2003).

It is now possible to find DVDs that ask the viewer to respond to questions and offer a narrative based on a psychoanalysis of the viewer's desires. This would seem to herald a new phase of interactivity where the viewer no longer even needs to select the elements of the product they want, but has it done for them. Now the television interacts with us rather than us with the television. TiVo also assesses viewers' preferences and records programmes of the kind they like without consulting the viewer. Interactive technology has even been accused of leading to a Brave New World scenario where the television is used as a surveillance device or for social control through spy-TV. 'Motricity', is a term devised by the French philosopher, Jean-François Lyotard, which implies that advances in technology are not always driven by the needs of the public but have their own momentum. This means that a technology may sometimes be developed and its potential acknowledged too early for it to be exploited. In 1977, the interactive television service Qube in Columbus, Ohio, was introduced by Warner Bros. only to be dropped because of the cost (<www.itvalliance.org>). Interactive television is poised to develop as a major new phenomenon, but how and when remains to be seen.

Adrian Page

RECOMMENDED READING

Curran, Steve (2003), *Convergence Design: Creating the User Experience for Interactive Television*, Gloucester, MA: Rockport.

Feinleib, David (1999), *The Inside Story of Interactive Television or Microsoft Web TV for Windows*, San Diego, CA: Morgan Kauffman.

Frenette, Michelene and Caron, André H. (1995), 'Children and Interactive Television', *Convergence: The Journal of Research into New Media Technologies*, vol. 1, no. 1, pp. 33–62.

Garnham, Nick (2000), *Emancipation, the Media and Modernity*, Oxford: Oxford University Press.

Gates, Bill (1996), *The Road Ahead*, London: Penguin.

Murray, Janet H. (1998), *Hamlet on the Holodeck: the Future of Narrative in Cyberspace*, Cambridge, MA: MIT Press.

Swann, Phillip (2000), *TV Dot Com: The Future of Interactive Television*, New York: TV Books.

Whitaker, Jerry (ed.) (2000), *Interactive Television Demystified*, New York, London: McGraw-Hill.

<www.itvalliance.org>.

<www.shaadionline.com/wedding-webcast.asp#>.

Conclusion

TV as Narrative: Looking Back and Looking Forward

Television adapted to narrative at first, even as early television tried non-narrative forms such as the variety show. But by about 1955 these early experiments had ended, Hollywood entered and narrative became the dominant form. This spilled over into all television forms. Sports were turned into stories. News was turned into stories. Musical shows such as *American Idol* were turned into stories.

Narrative is television. It is defined by its genres of storytelling. On 4 May 2003 *TV Guide*, then in its fiftieth year listing all the fare nationally, created a listing of the fifty greatest TV shows in the US of the first half-century. Narrative comedies of a limited set of characters led the way: first was the meta-narrative *Seinfeld* (31 May 1990–14 May 1998); and second was the narrative pace-setter *I Love Lucy* (15 October 1951–6 May 1957). Both are set around the stories of four characters, and both will run forever.

Soap operas are not musical but stories told over years, with instalments on a daily basis. Once NBC tried to show a US football game without announcers – the narrators – and the fans howled in protest; this experiment was never tried again. The news calls each of their segments 'stories', as in the lead story or a follow-up story. The classic of the narrative is the mystery story – a dead body, investigation, prosecution and closure as the perpetrator is caught and sentenced. We know the killer will be caught. The pleasure comes in the how – the style and flare.

Even *60 Minutes* – the longest hit show in the history of television in the US – had the narrative quality of news as its basic principle and promoted the on-screen star/reporter over the programme's lowly backstage field producers, who have always done most of the research and reporting for the programme – as Richard Campbell points out (1991). Drawn to news through his early love of 1930s' movie characters, the programme's creator, Don Hewitt, remembered in his autobiography:

> As a child of the movies, I was torn between wanting to be Julian Marsh, the Broadway producer in 42nd Street, who was up to his ass in showgirls, and Hildy Johnson, the hellbent-for-leather reporter in The Front Page, who

was up to his ass in news stories. Oh my God, I thought, in television, I could be both of them. (Hewitt, 2001, p. 75)

He thus took the Hollywood model and crafted a new form of television, running in the top ten most popular programmes for the final three decades of the 20th century.

In 1981, Hewitt told the *Chicago Tribune* that storytelling was the key to the programme's appeal: 'I'll bet if we made it multi-subject and we made it personal journalism – instead of dealing with issues we told stories; if we packaged reality as well as Hollywood packages fiction, I'll bet we could double the rating.'

But this commonality of TV in the US as narrative began in the late 1950s, when the three major television networks – ABC, CBS, and NBC – moved their entertainment divisions to Los Angeles, in part, because of its close proximity to Hollywood production studios. Network news operations, however, remained in New York. Symbolically, these cities came to represent the two major branches of TV programming: entertainment and information. Yet this geographical distance masked the separation. At the time, former radio reporter John Daly hosted the CBS game show *What's My Line?*. When he began moonlighting as the evening TV news anchor on ABC, the fledgling network blurred the so-called entertainment and information border, foreshadowing narration as the common thread.

CBS's *60 Minutes* involves adapting the classic narrative fictional form – the detective mystery – to TV journalism. Through this familiar cultural frame, the reporters of *60 Minutes* have performed over the years, not as detached journalists but as dramatic characters. Their mission: to locate themselves in the middle of an adventure and make sense of the world through their stories. Thus, '60 Minutes is the adventures of five reporters,' Hewitt has said, 'more fascinating to the American public being themselves than Robert Redford and Dustin Hoffman were playing Woodward and Bernstein [in the 1976 film *All the President's Men*].'

Even the production techniques on the programme have contributed to the image of the reporters as detective heroes. First, unlike on the conventional evening news, Hewitt's correspondents are featured characters in their dramas. They are usually in more shots than any of the subjects interviewed. Frequently, in reaction shots, interview subjects appear in extreme close-ups – usually with the top of the head cut from the frame. This is in contrast to the medium shots of the reporter, usually shown from mid-waist, with space revealed overhead. The greater space granted to the reporters may be read on one level as the TV narrative counterpart to print's neutral third-person point of view.

Detective stories celebrate individual heroes and condemn institutional villains. In this way, journalism in general suffers from this malady that plagues *60 Minutes* (as good as some of its best investigative pieces have been). Stories centring on the afflictions of individuals make the world seem like a place where problems are personal, not social – that require only private redress or remedy rather than any sort of collective engagement.

What is a narrative? It is a means of pleasure production where a chain of events occurs in time and space, linked by cause and effect. At its most basic, Lucy gets into a jam and then gets out of it (the chain of events), and the laughter is produced by the cause and effects she and her husband and their two neighbours use to get her to a happy ending with closure, so it can happen all over again.

Television learned this from Hollywood, which has set a world standard of a system so clear that it leaps over culture and time; shows like *I Love Lucy* are still understood around the world today, and in cultures from East to West, North to South.

TV is often accused of being a medium for idiots, but I argue that, while it is clear and simple to follow, at its best US television narrative can be complex on many levels. This can be seen on the top show as I write this – Viacom's *CSI: Crime Scene Investigation*. We know these scientists who work for the Las Vegas police will solve the crime, but it is the methods they use in the story that fascinate us. They use the most advanced science to solve the crimes and, coupled with the beauty of the cinematography in high-definition television, this makes for a popular and complex television experience.

We know the form, four 'acts' with breaks in between for advertisements. We look at hundreds of shots. Yet it all makes sense and challenges us to think while we enjoy ourselves. We must understand that the form of the television narrative is not a continuous entity; instead, it is a conglomeration of blocks, represented by shots and scenes. These blocks have the tendency to fall apart, thereby interrupting the continuity of the story in a decisive manner. In order to overcome these breaks, we must search for connecting elements within the story.

If the elements of the story overlap the breaks caused by the technical subdivisions, we can achieve connection. The narrative disruptions can occur either within a scene or at the transitions between scenes. But television adopted from

Hollywood ways of handling these problems: placing a distant framing of the action early in a scene to establish the locale and who is present in it. This general view may be preceded by or include a sign further specifying the locale. The analytical editing system of breaking the space into closer framings makes the action more comprehensible by enlarging the salient visual elements. Matches on action at the cuts promote a sense of temporal continuity.

Compositions usually centre the most important characters or objects, ensuring that the spectator will notice them. In a shot/reverse-shot conversation, the characters are often balanced in a gentle see-saw of slightly off-centre framings. Similar emphasis may be provided by design techniques like bright-coloured clothing or staging that calls attention to a moving character. Such clarity is still valued in television.

Taken together, such techniques constitute television storytelling. In general, the continuity system utilises style primarily to make the narrative events as clear as possible, though it also sometimes promotes additional aspects like humour and big production values (splendid sets, elaborate special effects). No doubt the music-video aesthetic has sped up the editing a bit in recent years with its fast cutting and yet little has really changed if one compares *I Love Lucy* from 1953 and *Everybody Loves Raymond* in 2004.

Lighting and tonality tend to be darker, noticeably outside the realm of the film noir – even in self-reflexive animation like *The Simpsons*, with its allusions to other works of television and film. Dissolves to soften scene transitions have all but disappeared, and fades are used only to mark the few most important scene changes. Startling sound bridges have become common. Dazzling developments in special effects have made flashy style much more prominent, especially in science-fiction and action films. Yet these techniques have not broken down the principle that style's most fundamental function is to promote narrative clarity.

This is why the establishing shot is so crucial for maintaining a clear sense of locale in television. *CSI* always begins with helicopter shots of Las Vegas, so beautiful, yet establishing that danger is near. The most basic source of temporal and causal clarity is the dangling cause.

One simple technique is to leave a cause open at the end of one scene and immediately pick it up in the next; such a transition is known as a 'hook'. From act to act, the hook must be strong enough so that the viewer will sit through the advertisements so as not to miss the beginning of the next scene – literally hooked. Frequently, at the end of a scene, a character will mention what he or she is going to do and then will immediately be seen doing it early in the next scene. Such a line is a 'dialogue hook'. Although dialogue hooks provide a high degree of clarity and redundancy, a too-frequent use of them would soon come to seem mechanical and contrived, and they are used only for some transitions.

All methods of achieving scene-to-scene clarity can be supplemented or replaced with a voice-over narration, though that relatively self-conscious narrational device is not common in classical narratives.

Finally, television in any form can achieve overall unity and clarity by means of motifs. These can be auditory or visual. It also provides a snappy means of exposition. Since the earliest days of classical film-making, Hollywood has been adept at using visual motifs to add emotional resonance to a narrative. David Bordwell and Kristin Thompson have sorted out the workings of the Hollywood narration techniques. Yet they have not explained their power and hold. That is considerable, so powerful that it defines the very use of living life in the US.

And these narratives will remain a core part of life in the US. Most American households spent at least a little time every evening relaxing in front of a screen. But with all the new choices, watching TV – about six hours a day – clearly dominates.

What is remarkable is the power of first-run narratives. Even with all the options, the major broadcast networks account for 45 per cent of viewing, a remarkable testament to the strength of the business model, given the proliferation of choices over the past quarter-century. This will continue – however the technology changes, however the social impact alters and however long the TV industry continues to dominate life in the US. Narrative defined TV's past and will continue to dominate its future.

Douglas Gomery

RECOMMENDED READING

Campbell, Richard (1991), *60 Minutes and the News*, Urbana: University of Illinois Press.

Hewitt, Don (2001), *Don Hewitt, Tell Me a Story*, New York: Public Affairs Press.

Thompson, Kristin (2003), *Storytelling in Film and Television*, Cambridge, MA: Harvard University Press.

Television – the Future, Little and Large

THE DEMISE OF ANALOGUE

Innovations in television technology have a curious and somewhat predictable pattern from which it is possible to make an informed guess about some of what the future of broadcasting may have in store for us as consumers and citizens. Two areas are of particular importance: the development of new technology and its acceptance and subsequent use in society.

Historically it has taken longer than might be expected to achieve high levels of market acceptance of new technologies; it is almost as though new technologies are brought to the market ahead of the consumers' demand and need for them. For example, the BBC's first experiments with colour television date back to the 1950s (interestingly they used the National Television Standards Committee (NTSC) system developed by the Radio Corporation of America (RCA) in the United States). At that time television sets in the UK used a 405-line system and the early experiments showed that this was not enough for acceptable colour quality. A new standard of 625 lines was set (incidentally, much of Europe was already using the 625-line standard for their black-and-white transmissions). The BBC abandoned NTSC in favour of Phase Alternation by Line (PAL), which, with exception of France, again assured a degree of standardisation across Europe. As might be expected, there was a transitional period in which the new 625 television sets where to be phased in before the old 405-line transmitters were switched off. How long was this? Almost twenty-one years.

DIGITAL TERRESTRIAL

The scenario may seem familiar. Currently the government in the UK is hoping to switch off the analogue television signal by 2010. The take-up of digital terrestrial television (DTT) across Europe is patchy but growing. The data from the European Radiocommunications Office for February 2004 shows that in the UK there are 2.8 million DTT set-top boxes; Finland has 400,000; Sweden and Germany 200,000 each. However, according to Freeview, there are more than 4 million DTT households in the UK alone. The prediction was that 59 per cent of UK households would be able to receive some form of DTV by the end of 2004, with the figure rising to 20 million by 2010. However, if we are to go by what has happened in the past, then 2015 or even 2020 look like more realistic dates. By extrapolation, we can predict something similar for other innovations in broadcasting. Some embryonic areas may develop more quickly, for example, the convergence between telecommunications and broadcasting. Yet in all cases, we would do well to remember that these changes are driven primarily by equipment manufacturers who have a commercial interest in ensuring the new products are brought to market, as older production lines reach their potential market saturation.

HIGH DEFINITION

The development of the high-definition television set market in the UK is interesting and part of the above pattern. The resolution of these sets, which are now widely available, is considerably higher than the quality of the current broadcast signal. (Most manufacturers offer a maximum quality of 1024 x 1024.) The benefits of the increased resolution come when watching DVDs, as they are able to reproduce the higher picture and sound quality offered by this format. It does not take a great leap of insight to see how this can be used to drive the demand for higher-quality broadcast transmissions, which will involve the replacement of all equipment in the broadcast production and transmission chain – clearly of benefit if you are a manufacturer of such products.

To achieve reasonable levels of HDTV sales, plasma screens and LCD panel displays or digital light processing-enabled projectors must be affordable. The previously high price point of these products is dropping rapidly particularly in the UK, Germany, France and Italy, with a related increase in sales. Estimates vary but typically suggest that there will be around 1 million HDTV viewers in Europe by 2006 and 7 million by 2008, with 10 per cent of all European homes able to receive HDTV. Agreement is still needed on transmission standards, hardware connectivity and HD business models. Europe's satellite operators are keen to use up their spare capacity and there is some dissatisfaction with current broadcast images compared to DVD, which is particularly noticeable on large high-resolution television screens, as listed above. It is therefore expected that domestic broadcasters will routinely be transmitting HDTV broadcasts by 2008 with domestic mass-market adoption by 2010.

Importantly, Europe's first high-definition satellite channel launched in January 2004. Euro1080 is the first channel to broadcast exclusively in high-definition throughout Europe. As part of its consumer launch proper, on 1 September, the channel rebranded itself HD1 (www.hd-1.tv/). In terms of content, it offers sports, music, shows and cultural events with surround sound. The company predicted that from 1 December 2004, there would be five languages available both via subtitling and on a commentary track, enabling fiction, documentaries and more sports.

Another part of the company's operation is the Event Channel, which distributes to cinemas and other large venues equipped with electronic projection and 5.1 surround sound. The intention is to broadcast events only once, and live into 'event cinemas', although repeats are already starting, with the second transmission of the concert by Elton John at the Covent Garden Opera House. Other events aired include the broadcasting of Jean Michel Jarre's concert in the Forbidden City Beijing on 10 October 2004 to cinemas in Amsterdam, Luxembourg and Longwy; Aida live from La Monnaie Opera House, Brussels; and a New Year's concert live from Vienna. It will be interesting to see the extent to which this venture develops. With the prospect of Hollywood distributing its

films digitally into cinemas with data, rather than film, projectors, it may be that some interesting changes occur in the way cinemas are used. This marks an unexpected change in the social patterns for the consumption of digital media, which, up to this point, have been predominantly personal and domestic. Here, the notion of media event as spectacle and commodity is finding a new lease of life. As Guy Debord notes:

> The spectacle corresponds to the historical moment at which the commodity completes its colonization of social life. It is not just that the relationship to commodities is now plain to see – commodities are now *all* that there is to see; the world we see is the world of the commodity. (Debord, 1995)

You might be tempted to think that there's no end to the constant process of technological innovation and commodification, and the world of digital media gives little cause to doubt this state of affairs. The comments about product life-cycle apply here; whether there's a need or not, new products (textual and technological) and whole new generations of technology will continue to ensure that our existing television equipment is out of date, that new commodities are 'needed'. The latest technology to emerge in this field is called Ultra High Definition Video (UHDV), which can display 7680 x 4320 lines of resolution. Such is the quality of this image that it will be like looking out of a window. As the technology develops, the price of the 'old' plasma and LCD screens will drop. How long before such technology becomes affordable? Estimates suggest at least twenty years. However long it takes, you can be sure that its arrival will coincide with the demise and mass-market adoption of HDTV.

CONVERGED CHANNELS

Interestingly, these developments in ever higher-definition images are being mirrored by the emergence of low-resolution video images. These images are not produced by traditional cameras, nor are they edited in the standard broadcast manner. Instead, they are one aspect of the much vaunted convergence between telecommunications and broadcasting, which has been enabled by digital media technology.

The videos I have in mind are originated on cameras that are integrated into mobile phones. The main appeal of these devices was clearly for the domestic market, with telecommunications providers seeing clear money-making potential in building on the somewhat unexpected success of text-messaging with photo and video messaging services. Perhaps more surprising was the use of these devices in electronic news gathering (ENG). Recently the graphic video of Nicholas Berg, an American in Iraq, was dramatically broadcast to the world via an al Qaeda-linked website. The BBC has recently given forty of its reporters Nokia mobile videophones. These phones have specially designed software from Phillips, which allows up to fifteen minutes of video to be stored. The Nokia 7610 can record video, edit scenes, add special-effects music, text email images or transmit them via Bluetooth to computers, printers or Web albums. In theory, anyone with a mobile videophone can be a journalist; put another way, anyone with a digital camera, website and the ability to stream images can command global attention. However, there is a difference between professional journalists working for news organisations, offering comment and analysis, and just 'broadcasting' something on the Net. While the potential to democratise the journalistic process is welcome, it is becoming more vital than ever that viewers have the media literacy skills to distinguish between different types of digital media content, something that is not straightforward.

CONCLUSION

On the one hand, the above developments in the technology that surrounds the television industry might be characterised as a process of technological determinism. Media companies' research and development teams develop new products, which, in turn, offer new social opportunities. In this mode of analysis it is assumed that each technology is essentially better than its predecessor – that matters are getting progressively better.

Another way of analysing these developments is to see technology and technological developments as part of a complex, interrelated cultural system that is in some way symptomatic of society. In this model, technological change comes about as part of other cultural changes. Technology is not deterministic but subsumed within a complex cultural flux. However, we would do well to remember a third and more integrated model presciently suggested by Raymond Williams in 1975:

But in the case of television it may be possible to outline a different kind of interpretation, which would allow us not only to see its [television's] history but also its uses in a more radical way. Such an interpretation would differ from technological determinism in that it would restore *intention* to the process of research and development. The technology would be seen, that is to say, as being looking for and developed with certain purposes and practices already in mind. At the same time the interpretation would differ from symptomatic technology in that these purposes and practices would be seen as *direct*: as known social needs, purposes and practices to which the technology is not marginal but central. (Williams, 1997)

The twin notions of *intention* and *direction* seem crucial if we are to come to an informed view about the ways in which television technology functions at social and cultural levels. The axis that Williams draws our attention to reminds us that, in tracking these changes, it is important to be mindful of the business imperatives that drive equipment providers and the research (both social and technological) that they conduct. At the same time there is a need to be explicit about the role of technology in society, to understand its relation to business and to cultural life in general. With ever converging digital technologies, now, more than ever, there is a real need for everyone to be highly media-literate and to understand how the media, and audiovisual media in particular, are produced, regulated, owned and controlled.

Luke Hockley

RECOMMENDED READING

Debord, Guy (1995), *The Society of the Spectacle*, trans. Donald Nicholson-Smith, New York: Zone Books, para. 42.

Williams, Raymond (1997 [1975]), *Television Technology and Cultural Form*, London: Routledge, p. 14.

BIBLIOGRAPHY

Television as Business

Aksoy, Asu and Robins, Kevin (1992), 'Hollywood for the 21st Century: Global Competition for Critical Mass in Image Markets', *Cambridge Journal of Economics*, vol. 16, pp. 1–22.

Alexander, Alison, Owers, James and Carvath, Rod (1998), *Media Economics: Theory and Practice* (2nd edition), Mahwah, NJ: Lawrence Erlbaum Associates Publishers.

Aufderheide, Patricia (1999), *Communications Policy and the Public Interest: The Telecommunications Act of 1996*, New York: Guilford Press.

Bagdikian, Ben H. (2004), *The Media Monopoly*, Boston, MA: Beacon.

Barnouw, Erik (1975), *Tube of Plenty: The Evolution of American Television*, New York and Oxford: Oxford University Press.

Barnouw, Erik (1978), *The Sponsor: Notes on a Modern Potentate*, New York and Oxford: Oxford University Press.

Bogart, Leo (2000), *Commercial Culture: The Media System and the Public Interest*, New Brunswick, NJ: Transaction Publishers.

Campbell, Richard (1991), *60 Minutes and the News*, Urbana: University of Illinois Press.

Cantor, Muriel (1980), *Prime Time TV: Content and Control*, Beverly Hills, CA: Sage Publications.

Creators' Rights Alliance (2004), Submission to DCMS Review of the Royal Charter.

Economist (1989), 'There's No Bigness like Show Bigness', 25 March.

Edgerton, Gary R. (2001), *Ken Burn's America*, New York: Palgrave.

Eisner, Michael (1998), *Work in Progress*, New York: Random House.

Engelman, Robert (1996), *Public Radio and Television in America*, Thousand Oaks, CA: Sage.

Gomery, Douglas (1996), 'Mass Media Merger Mania', *American Journalism Review*, vol. 18, no. 9.

Gomery, Douglas (2002), *The FCC's Newspaper-Broadcast Cross Ownership Rule: An Analysis*, Washington, DC: Economic Policy Institute.

Gomery, Douglas (2003), 'The Role of the MPAA', in Thomas Paris and Pierre-Jean Benghozi (eds), *Hollywood and the Rest of the World: Which Approach for the 21st Century?*, Paris: CineAction!.

Gomery, Douglas (2004), 'Television Industry', in Neil J. Smelser and Paul B. Bates (eds), *International Encyclopedia of the Social and Behavioral Sciences*, Amsterdam: Pergamon.

Gomery, Douglas (2005), *The Hollywood Studio System*, London: BFI.

Gray, Lois S. and Seeber, Ronald L. (eds) (1996), *Under the Stars: Essays on Labor Relations in Arts and Entertainment*, Ithaca, NY: Cornell University Press.

Greco, Albert N. (ed.) (2000), *The Media and Entertainment Industries*, Boston, MA: Allyn and Bacon.

ITV Press Release, 4 July 2002.

McCarthy, Anna (2001), *Ambient Television*, Durham, NC: Duke University Press.

Miles, Raymond (1989), 'Adapting to Technology and Competition: A New Industrial Relations System for the 21st Century', *California Management Review*, Winter: pp. 9–28.

Miller, James (1985), 'How Much Is Not Enough?', in *Back to the Future: Prognostications on the Motion Picture and Television Industries, Proceedings of the Tenth Annual UCLA Entertainment Symposium*, Los Angeles, California: pp. 79–86.

Mittleman, Sheldon (1987), 'Residuals under the Guild Agreements – WGA, DGA, IATSE, SAG and AFM: Accommodating the New Media', in *Reel of Fortune: A Discussion of Critical Issues Affecting Film and Television Today, Proceedings of the Twelfth Annual UCLA Entertainment Symposium*, Los Angeles, California: pp. 83–92.

Napoli, Philip M. (2003), *Audience Economics: Media Institutions and the Audience Marketplace*, New York: Columbia University Press.

Newcomb, Horace (ed.) (1997), *Encyclopedia of Television*, Chicago, IL: Fitzroy-Dearborn.

Noam, Eli and Millonzi, J. C. (eds) (1993), *The International Market in Film and Television Programs*, Westport, CT: Greenwood Press.

Observer, 29 July 2001.

Owen, Bruce M. and Wildman, Steven S. (1992), *Video Economics*, Cambridge, MA: Harvard University Press.

Redstone, Sumner (2000), *A Passion to Win*, New York: Simon and Schuster.

Smith, Anthony (ed.) (1998), *Television: An International History* (2nd edition), Oxford: Oxford University Press.

Tolette, J. P. (2004), *Disney TV*, Detroit, MI: Wayne State University Press.

Waterman, David and Weis, Andrew (1997), *Vertical Integration in Cable Television*, Cambridge, MA: MIT Press.

Wirth, Michael O. (2002), 'Economics of Multichannel Video Program Distribution Industry', *Journal of Media Economics*, vol. 15, no. 3.

Vogel, Harold L. (1994), *Entertainment Industry Economics: A Guide for Financial Analysis*, New York: Cambridge University Press.

ONLINE RESOURCES

Broadcasting and Cable, <www.broadcastingandcable.com>.

Cable Television Advertising Bureau, <www.cabletvadbureau.com>.

Communications Bill, <www.communicationsbill.gov.uk/pdf/>.

Dodson, Sean; *Guardian* newspaper, 2004, <www.guardian.co.uk/online/story/0,3605,1155700,00.html>.

Federal Communications Commission, <www.fcc.gov>.

Granada Annual Report 2002, <www.itvplc.com/itv/merger/granadaarchive>.

Independent TV (Industrial Report), Mintel, 2004, <http://reports.mintel.com/>.

Mediaweek, <www.mediaweek.com>.

Motion Picture Association of America, <www.mpaa.org>.

Museum of Broadcast Communications, <www.museum.tv/archives/etv/P/htmlP/payperview/payperview.htm>.

National Association of Broadcasters, <www.nab.org>.

Northern California Translators Association, <www.ncta.org>.

Television Week, <www.TVweek.com>.

Variety, <www.variety.com>.

WikiPedia, <en.wikipedia.org/wiki/Pay_Per_View>.

Television Technology

Atkin, D. J. (2003), 'Predictors of Audience Interest in Adopting Digital Television', *Journal of Media Economics*, vol. 16, no. 3.

Bartlett, Eugene R. (1999), *Cable Television Handbook*, New York: McGraw-Hill.

Caldwell, John Thompson (ed.) (2000), *Electronic Media and Technostructure*, New Brunswick, NJ: Rutgers University Press.

Chan-Olmsted, Sylvia M. and Kang, Jae-Won (2003), 'Theorizing the Strategic Architecture of a Broadband Television Industry', *Journal of Media Economics*, vol. 16, no. 4.

Ciciora, Walter, Farmer, James and Lange, David (1999), *Modern Cable Television Technology*, New York: Morgan Kaufmann.

Compaine, Benjamin M. and Gomery, Douglas (2000), *Who Owns the Media?: Competition and Concentration in the Mass Media Industry* (3rd edition), Mahwah, NJ: Lawrence Erlbaum Associates, Publishers.

Engelman, Robert (1996), *Public Radio and Television in America*, Thousand Oaks, CA: Sage.

Gomery, Douglas (2004), 'Film and Video Industry', in Neil J. Smelser and Paul B. Bates (eds), *International Encyclopedia of the Social and Behavioral Sciences*, Amsterdam: Pergamon.

Gomery, Douglas (2004), 'Television Industry', in Neil J. Smelser and Paul B. Bates (eds), *International Encyclopedia of the Social & Behavioral Sciences*, Amsterdam: Pergamon.

Jack, Keith and Tsatsoulin, Vladimir (2002), *Dictionary of Video & Television Technology*, New York: Newes.

Kang, Myung (2002), 'Digital Cable: Exploring Factors Associated with Early Adoption', *Journal of Media Economics*, vol. 15, no. 3.

Newcomb, Horace (ed.) (1997), *Encyclopedia of Television*, Chicago: Fitzroy-Dearborn.

O'Driscoll, Gerard (1999), *The Essential Guide to Digital Set-top Boxes and Interactive TV*, Englewood Cliffs, NJ: Prentice-Hall.

Ovadia, Shlomo (2001), *Broadband Cable TV Access Networks: From Technologies to Applications*, Englewood Cliffs, NJ: Prentice-Hall.

Owen, Bruce M. and Wildman, Steven S. (1992), *Video Economics*, Cambridge, MA: Harvard University Press.

Rizzuto, Ronald J. (2002), 'The Economics of Video on Demand', *Journal of Media Economics*, vol. 15, no. 3.

Robin, Michael and Poulin, Michael (2000), *Digital Television Fundamentals*, New York: McGraw-Hill.

Smith, Anthony (ed.) (1998), *Television: An International History* (2nd edition), Oxford: Oxford University Press.

ONLINE RESOURCES

BBC Micro, Wikipedia: The Free Encyclopaedia, 4 August 2003, <en.wikipedia.org/wiki/BBC_Micro>.

BBC Online – Review against the terms of the 1997 and 1998 approvals for the BBC's online service, <www.bbc.co.uk>.

BIPA welcomes the Graf Report on the BBC's online services, 6 August 2004, <www.bipa.co.uk/getArticle.php?ID=313>.

Cable Television Advertising Bureau, <www.cabletvadbureau.com>.

Communications Act 2003, <www.legislation.hmso.gov.uk/acts/acts2003/20030021.htm>.

Department for Culture, Media and Sports Press Release, 23 August 2003, <www.culture.gov.uk>.

Department for Culture, Media and Sports Press Release, 5 July 2004, <www.culture.gov.uk/global/press_notices/archive_2004/dcms085_2004.htm>.

Federal Communications Commission, <www.fcc.gov>.

Internet DVD Database, <www.dvdloc8.com>.

Mediaweek, <www.mediaweek.com>.

Motion Picture Association of America, <www.mpaa.org>.

Northern California Translators Association, <www.ncta.org>.

Office of Communications, <www.ofcom.org.uk>.

PC Technology Guide, <www.pctechguide.com>.

Screen Digest, <www.screendigest.com>.

Screen International, <www.newsdaily.com>.

Society of Cable Telecommunications Engineers, <www.scte.org>.

Society of Motion Picture and Television Engineers, <www.smpte.org>.

Television Week, <www.TVweek.com>.

TV Shows on DVD, <www.tvshowsondvd.com>.

Television Infrastructures

Aufderheide, Patricia (1991), 'Cable Television and the Public Interest', *Journal of Communication*, vol. 42, no. 1.

Aufderheide, Patricia (2000), *The Daily Planet: A Critic on the Capitalist Culture Beat*, Minneapolis: University of Minnesota Press.

Bagdikian, Ben H. (2004), *The Media Monopoly*, Boston, MA: Beacon.

Blumler, Jay (ed.) (1992), *Television and the Public Interest*, London: Sage.

Bogart, Leo (2000), *Commercial Culture: The Media System and the Public Interest*, New Brunswick, NJ: Transaction Publishers.

Briggs, Asa and Burke, Peter (2002), *A Social History of the Media: From Gütenberg to the Internet*, Cambridge: Polity.

Brinkley, Joel (1997), *Defining Vision: The Battle for the Future of Television*, New York: Harcourt Brace.

Communications Act 2003 (2003), London: The Stationery Office.

Compaine, Benjamin M. and Gomery, Douglas (2000), *Who Owns the Media?: Competition and Concentration in the Mass Media Industry* (3rd edition), Mahwah, NJ: Lawrence Erlbaum Associates, Publishers.

Croteau, David and Hoynes, William (2001), *The Business of Media: Corporate Media and the Public Interest*, Thousand Oaks, CA: Sage.

Economist (1989), 'There's No Bigness like Show Bigness', 25 March.

Epstein, Mara (2004), 'The Financial Interest and Syndication Rules and Changes in Program Diversity', *Journal of Media Economics*, vol. 17, no. 1.

Gomery, Douglas (2002), *The FCC's Newspaper–Broadcast Cross Ownership Rule: An Analysis*, Washington, DC: Economic Policy Institute.

Gomery, Douglas (2003), 'The Role of the MPAA', in Thomas Paris and Pierre-Jean Benghozi (eds), *Hollywood and the Rest of the World: Which Approach for the 21st Century?*, Paris: CineAction!.

Gomery, Douglas (2004), 'Television and American Culture', in Carroll Pursell (ed.), *A Companion to American Technology*, London: Blackwell Publishing.

Gomery, Douglas (2004), 'Television Industry', in Neil J. Smelser and Paul B. Bates (eds), *International Encyclopedia of the Social and Behavioral Sciences*, Amsterdam: Pergamon.

Gomery, Douglas (2005), *The Hollywood Studio System*, London: BFI.

Goodwin, Peter (1998), *Television under the Tories: Broadcasting Policy 1979–1997*, London: BFI.

Gray, Lois S. and Seeber, Ronald L. (eds) (1996), *Under the Stars: Essays on Labor Relations in Arts and Entertainment*, Ithaca, NY: Cornell University Press.

Greco, Albert N. (ed.) (2000), *The Media and Entertainment Industries*, New York: Allyn and Bacon.

Hilmes, Michele (ed.) (2003), *The Television History Book*, London: BFI.

Hood, Stuart (ed.) (1994), *Behind the Screens: The Structure of British Television in the Nineties*, London: Lawrence and Wishart.

LeDuc, Don L. (1973), *Cable Television and the FCC*, Philadelphia, PA: Temple University Press.

Leys, Colin (2001), *Market-driven Politics: Neoliberal Democracy and the Public Interest*, London: Verso.

McQuail, Denis and Siune, Karen (eds) (1998), *Media Policy: Convergence, Concentration and Commerce*, London : Sage.

Miles, Raymond (1989), 'Adapting to Technology and Competition: A New Industrial Relations System for the 21st Century', *California Management Review*, Winter: 9–28.

Miller, James (1985), 'How Much Is Not Enough?', in *Back to the Future: Prognostications on the Motion Picture and Television Industries. Proceedings of the Tenth Annual UCLA Entertainment Symposium*, Los Angeles, California: 79-86.

Negrine, Ralph (1994), *Politics and the Mass Media in Britain* (second edition), London: Routledge.

Newcomb, Horace (ed.) (1997), *Encyclopedia of Television*, Chicago, IL: Fitzroy-Dearborn.

Owen, Bruce M. and Wildman, Steven S. (1992), *Video Economics*, Cambridge, MA: Harvard University Press.

Smith, Anthony (ed.) (1974), *British Broadcasting*, Newton Abbot: David and Charles.

Smith, Anthony (ed.) (1998), *Television: An International History* (second edition), Oxford: Oxford University Press.

Steemers, Jeanette (ed.) (1998), *Changing Channels: The Prospects for Television in a Digital World*, Luton: John Libbey Media.

Stevenson, Wilf (ed.) (1993), *All Our Futures*, London: BFI.

Tambini, Damian and Cowling, Jamie (eds) (2004), *From Public Service Broadcasting to Public Service Communications*, London: Institute for Public Policy Research.

Tracey, Michael (1998), *The Decline and Fall of Public Service Broadcasting*, Oxford: Oxford University Press.

Vogel, Harold L. (1994), *Entertainment Industry Economics: A Guide for Financial Analysis*, New York: Cambridge University Press.

ONLINE RESOURCES

Broadcasting and Cable, <www.broadcastingandcable.com>.

Cable Television Advertising Bureau, <www.cabletvadbureau.com>.

Federal Communications Commission, <www.fcc.gov>.

Mediaweek, <www.mediaweek.com>.

Television Week, <www.TVweek.com>.

Variety, <www.variety.com>.

Making Programmes

BBC (2004), *Building Public Value*, 29 June.

Bielby, William T. and Bielby, Denise D. (1998), *The 1989 Hollywood Writers' Report: Unequal Access, Unequal Pay*, West Hollywood, CA: Writers Guild of America, West.

Brinkley, Joel (1997), *Defining Vision: The Battle for the Future of Television*, New York: Harcourt Brace.

Broadcasters Audience Research Board (2004), for week ending 22 June.

Broadcasting (1998), 'The Discovery Channel Looks for the Next Frontier', 11 June.

Broadcasting Act 1980 (1980), Chapter 64, Part III, 4 (3b).

Brookes, Martin (2004), *Watching Alone: Social Capital in Public Service Broadcasting*, London: The Work Foundation/BBC.

Campbell, Richard (1991), *60 Minutes and the News*, Urbana: University of Illinois Press.

Compaine, Benjamin M. and Gomery, Douglas (2000), *Who Owns the Media?: Competition and Concentration in the Mass Media Industry* (third edition), Mahwah, NJ: Lawrence Erlbaum Associates, Publishers.

Crisell, A (2002), *An Introductory History of British Broadcasting*, (second edition), London and New York: Routledge, p. 208.

Directors Guild of America (1991), *Constitution and Bylaws*, Rev. Hollywood, CA:

Eastman, Susan T. and Furgeson, Douglas A. (1997), *Broadcasting and Cable Programming*, Belmont, CA: Wadsworth.

Eastman, Susan T., Furgeson, Douglas A. and Klein, Robert A. (eds) (1999), *Promotion and Marketing for Broadcasting and Cable* (third edition), Boston, MA: Focal Press.

Edgerton, Gary R. (2001), *Ken Burn's America*, New York: Palgrave.

Engelman, Ralph (1996), *Public Radio and Television in America: A Political History*, Thousand Oaks, CA: Sage Publications.

Fanthome, Christine (2004a), Interview with the author, 20 May.

Fanthome, Christine (2004b), Interview with the author, 25 May.

Fanthome, Christine (2004c), Email to the author, 3 June.

Fanthome, Christine (2004d), Interview with the author, 3 June.

Fanthome, Christine (2004e), Janet Root (BBC Controller January 1999– June 2004) interview with the author, 4 June.

Fanthome, Christine (2004f), Telephone interview with the author, 6 June.

Fanthome, Christine (2004g), Email to the author, 8 June.

Fanthome, Christine (2004h), Telephone interview with the author, 11 June.

Fanthome, Christine (2004i), Email to the author, 14 June.

Fanthome, Christine (2004j), Email to the author, 22 June.

Gomery, Douglas (2004), 'Television and American Culture', in Carroll Pursell (ed.), *Companion to American Technology*, London: Blackwell.

Goodwin, Peter (1998), *Television under the Tories, Broadcasting Policy 1979–1997*, London: BFI, p. 34.

Greenberg, Bradley S. (2001), *The Alphabet Soup of Television Program Ratings*, Cresskill, NJ: Hampton Press, Inc.

Hart, Colin (1999), *Television Program Making*, Boston, MA: Focal Press.

Kubey, Robert (2004), *Creating Television*, Mahwah, NJ: Lawrence Erlbaum Publishers.

Lavery, David (ed.) (1994), *Full of Secrets: Critical Approaches to Twin Peaks*, Detroit, MI: Wayne State University Press.

Montgomery, Kathryn C. (1989), *Target: Prime Time. Advocacy Groups and the Struggle over Entertainment Television*, New York and Oxford: Oxford University Press.

Murray, Susan, and Ouellette, Laurie (eds) (2004), *Reality TV: Remaking Television Culture*, New York: New York University Press.

Newcomb, Horace (ed.) (1997), *Encyclopedia of Television*, Chicago, IL: Fitzroy-Dearborn.

Peacock, Professor Alan (1986), *Report of the Committee on the Financing of the BBC*, London: HMSO, Cmnd. 9824.

Price, Monroe E. (ed.) (1998), *The V-Chip Debate: Content Filtering from Television to the Internet*, Mahwah, NJ: Lawrence Erlbaum Associates.

Prindle, David F. (1988), *The Politics of Glamour: Ideology and Democracy in the Screen Actors Guild*, Madison: University of Wisconsin Press.

Smith, Anthony (ed.) (1998), *Television: An International History* (second edition), Oxford: Oxford University Press.

Sohn, Ardyth Broadrick, Wicks, Jan LeBlanc, Lacy, Stephen and Sylvie, George (1999), *Media Management: A Casebook Approach*, Mahwah, NJ: Lawrence Erlbaum Associates.

Tolette, J. P. (2004), *Disney TV*, Detroit, MI: Wayne State University Press.

White, E. B. (1966), Letter to Carnegie Commission on Public Television, September.

ONLINE RESOURCES

American Federation of Television and Radio Artists, <www.aftra.com>.

BBC, <www.bbc.co.uk/commissioning/tv/business/tariffs.shtml>.

Channel Four, <www.channel4.com/corporate/4producers/resources/documents/C4%20Code%20of%20Practice%20Feb%202005.pdf>.

Five, <www.five.tv/fivepdf/codeofpractice.pdf>.

Communications Workers of America, <www.cwa.org>.

Directors Guild of America, <www.dga.org>.

International Alliance of Theatrical Stage Employes, <www.iatse-intl.org>.

ITV, <www.itvplc.com>.

Motion Picture Association of America, <www.mpaa.org>.

National Association of Broadcast Employees and Technicians, <www.nabetcwa.org>.

Office of Communications, <www.ofcom.org.uk>.

PACT <www.pact.co.uk>.

Writers Guild of America, East, <www.wgae.org>.

Writers Guild of America, West, <www.wgaw.org>.

Selling and Television

Bagdikian, Ben H. (2004), *The Media Monopoly*, Boston, MA: Beacon.

Banks, M. J. (1981), 'History of broadcast audience research in the United States, 1920–1980 with an emphasis on the rating services', unpublished doctoral dissertation, University of Tennessee, Knoxville, TN.

BBC press release (2000), 'BBC News to Move to 10pm, Says BBC Director-General', 25 August.

Beville, Hugh M. (1988), *Audience Ratings*, Hillsdale, NJ: Lawrence Erlbaum Associates, Inc.

Bogart, Leo (2000), *Commercial Culture: The Media System and the Public Interest*, New Brunswick, NJ: Transaction Publishers.

Brown, Maggie (2004), 'War of the News Walls', *Guardian*, 26 January.

Buzzard, Karen S. (1990), *Electronic Media Ratings: Turning Audiences into Dollars and Sense*, Boston, MA: Focal Press.

Buzzard, Karen S. (2002), 'The People Meter Wars: A Case Study of Technological Innovation and Diffusion in the Ratings Industry', *Journal of Media Economics*, vol. 15, no. 4.

Capo, Joe (2003), *The Future of Advertising*, New York: McGraw Hill.

Communications Act 2003 (2003), London: HMSO, clause 267 (1) and (2) (a) and (b).

Compaine, Benjamin M. and Douglas Gomery (2000), *Who Owns the Media?: Competition and Concentration in the Mass Media Industry* (third edition), Mahwah, NJ: Lawrence Erlbaum Associates, Publishers.

Croteau, David and Hoynes, William (2001), *The Business of Media: Corporate Media and the Public Interest*, Thousand Oaks, CA: Sage.

Eastman, Susan T. and Furgeson, David A. (1997), *Broadcasting and Cable Programming*, Belmont, CA: Wadsworth.

Eastman, Susan T., Furgeson, Douglas A. and Klein, Robert A. (eds) (1999), *Promotion and Marketing for Broadcasting and Cable* (third edition), Boston, MA: Focal Press.

Ettma, James and Whitney, D. Charles (eds) (1994), *Audience Making: How the Media Creates the Audience*, Thousand Oaks, CA: Sage.

Fanthome, Christine (2004a), Email to the author, 14 May.

Fanthome, Christine (2004b), Telephone interview with the author, 13–17 May.

Fanthome, Christine (2004c), Email from Sandy Maer, Controller for Scheduling, Planning and Presentation, BBC, to the author, 14 May.

Flournay, Don and Stewart, Robert (1997), *CNN: Making News in the Global Market*, Luton: University of Luton Press.

Friedland, Lewis A. (1992), *Covering the World*, New York: Twentieth Century Fund.

Gomery, Douglas (2004), 'Television Industry', in Neil J. Smelser and Paul B. Bates (eds), *International Encyclopedia of the Social and Behavioral Sciences*, Amsterdam: Pergamon.

Jung, Jaemin (2004), 'Acquisition or Joint Ventures: Foreign Market Entry Strategy of U.S. Advertising Agencies', *Journal of Media Economics*, vol. 17, no. 1.

Kung-Shankleman, Lucy (2000), *Inside the BBC and CNN: Managing Media Organisations*, London: Routledge.

Levine, Robert (2003), *The Power of Persuasion*, New York: Wiley.

McCarthy, Anna (2001), *Ambient Television*, Durham, NC: Duke University Press.

Moran, Albert (2003), *Copycat TV: Globalisation, Program Formats and Cultural Identity*, Luton: University of Luton Press.

Murray, Susan and Ouelette, Laurie (eds) (2004), *Reality TV: Remaking Television Culture*, New York: New York University Press.

Newcomb, Horace (ed.) (1997), *Encyclopedia of Television*, Chicago, IL: Fitzroy-Dearborn.

Ofcom (2004), *Ofcom Review of Public Service Television Broadcasting: Phase 1 – Is Television Special?*, p.18

Owen, Bruce M. and Steven S. Wildman (1992), *Video Economics*, Cambridge, MA: Harvard University Press.

Parks, Lisa and Kumar, Shanti (eds) (2002), *Planet TV: A Global Television Reader*, New York: New York University Press.

Phalen, Patricia F. (1996), 'Information and Markets and the Market for Information: An Analysis of the Market for Television Audiences', unpublished doctoral dissertation, Northwestern University, Evanston, IL.

Picard, Robert G. (1993), *The Cable Networks Handbook*, Riverside, CA: Carpelan Publishing Company

Robinson, Piers (2002), *The CNN Effect: The Myth of News Media, Foreign Policy and Intervention*, London: Routledge.

Schroder, K., Drotner, K., Kline, S. and Murray, C. (2003), *Researching Audiences*, London: Arnold.

Sinclair, John, Jacka, Eilizabeth and Cunningham, Stuart (eds) (2003), *New Patterns in Global Television*, New York: Oxford University Press.

Smith, Anthony (ed.) (1998), *Television: An International History* (second edition), Oxford: Oxford University Press.

Tolette, J. P. (2004), *Disney TV*, Detroit, MI: Wayne State University Press.

Wang, Georgette, Goonasekera, Anura and Servaes, Jan (eds) (2000), *The New Communications Landscape: Demystifying Media Globalization*, London and New York: Routledge.

ONLINE RESOURCES

Advertising Age, <www.adage.com>.

Broadcasting and Cable, <www.broadcastingandcable.com>.

Cable Television Advertising Bureau, <www.cabletvadbureau.com>.

Creativity, <www.adcritic.com>.

Federal Trade Commission, <www.ftc.gov>.

Mediaweek, <www.mediaweek.com>.

Television Week, <www.TVweek.com>.

Variety, <www.variety.com>.

Television Culture

Alberti, John (ed.) (2004), *Leaving Springfield*, Detroit, MI: Wayne State University Press.

Andrews, David L. (2003), 'Sport and the Transnationalizing Media Corporation', *Journal of Media Economics*, vol. 16, no. 4.

Aufderheide, Patricia (1991), 'Cable Television and the Public Interest', *Journal of Communication*, vol. 42, no. 1.

Aufderheide, Patricia (1999), *Communications Policy and the Public Interest*, New York: Guilford Press.

Bogart, Leo (2000), *Commercial Culture: The Media System and the Public Interest*, New Brunswick, NJ: Transaction Publishers.

Brown, Keith S. and Cavazos, Roberto J. (2002), 'Network Revenues and African American Broadcast Television Revenues', *Journal of Media Economics*, vol. 15, no. 4.

Campbell, Richard (1991), *60 Minutes and the News*, Urbana: University of Illinois Press.

Dayan, Daniel and Katz, Elihu (1987), 'Performing Media Events', in James Curran, Anthony Smith and Pauline Wingate (eds), *Impacts and Influences: Essays on Media Power in the Twentieth Century*, London: Methuen, pp. 174–97.

Dayan, Daniel and Katz, Elihu (1994), *Media Events: The Live Broadcasting of History*, Cambridge, MA: Harvard University Press.

Debord, Guy (1995), *The Society of the Spectacle*, New York: Zone Books.

Eastman, Susan T. and Furgeson, Douglas A. (1997), *Broadcasting and Cable Programming*, Belmont, CA: Wadsworth.

Eastman, Susan T., Furgeson, Douglas A. and Klein, Robert A. (eds) (1999), *Promotion and Marketing for Broadcasting and Cable* (third edition), Boston, MA: Focal Press.

Edgerton, Gary R. (2001), *Ken Burn's America*, New York: Palgrave.

Engelman, Robert (1996), *Public Radio and Television in America*, Thousand Oaks, CA: Sage.

Fiske, John (1988) *Television Culture*, London: Methuen.

Gomery, Douglas (2004), 'Television and American Culture' in Carroll Pursell (ed.), *Companion to American Technology*, London: Blackwell.

Haralovich, Mary Beth and Rabinovitz, Lauren (1999), *Television, History, and American Culture: Feminist Critical Readings*, Durham, NC: Duke University Press.

Heider, Don (2000), *White News: Why Local News Programs Don't Cover People of Color*, Mahwah, NJ: Lawrence Erlbaum Associates, Publishers.

Kellner, Douglas (2003), *Media Spectacle*, New York: Routledge.

Kung-Shankleman, Lucy (2000), *Inside the BBC and CNN: Managing Media Organisations*, London: Routledge.

Lavery, David (ed.) (1994), *Full of Secrets: Critical Approaches to Twin Peaks*, Detroit, MI: Wayne State University Press.

Lipschultz, Jeremy H. and Hilt, Michael L. (2002), *Crime and Local Television News*, Mahwah, NJ: Lawrence Erlbaum Associates, Publishers.

McCarthy, Anna (2001) *Ambient Television*, Durham, NC: Duke University Press.

Murray, Susan and Ouellette, Laurie (eds) (2004), *Reality TV: Remaking Television Culture*, New York: New York University Press.

Newcomb, Horace (ed.) (1997), *Encyclopedia of Television*, Chicago, IL: Fitzroy-Dearborn.

Powers, Angela (2001), 'Toward a Monopolistic Competition in U.S. Local Television News', *Journal of Media Economics*, vol. 14, no. 2.

Price, Monroe E. (ed.) (1998), *The V-Chip Debate: Content Filtering from Television to the Internet*, Mahwah, NJ: Lawrence Erlbaum Associates.

Staiger, Janet (2003), *Blockbuster TV: Must-See Sitcoms in the Network Era*, New York: New York University Press.

Thompson, Kristin (2003), *Storytelling in Film and Television*, Cambridge, MA: Harvard University Press.

ONLINE RESOURCES

Broadcasting and Cable, <www.broadcastingandcable.com>.

Cable Television Advertising Bureau, <www.cabletvadbureau.com>.

Federal Communications Commission, <www.fcc.gov>.

Federal Trade Commission, <www.ftc.gov>.

Mediaweek, <www.mediaweek.com>.

Variety, <www.variety.com>.

Conclusion

Aksoy, Asu and Robins, Kevin (1992), 'Hollywood for the 21st Century: Global Competition for Critical Mass in Image Markets', *Cambridge Journal of Economics*, issue 16, pp. 1–22.

Alexander, Alison, Owers, James and Carvath, Rod (1998), *Media Economics: Theory and Practice* (second edition), Mahwah, NJ: Lawrence Erlbaum Associates, Publishers.

Aufderheide, Patricia (1999), *Communications Policy and the Public Interest*, New York: Guilford Press.

Bagdikian, Ben H. (2004), *The Media Monopoly*, Boston, MA: Beacon.

Bogart, Leo (2000), *Commercial Culture: The Media System and the Public Interest*, New Brunswick, NJ: Transaction Publishers.

Campbell, Richard (1991), *60 Minutes and the News*, Urbana: University of Illinois Press.

Compaine, Benjamin M. and Gomery, Douglas (2000), *Who Owns the Media?: Competition and Concentration in the Mass Media Industry* (third edition), Mahwah, NJ: Lawrence Erlbaum Associates, Publishers.

Gomery, Douglas (2003), 'The Role of the MPAA', in Thomas Paris and Pierre-Jean Benghozi (eds), *Hollywood and the Rest of the World: Which Approach for the 21st Century?*, Paris: CineAction!.

Gomery, Douglas (2004), 'Television and American Culture', in Carroll Pursell (ed.), *Companion to American Technology*, London: Blackwell.

Gomery, Douglas (2004), 'Television Industry', in Neil J. Smelser and Paul B. Bates (eds), *International Encyclopedia of the Social and Behavioral Sciences*, Amsterdam: Pergamon.

Gomery, Douglas (2005), *The Hollywood Studio System*, London: BFI.

Gray, Lois S. and Seeber, Ronald L. (eds) (1996), *Under the Stars: Essays on Labor Relations in Arts and Entertainment*, Ithaca, NY: Cornell University Press.

Greco, Albert N. (ed.) (2000), *The Media and Entertainment Industries*, New York: Allyn & Bacon.

Greenberg, Bradley S. (2001), *The Alphabet Soup of Television Program Ratings*, Cresskill, NJ: Hampton Press, Inc.

Heins, Marjorie (2001), *Not in Front of the Children: 'Indecency', Censorship, and the Innocence of Youth*, New York: Hill and Wang.

Hilmes, Michele (2002), *Only Connect: A Cultural History of Broadcasting*, Belmont, CA: Wadsworth Publishing.

Kung-Shankleman, Lucy (2000), *Inside the BBC and CNN: Managing Media Organisations*, London: Routledge.

McCarthy, Anna (2001), *Ambient Television*, Durham, NC: Duke University Press.

Montgomery, Kathryn C. (1989), *Target: Prime Time, Advocacy Groups and the Struggle over Entertainment Television*, New York and Oxford: Oxford University Press.

Newcomb, Horace (ed.) (1997), *Encyclopedia of Television*, Chicago, IL: Fitzroy-Dearborn.

Owen, Bruce M. and Wildman, Steven S. (1992), *Video Economics*, Cambridge, MA: Harvard University Press.

Picard, Robert G. (1993), *The Cable Networks Handbook*, Riverside, CA: Carpelan Publishing Company.

Price, Monroe E. (ed.) (1998), *The V-Chip Debate: Content Filtering from Television to the Internet*, Mahwah, NJ: Lawrence Erlbaum Associates.

Thompson, Kristin (2003), *Storytelling in Film and Television*, Cambridge, MA: Harvard University Press.

Waterman, David and Weis, Andrew (1997), *Vertical Integration in Cable Television*, Cambridge, MA: MIT Press.

Vogel, Harold L. (1994), *Entertainment Industry Economics: A Guide for Financial Analysis*, New York: Cambridge University Press.

List of Illustrations

Whilst considerable effort has been made to correctly identify the copyright holders, this has not been possible in all cases. We apologise for any apparent negligence and any omissions or corrections brought to our attention will be remedied in any future editions.

Television as Business: *Big Brother*, Endemol UK Productions; *Coronation Street*, Granada Television; **Television Technology:** *Smallville*, Warner Bros. Televison/Tollin/Robins Productions; *Friends*, Warner Bros. Television/Bright/Kauffman/Crane Productions; *The Office*, BBC; **Making Programmes:** *Margin for Error*, © Twentieth Century-Fox Film Corporation; *Dallas*, Lorimar Productions; CSI, Alliance Atlantis Communications/Arc Entertainment/CBS Productions/Jerry Bruckheimer Television/Jerry Bruckheimer Films; *Love Thy Neighbour*, Thames Television; *Desmond's*, Humphrey Barclay Productions; **Selling and Television:** *Nine O'Clock News*, BBC; *News at Ten*, ITN; *Sex and the City*, HBO; *I Love Lucy*, CBS Television/Desilu Productions Inc.; *American Idol*, Fremantle Media Ltd/Fremantle Media North America/19 Television/American Idol Productions/Fox Television Network; *Big Brother South Africa*, M-Net/MagicWorks Co-production; **Television Culture:** *The Simpsons*, Gracie Films/20th Century Fox TV; *Pop Idol*, 19 Television/Thames Television.

INDEX

Page numbers in bold denote detailed treatment in a 'grey box' study; page numbers in italic denote illustrations (may be textual material on same page); t = table